D0088200

PLAYS BY RENAISSANCE AND RESTORATION DRAMATISTS

General Editor: Graham Storey

FORD

VOLUMES IN THIS SERIES

PUBLISHED

The plays of Cyril Tourneur, edited by George Parfitt: *The Revenger's Tragedy*; *The Atheist's Tragedy*

The selected plays of Philip Massinger, edited by Colin Gibson: *The Duke of Milan*; *The Roman Actor*; *A New Way to Pay Old Debts*; *The City Madam*

The selected plays of Thomas Middleton, edited by David L. Frost: *A Mad World, My Masters*; *A Chaste Maid in Cheapside*; *Women Beware Women*; *The Changeling* (with William Rowley)

The plays of William Wycherley, edited by Peter Holland: *Love in a Wood*; *The Gentleman Dancing Master*; *The Country Wife*; *The Plain Dealer*

The comedies of William Congreve, edited by Anthony Henderson: *The Old Batchelor*; *The Double-Dealer*; *Love for Love*; *The Way of the World*

The plays of Sir George Etherege, edited by Michael Cordner: *The Comical Revenge*; or *Love in a Tub*; *She Would If She Could*; *The Man of Mode*; or *Sir Fopling Flutter*

The selected plays of John Webster, edited by Jonathan Dollimore and Alan Sinfield: *The White Devil*; *The Devil's Law Case*; *The Duchess of Malfi*

The selected plays of John Marston, edited by MacDonald P. Jackson and Michael Neill: *Antonio and Mellida*; *Antonio's Revenge*; *The Malcontent*; *The Dutch Courtesan*; *Sophonisba*

FORTHCOMING

The selected plays of Ben Jonson, edited by Johanna Procter: *Sejanus*; *Epicoene*, or *The Silent Woman*; *Volpone*

The selected plays of Ben Jonson, edited by Martin Butler: *The Alchemist*; *Bartholomew Fair*; *The New Inn*; *A Tale of a Tub*

THE SELECTED PLAYS OF JOHN FORD

The Broken Heart

'Tis Pity She's a Whore

Perkin Warbeck

EDITED BY
COLIN GIBSON

Donald Collie Professor of English, University of Otago, Dunedin, New Zealand

CAMBRIDGE UNIVERSITY PRESS

CAMBRIDGE
LONDON NEW YORK NEW ROCHELLE
MELBOURNE SYDNEY

Published by the Press Syndicate of the University of Cambridge
The Pitt Building, Trumpington Street, Cambridge CB2 1RP
32 East 57th Street, New York, NY 10022, USA
10 Stamford Road, Oakleigh, Melbourne 3166, Australia

First published 1986

Printed in Great Britain at
the University Press, Cambridge

British Library cataloguing in publication data

Ford, John, *b. ca 1586*
The selected plays of John Ford. – (Plays by
Renaissance and Restoration dramatists)
I. Title II. Gibson, Colin, *1933–* III. Ford,
John, *b. ca 1586* The broken heart IV. Ford, John,
b. ca 1586 'Tis pity she's a whore V. Ford,
John, *b. ca 1586* Perkin Warbeck VI. Series
822'.3 PR2521.5

Library of Congress cataloguing in publication data

Ford, John, 1586–*ca*. 1640.
The selected plays of John Ford.
(Plays by Renaissance and Restoration dramatists)
Contents: The broken heart – 'Tis pity she's a
whore – Perkin Warbeck.
I. Gibson, Colin. II. Title. III. Series.
PR2522.G53 1986 822'.3 86–6058

ISBN 0 521 22543 4 hard covers
ISBN 0 521 29545 9 paperback

GG

PREFACE TO THE SERIES

This series provides the best plays (in some cases, the complete plays) of the major English Renaissance and Restoration dramatists, in fully-annotated, modern-spelling texts, soundly edited by scholars in the field.

The introductory matter in each volume is factual and historical rather than critical: it includes, where appropriate, a brief biography of the playwright, a list of his works with dates of plays' first performances, the reasons for the volume editor's choice of plays, a short critical bibliography and a note on the texts used. An introductory note to each play then gives the source material, a short stage-history, and details of the individual editions of that play.

Short notes at the foot of the page are designed to gloss the text or enlarge on its literary, historical or social allusions. Editors have added explanatory notes and have commented on textual variants.

The volumes are intended for anyone interested in English drama in two of its richest periods, but they will prove especially useful to students at all levels who want to enjoy and explore the best work of these dramatists.

Graham Storey

CONTENTS

INTRODUCTION

This selection consists of the three plays which are generally recognised to be Ford's finest work. *The Broken Heart* (1633) is a Racinian tragedy of suffering, appropriately described in the prologue as its author's 'best of art'. *'Tis Pity She's a Whore* (1633), a tragedy of ambition and rivalry expressed in sexual terms, is Ford's most famous (or infamous) play, one which has proved its ability to engage modern readers and audiences. *The Chronicle History of Perkin Warbeck* (1634) is the last great English history play, exhibiting a Shakespearian range of character in action and fully vindicating its prologue's promise of 'truth and state'.

Although they do not exhaust Ford's range as a playwright, the three plays exemplify his concentration of thematic interests and the unique tone of his drama, in which passion, gravity and deliberate composure are united with a poetic sense of theatre.

Life and works

John Ford was born into an old Devonshire family with manors at Ilsington and Bagtor. He was baptised on 17 April 1586, the second son in a family of three brothers and two sisters. His father, Thomas Ford, was a prosperous country gentleman who married the niece of the great Elizabethan judge Sir John Popham, later Lord Chief Justice of England (1592–1607).

Like his older brother Henry, Ford was intended for a career at law. He may first have spent some months at Exeter College, Oxford, since a 'John Ford Devon gent.' matriculated there on 26 March 1601, but in the following year he was placed at one of the Inns of Court to be educated as a gentleman and receive a legal training. On 16 November 1602, he was admitted to the Middle Temple – the Inn of which both his great-uncle Sir John Popham and his father's cousin, Thomas Ford of Ashburton, were members.

Ford probably remained in chambers there for most of the rest of his life. In 1638, in a commendatory poem prefixed to his play *The Fancies Chaste and Noble*, he is still addressed as 'Master John Ford of the Middle Temple'. He figures in the records of the Inn only in connection with two minor offences. In the

Hilary term of 1605/6 he was suspended for the common offence of not paying his buttery bill and was not reinstated until 10 June 1608; in 1617 he was reprimanded for joining an organised protest against the Inn's rules for dress. There is no evidence that Ford was ever called to the bar, but his continued residence in the Middle Temple suggests that he pursued some kind of legal career, perhaps in the management of property for members of the landed gentry.

The lively cultural and intellectual milieu of the Inns of Court, well described in P. J. Finkelpearl's *John Marston of the Middle Temple* (Cambridge, Mass.: Harvard University Press, 1969), must have encouraged Ford to take up writing; shortage of money may have been an added inducement. He began the search for patronage and recognition as a pamphleteer and poet.

Honour Triumphant (1606) is a prose pamphlet dedicated to the Countess of Pembroke and the Countess of Montgomery, responding to a writing competition associated with the visit to England of the King of Denmark in the summer of 1606. It wittily defends four courtly love propositions, and includes poetry celebrating the royal visit. *Fame's Memorial*, written in the same year, is an elegy on Charles Blount, Earl of Devonshire, dedicated to his widow Lady Penelope (née Devereux), whose betrothal to Blount and forced marriage to Lord Rich may have contributed something to the plot of *The Broken Heart* (see Katherine Duncan-Jones, 'Ford and the Earl of Devonshire', *Review of English Studies*, 29 (1978), 447–52).

In 1613 Ford addressed *The Golden Mean*, a prose work advocating stoic endurance of all adversity, to the imprisoned Earl of Northumberland. An enlarged second edition appeared in 1614, and a third in 1638. Also in 1613 a long poem entitled *Christ's Bloody Sweat* and dedicated to the Earl of Pembroke was published by 'I.F.'. It is almost certainly Ford's work, and argues insistently that heartfelt repentance for sin will bring salvation through the atonement of Christ. There are signs of a Calvinist doctrine of election, and the poem includes a strong attack on the glorification of sexual love outside marriage.

A biographical account of the Overbury affair, *Sir*

Thomas Overbury's Ghost, was licensed in 1615 (though no copy has survived), and in 1616 Ford contributed a poem to *Sir Thomas Overbury His Wife*; Overbury had been a fellow member of the Middle Temple. In 1620 Ford published the pamphlet *A Line of Life*, dedicated to one of James's favourites, Sir James Hay, Viscount Doncaster, then working for the release of his father-in-law, the Earl of Northumberland. It paraphrases some of the material in *The Golden Mean*, and praises a life of virtuous action. In addition to these pieces, Ford contributed commendatory poems to plays by Webster (1623), Massinger (1629 and 1636), Shirley (1629) and Brome (1632), to Jonson's memorial, *Jonsonus Virbius* (1638), and to prose works by Barnes (1606), Cockeram (1623) and Saltonstall (1636). Commendatory verses in *Dia Poemata* (1655) and a verse-anagram, 'A Contract of Love and Truth', on the marriage of the daughter of Viscount Campden to Sir Erasmus de la Fountaine, are also attributed to him: see Peter Beal, *Index of English Literary Manuscripts*, vol. 1: 1450–1625 (London: Mansell, 1982), where a number of manuscript copies of lyrics from the plays are also recorded.

Ford's prose and verse works have no great literary merit, but they throw much light on his dramatic preoccupations, and on occasion their ideas and vocabulary appear in the plays.

It is not known when Ford began writing for the stage, and the shape of his career as a dramatist is obscured by the number of lost works and by uncertainty about collaborative involvement and the date of composition of most of the surviving plays. Eighteen plays, including seven lost texts, are usually attributed to him as sole author or major partner. (See G.E. Bentley, *The Jacobean and Caroline Stage*, vol. 3 (Oxford: Clarendon Press, 1956), pp. 433–64, and Clifford Leech, *John Ford and the Drama of His Time* (London: Chatto and Windus, 1957), pp. 124–32, for discussion of these attributions.) Several of the plays were produced by the King's Men at the Blackfriars theatre; a number of others were presented at the Phoenix theatre by the Queen's Men.

The lost plays are:

The Royal Combat (date unknown)
An Ill Beginning has a Good End (?1613)

The Bristow Merchant (1624) with Dekker
The Fairy Knight (1624) with Dekker
A Late Murder of the Son upon the Mother (1624) with Dekker, Rowley and Webster
The London Merchant (?1624)
Beauty in a Trance (1630)

Between 1621 and 1625, Ford collaborated in a number of plays, principally with Dekker, but also with Middleton, Rowley and Webster, and possibly with Massinger and Fletcher. The surviving plays are:

The Witch of Edmonton (1621) with Dekker and Rowley
The Sun's Darling (1624), a masque, with Dekker
? *The Laws of Candy* (1619–23) with Fletcher and Massinger
The Spanish Gipsy (1623) with Middleton and Rowley
? *The Welsh Ambassador* (1623) with Dekker
? *The Fair Maid of the Inn* (1626) with Fletcher, Massinger and Webster

Ford's independent plays were published between 1629 and 1639, but their sequence and the dates of composition for all but two of them remain uncertain. In order of publication they are:

The Lover's Melancholy (1629; licensed in 1628)
Love's Sacrifice (1633)
'Tis Pity She's a Whore (1633)
The Broken Heart (1633)
The Chronicle History of Perkin Warbeck (1634)
The Fancies Chaste and Noble (1638)
The Lady's Trial (1639; licensed in 1638)

To these should be added *The Queen*, which was not published until 1653.

Almost nothing factual is known of Ford's personal life. In *Fame's Memorial* he twice speaks (in conventional terms) of his rejected love for Lycia (or Lucia), and the preface to *Christ's Bloody Sweat* refers to a religious conversion or serious change of life. However, William Heminges's well-known lines about Ford in his elegy *On Randolph's Finger* (?1632),

Deep In a dumpe Iacke forde alone was gott
W[th] folded Armes and Melancholye hatt (81–2)

are more likely to be a witty allusion to Ford's play *The Lover's Melancholy* than a description of his temperament. Ford's friends and acquaintances, many of them associated with the Inns of Court, included a number of writers: Barnabe Barnes, Brome, Davenant, Dekker, Massinger, Rowley, Shirley and Webster. The publication early in 1639 of *The Lady's Trial* with a signed dedication is the last certain record of his working life, and it is generally assumed that he died shortly afterwards, but neither the place nor the date of his death is known.

A select bibliography

S.A. Tannenbaum's *John Ford (A Concise Bibliography)* (New York, 1941), supplemented by C.A. Pennel and W.P. Williams's *Elizabethan Bibliographies Supplements*, vol. 8 (London: Nether Press, 1968), is still useful, but the fullest modern bibliography of Ford's work is *A Bibliography of Writings by and about John Ford and Cyril Tourneur*, by Kenneth Tucker (Boston, Mass.: G.K. Hall, 1977). More recent scholarly work can be traced in *The Annual Bibliography of English Language and Literature* and the MLA bibliographies, and there is a useful survey of Ford criticism and scholarship by D.K. Anderson in T.P. Logan and D.S. Smith (eds.), *The Later Jacobean and Caroline Dramatists* (Lincoln: University of Nebraska Press, 1978).

The standard edition of Ford is still Alexander Dyce's three-volume revision of William Gifford's *The Works of John Ford* (London: J. Toovey, 1869). There are annotated, modernised texts of *The Broken Heart*, *'Tis Pity She's a Whore* and *Perkin Warbeck* in Keith Sturgess (ed.), *John Ford: Three Plays* (Harmondsworth: Penguin English Library, 1970), and these plays, together with *The Lover's Melancholy*, are included in the Revels Plays series. Other modern editions are noticed in the individual introductions to the present edition, and a complete edition of Ford's non-dramatic writing is in preparation under the general editorship of Professor L.E. Stock of the University of Ontario.

Joan M. Sargeaunt's primary survey of Ford's life

and works, *John Ford* (Oxford: Basil Blackwell, 1935), is supplemented by Donald K. Anderson, *John Ford* (New York: Twayne, 1972), and G.E. Bentley, *The Jacobean and Caroline Stage*, 7 vols. (Oxford: Clarendon Press, 1941–68), deals with many aspects of Ford's drama and its theatrical milieu. See also *The Revels History of Drama in English*, vol. 4 (London and New York: Methuen, 1981).

There are a number of illuminating book-length studies of Ford, beginning with S.B. Ewing's *Burtonian Melancholy in the Plays of John Ford* (Princeton: Princeton University Press, 1940). G.F. Sensabaugh presents Ford as a social rebel, in *The Tragic Muse of John Ford* (Stanford: Stanford University Press, 1944); Mark Stavig, *John Ford and the Traditional Moral Order* (Madison and London: University of Wisconsin Press, 1968), finds in him a conservative moralist. H.J. Oliver, *The Problem of John Ford* (Melbourne, London and New York: Melbourne University Press, 1955), Robert Davril, *Le Drame de John Ford* (Paris: Librairie Marcel Didier, 1954) and Clifford Leech, *John Ford and the Drama of his Time* (London: Chatto and Windus, 1957), offer scholarly readings of his whole work. Orbison Tucker, *The Tragic Vision of John Ford* (Salzburg: University of Salzburg, 1974), Ronald Huebert, *John Ford: Baroque English Dramatist* (Montreal and London: McGill and Queen's University Press, 1977) and Dorothy M. Farr, *John Ford and the Caroline Theatre* (London: Macmillan, 1979), stress the cultural and theatrical contexts of his drama.

The seminal critical estimates of Ford are those of Charles Lamb, *Specimens of English Dramatic Poets who lived about the time of Shakspeare* (London: Bell, 1808), William Hazlitt, *Lectures Chiefly on the Dramatic Literature of the Age of Elizabeth* (London: Bell, 1820), T.S. Eliot, *Selected Essays* (London: Faber, 1932), and Una Ellis-Fermor, *Jacobean Drama: An Interpretation* (London: Methuen, 1936). The range of modern critical approaches to Ford is illustrated in Peter Ure, 'Marriage and the domestic drama in Heywood and Ford', *English Studies*, 32 (1951), 200–16; Cyrus Hoy, ' "Ignorance in knowledge": Marlowe's Faustus and Ford's Giovanni', *Modern Philology*, 57

(1960), 145–54; Donald K. Anderson, 'The heart and the banquet: imagery in Ford's *'Tis Pity* and *The Broken Heart*', *Studies in English Literature*, 2 (1962), 209–17; Philip Edwards, 'The royal pretenders in Massinger and Ford', *Essays and Studies*, 27 (1974), 18–36; Carol C. Rosen, 'The language of cruelty in Ford's *'Tis Pity She's a Whore*', *Comparative Drama*, 8 (1974), 356–68; Anne Barton, ' "He that plays the king": Ford's *Perkin Warbeck* and the Stuart history play', in Marie Axton and Raymond Williams (eds.), *English Drama: Forms and Development* (Cambridge: Cambridge University Press, 1977), pp. 69–93; Michael Neill, 'Ford's unbroken art: the moral design of *The Broken Heart*', *Modern Language Review*, 75 (1980), 249–68; and Joseph Candido, 'The "strange truth" of *Perkin Warbeck*', *Philological Quarterly*, 59 (1980), 300–16. To these should be added the close readings of individual plays given in the Revels, New Mermaid and Regents Renaissance Drama series, and Michael Scott's *Renaissance Drama and a Modern Audience* (London: Macmillan, 1982). Two volumes of essays on Ford are in preparation, one edited by Michael Neill for Cambridge University Press, the other edited by Donald K. Anderson for AMS Press, New York.

Treatment of the text

This edition offers modernised texts of three plays, prepared from the original Quartos. The copy-text for *The Broken Heart* was the Bodleian copy Malone 205 (6), for *'Tis Pity She's a Whore*, Bodleian Malone 238 (3) with British Library 1481.bb.18 for the commendatory poem by Thomas Ellice, and for *The Chronicle History of Perkin Warbeck*, a copy, C.7.2, in the library of King's College, Cambridge. Although I have recollated all Bodleian and British Library copies of the three plays, I have been able to consult the extensive collations made by the Regents Renaissance Drama and Revels Plays editors, covering ten copies of *The Chronicle History of Perkin Warbeck* and virtually all the known copies of *The Broken Heart* and *'Tis Pity She's a Whore*. The Textual Notes for this edition record all substantial variants between uncorrected and corrected formes, all substantive emendations accepted into the texts and alterations in the substance or position of stage directions, but there is no attempt to provide a complete textual history by listing substantive emendations proposed by previous editors and rejected here.

The modernisation of the texts includes the silent replacement of italic passages with roman type (in the Prologue to *The Broken Heart*, for example, and Bergetto's letter in *'Tis Pity She's a Whore*, II.iv) and the disappearance of the sometimes elaborate system of capitals and italics used for rhetorical purposes in the play-texts and their supporting material. The spelling of all words has been modernised, and archaic forms have not been retained. This practice has been extended to unusual colloquial forms characteristic of Ford's writing, such as *'a* (he), *'ee* (ye), *shu'd* (should), *wu't* (wilt) and *y'are* (you're), in the interests of general readers and actors. The original punctuation has been altered where necessary, but the pointing of the Quartos has been left undisturbed where it provided a satisfactory and comprehensible guide to the reading or speaking of the text.

Changes in the original lineation of prose passages and translations of Latin stage directions other than the familiar *exit* and *exeunt* have been made silently, and the practice of elision in Ford's verse and prose is regularised. The usual distinction in the play-texts between non-syllabic and syllabic endings in preterites and past participles is preserved by an *-'d/-ed* system. Editorial additions and emendations to existing stage directions are enclosed in square brackets.

In the Textual Notes, emendations are attributed usually by name to their first proposer, followed by the original Quarto reading. With the following exceptions, the names refer to editors or editions mentioned in the general or individual introductions:

Dodsley	Robert Dodsley (ed.), *A Select Collection of Old English Plays* vol. 5 (London, 1744)
Ellis	Havelock Ellis (ed.), *The Best Plays of . . . John Ford* (London: Vizetelly, 1888)

Maxwell	J.C. Maxwell, review of Brian Morris's 1965 edition of *The Broken Heart*, *Notes and Queries*, 211 (1966), 308–9
Merivale	J.H. Merivale, review of Weber's edition of Ford's works, *Monthly Review*, 67 (1812), p. 373
Mitford	*A Letter to Richard Heber* [by John Mitford] (London, 1812)
Modern British Drama	Walter Scott (ed.), *The Modern British Drama*, vol. 1 (London: William Miller, 1811)
Reed	*A Select Collection of Old Plays*, revised second edition by Isaac Reed, vol. 8 (London, 1780)
Weber	William Weber (ed.), *The Dramatic Works of John Ford*, 2 vols. (Edinburgh: Constable, 1811)

THE
BROKEN
HEART.

A Tragedy.

ACTED
By the KING'S Majeſties Seruants
at the priuate Houſe in the
BLACK-FRIERS.

Fide Honor.

LONDON:
Printed by I. B. for HVGH BEESTON, and are to
be ſold at his Shop, neere the *Caſtle* in
Corne-hill. 1633.

Title-page of the 1633 Quarto of *The Broken Heart*, reproduced by permission of the Bodleian Library, Oxford (shelfmark Mal. 238 (2)). The Latin motto, *Fide Honor*, meaning 'honour achieved through faith' or 'through fidelity', is also an anagram of the author's name, John Forde, and appears on the title-pages of three other of his plays, including *The Chronicle History of Perkin Warbeck*.

INTRODUCTORY NOTE

Sources

No single principal source for *The Broken Heart* has been discovered, despite the tantalising statement in the Prologue that 'What may be here thought a fiction, when time's youth / Wanted some riper years, was known a truth' (15–16).

In 668 B.C. the Spartans celebrated a victory over Messenia of the kind which brings Ithocles and Calantha together, and Calantha's fortitude on receiving the news of a triple disaster during the wedding dance (V.ii) has a parallel in Plutarch's account of the Spartans' refusal to interrupt their festive dances and sports at the news of their total defeat at Leuctra (371 B.C.).

Various analogues to Penthea's enforced marriage and eventual suicide have been traced, in the tale of Argalus and Parthenia in Sidney's *Arcadia* (1593), Book I, chapters 5–8, and Book III, chapters 12–16; in Castiglione's story in the third book of *The Courtier* of the devoted sufferings of a young Italian woman; and in the circumstances of the death in 1600 of Margaret Ratcliffe, one of Queen Elizabeth's maids of honour. None of these amounts to a confirmed source, though any one of them might have stirred the dramatist's imagination. The Arcadian story offers a number of plot parallels; it also has a Spartan setting and emphasises heroic virtue and constancy in tragic circumstances. But it is difficult to resist the conclusion that the germ of the Ithocles–Orgilus–Penthea plot lies in Ford's recollection of the marriage troubles of Penelope Devereux, the dedicatee of his first published work. Like Penthea, Penelope was compelled in 1581 to marry an older man, Lord Rich, a marriage which was endorsed (if not arranged) by her brother, the Earl of Essex, and which ignored a pre-contract to Charles Blount, Lord Mountjoy, who later became her lover and married her in 1605.

Parallels have also been found, in real life and in literature, to the episode in which Ithocles is trapped and murdered in a trick chair. One of these links Ford's tragedy to an earlier play, *The Devil's Charter* (1607), by Barnabe Barnes, one of the dramatist's associates; and the theatrical as well as the historical and literary indebtedness of *The Broken Heart* may be underscored by the fact that William Davenant's play, *The Cruel Brother*, performed in 1627 at the Blackfriars theatre by the same company which produced *The Broken Heart* there, contained a sensational scene in which a woman is tied to a chair and bled to death.

Stage history

Nothing is known of the first performances of *The Broken Heart*, except that they were very probably given by the same company named on the title-page of the 1633 Quarto, the King's Men, London's leading company, playing at their private theatre in Blackfriars. There are none of the ordinary indications of a theatrical success, and the tragedy may have been released for publication soon after the initial production.

It was not revived again until 1898, when William Poel directed it for the Elizabethan Stage Society in St George's Hall, London. The production was austere and dignified, but there were considerable cuts in the text, including the whole scene of Orgilus's suicide.

In 1904 *The Broken Heart* had a short run at the Royalty Theatre, London, under the direction of Philip Carr for the Mermaid Society, and in 1959 the Dramatic Society of the Queen's University of Belfast performed the play at Belfast and, in an outdoor theatre, at Stratford-upon-Avon, under the auspices of the Shakespeare Memorial Theatre.

In July 1962, Laurence Olivier produced Ford's tragedy for the opening season of the Chichester Festival Theatre. A notable cast included Olivier himself as Bassanes, Joan Greenwood (Calantha), Rosemary Harris (Penthea), John Neville (Orgilus), Keith Michell (Ithocles), Fay Compton (Grausis) and Alan Howard (Nearchus). The play was given a classical Greek setting and performed on a two-level fixed stage set. The power of Olivier's performance was recognised, but there were criticisms of the restlessness and rhetoric of the production style. Fuller descriptions of this and the Poel production may be found in Robert Speaight's *William Poel and the Elizabethan Revival* (London: Heinemann,

1954) and in the July and September issues of *Plays and Players* (1962).

The BBC broadcast adaptations of *The Broken Heart* for radio in 1955, 1956 and 1970, and a French television adaptation of the tragedy was shown in 1967.

Individual editions of the play

There are early single editions of *The Broken Heart* by Clinton Scollard (New York, 1895) and Oliphant Smeaton (London, 1906). Stuart P. Sherman brought out an old-spelling, annotated edition of *The Broken Heart* and *'Tis Pity She's a Whore* (Boston, 1915).

Brian Morris edited the play in 1965 for the New Mermaid series, giving a sensitive account of its themes, structure and poetry; Donald K. Anderson's 1968 Regents Renaissance Drama edition comments particularly on the dramaturgy of the play, and offers a chronology of Ford's life and works within the context of contemporary literary and political events. The principal individual edition of *The Broken Heart* is by T.J.B. Spencer, published in 1980 in the Revels Plays series. The text is fully annotated, and the introduction discusses the nature of the text, date of composition, stage history and sources, and offers a detailed reading of the play. Spencer prints Thomas Jordan's verse adaptation of *The Broken Heart* (?1664) and has an appendix on real and fictitious trick chairs of the kind Orgilus uses to trap Ithocles.

There are also annotated texts of the play in a number of anthologies of seventeenth-century drama. *The Broken Heart* appears in W.A. Neilson's *The Chief Elizabethan Dramatists* (Boston, 1911), E.H.C. Oliphant's *Shakespeare and his Fellow Dramatists* (New York, 1929) and *Elizabethan Dramatists other than Shakespeare* (New York, 1931), Felix E. Schelling and Matthew W. Black's *Typical Elizabethan Plays* (New York, 1931), C.F. Tucker Brooke and Nathaniel B. Paradise's *English Drama, 1580–1642* (Boston, 1933), Hazelton Spencer's *Elizabethan Plays* (Boston, 1933), and *Elizabethan and Stuart Plays*, edited by C.R. Baskervill and others (New York, 1934).

It is included in several more recent anthologies: R.C. Bald (ed.), *Six Elizabethan Plays* (Boston, 1963),

Richard C. Harrier (ed.), *An Anthology of Jacobean Drama*, an old-spelling text (New York, 1963), Robert Ornstein (ed.), *Elizabethan and Jacobean Tragedy* (Boston, 1964), Martin L. Wine (ed.), *Drama of the English Renaissance* (New York, 1969), Arthur H. Nethercot (ed.), *Stuart Plays* (New York, 1971), Russell A. Fraser and Norman Rabkin (eds.), *Drama of the English Renaissance* (New York and London, 1976) and Bernard Beckerman (ed.), *5 Plays of the English Renaissance* (New York, 1983).

[DEDICATORY EPISTLE]

To the most worthy deserver of the noblest titles in honour, William, Lord Craven, Baron of Hamstead Marshall.

My Lord,

The glory of a great name, acquired by a greater glory of action, hath in all ages lived the truest chronicle to his own memory. In the practice of which argument, your growth to perfection (even in youth) hath appeared so sincere, so unflattering a penman, that posterity cannot with more delight read the merit of noble endeavours, than noble endeavours merit thanks from posterity to be read with delight. Many nations, many eyes, have been witnesses of your deserts, and loved them. Be pleased, then, with the freedom of your own nature, to admit one amongst all, particularly, into the list of such as honour a fair example of nobility. There is a kind of humble ambition, not uncommendable, when the silence of study breaks forth into discourse, coveting rather encouragement than applause. Yet herein censure commonly is too severe an auditor, without the moderation of an able patronage. I have ever been slow in courtship of greatness, not ignorant of such defects as are frequent to opinion; but the justice of your inclination to industry emboldens my weakness of confidence to relish an experience of your mercy, as many brave dangers have tasted of your courage. Your Lordship strove to be known to the world (when the world knew you least) by voluntary but excellent attempts. Like allowance I plead of being known to your Lordship in this low

---

Title *William . . . Marshall*: see Additional Notes, p. 347.
23 *censure*: criticism.
26–7 *frequent to opinion*: commonly considered mine.

presumption, by tendering to a favourable entertainment a devotion offered from a heart that can be as truly sensible of any least respect as ever profess the owner, in my best, my readiest services, a lover of your natural love to virtue.

John Ford.

36 *entertainment*: reception.
37 *respect*: sign of favour.

THE PROLOGUE

Our scene is Sparta. He whose best of art
Hath drawn this piece calls it *The Broken Heart*.
The title lends no expectation here
Of apish laughter, or of some lame jeer
At place or persons; no pretended clause
Of jests fit for a brothel courts applause
From vulgar admiration. Such low songs,
Tun'd to unchaste ears, suit not modest tongues.
The Virgin Sisters then deserv'd fresh bays
When innocence and sweetness crown'd their lays.
Then vices gasp'd for breath, whose whole commerce
Was whipp'd to exile by unblushing verse.
This law we keep in our presentment now,
Not to take freedom more than we allow.
What may be here thought a fiction, when time's youth
Wanted some riper years, was known a truth;
In which, if words have cloth'd the subject right,
You may partake a pity with delight.

---

5 *pretended*: offered.
6 See Textual Notes, p. 339.
9 *Virgin Sisters*: the Muses.
bays: garlands of laurel as prizes for excellence.
13 *presentment*: dramatic presentation.
14 *allow*: approve of.
16 *Wanted*: lacked.

The Scene,
SPARTA

THE SPEAKERS' NAMES
fitted to their qualities

AMYCLAS (*common to the kings of Laconia*)
[King of Sparta]
ITHOCLES (*Honour of Loveliness*) A favourite
ORGILUS (*Angry*) Son to Crotolon
BASSANES (*Vexation*) A jealous nobleman
ARMOSTES (*an Appeaser*) A counsellor of state
CROTOLON (*Noise*) Another counsellor
PROPHILUS (*Dear*) Friend to Ithocles
NEARCHUS (*Young Prince*) Prince of Argos
TECNICUS (*Artist*) A philosopher
LEMOPHIL (*Glutton*) } Two courtiers
GRONEAS (*Tavernhaunter*) }
AMELUS (*Trusty*) Friend to Nearchus
PHULAS (*Watchful*) Servant to Bassanes

CALANTHA (*Flower of Beauty*) The king's daughter
PENTHEA (*Complaint*) Sister to Ithocles
EUPHRANIA (*Joy*) A maid of honour
CHRYSTALLA (*Crystal*) } Maids of honour
PHILEMA (*a Kiss*) }
GRAUSIS (*Old Beldam*) Overseer of Penthea

Persons included

THRASUS (*Fierceness*) Father of Ithocles
APLOTES (*Simplicity*) Orgilus so disguised

[Lords, courtiers, officers, servants, musicians]

See Textual Notes, p. 339, and Additional Notes, p. 347.

THE BROKEN HEART

ACT 1

SCENE I

Enter CROTOLON *and* ORGILUS.

CROTOLON. Dally not further. I will know the reason
That speeds thee to this journey.
ORGILUS. Reason? Good sir,
I can yield many.
CROTOLON. Give me one; a good one.
Such I expect, and ere we part must have.
Athens? Pray why to Athens? You intend not
To kick against the world, turn Cynic, Stoic,
Or read the logic lecture, or become
An Areopagite, and judge in causes
Touching the commonwealth? For as I take it,
The budding of your chin cannot prognosticate
So grave an honour.
ORGILUS. All this I acknowledge.
CROTOLON. You do? Then, son, if books and love of knowledge
Inflame you to this travel, here in Sparta
You may as freely study.
ORGILUS. 'Tis not that, sir.
CROTOLON. Not that, sir? As a father I command thee
To acquaint me with the truth.
ORGILUS. Thus I obey ye.
After so many quarrels as dissension,
Fury, and rage had broach'd in blood, and sometimes

---

6 *Cynic, Stoic*: schools of ancient philosophy.
7 *read . . . lecture*: study logic.
8 *Areopagite*: member of the highest judicial court of Athens.
15 See Textual Notes, p. 339.
18 *broach'd*: pierced open; a striking metaphorical anticipation of the later action of the play (cf. V.ii.125).
18 See Textual Notes, p. 339.

With death to such confederates as sided
With now dead Thrasus and yourself, my lord,
Our present king, Amyclas, reconcil'd
Your eager swords and seal'd a gentle peace.
Friends you profess'd yourselves; which to
confirm,
A resolution for a lasting league
Betwixt your families was entertain'd,
By joining in a Hymenean bond
Me, and the fair Penthea, only daughter
To Thrasus.

CROTOLON. What of this?

ORGILUS. Much, much, dear sir.
A freedom of converse, an interchange
Of holy and chaste love, so fix'd our souls
In a firm growth of union, that no time
Can eat into the pledge. We had enjoy'd
The sweets our vows expected, had not cruelty
Prevented all those triumphs we prepar'd for,
By Thrasus his untimely death.

CROTOLON. Most certain.

ORGILUS. From this time sprouted up that
poisonous stalk
Of aconite, whose ripen'd fruit hath ravish'd
All health, all comfort of a happy life.
For Ithocles her brother, proud of youth,
And prouder in his power, nourish'd closely
The memory of former discontents.
To glory in revenge, by cunning partly,
Partly by threats, he woos at once, and forces
His virtuous sister to admit a marriage
With Bassanes, a nobleman, in honour
And riches, I confess, beyond my fortunes.

CROTOLON. All this is no sound reason to
importune

---

26 *Hymenean bond*: marriage.
31 See Textual Notes, p. 339.
34 *triumphs*: celebrations.
37 *aconite*: the plant monkshood or wolfsbane, which produced a deadly poison.
40 *closely*: secretly.
43 *at once*: suddenly.
44 *admit*: consent to.

My leave for thy departure.
ORGILUS. Now it follows.
Beauteous Penthea, wedded to this torture
By an insulting brother, being secretly
Compell'd to yield her virgin freedom up
To him who never can usurp her heart,
Before contracted mine, is now so yok'd
To a most barbarous thraldom, misery,
Affliction, that he savours not humanity
Whose sorrow melts not into more than pity
In hearing but her name.
CROTOLON. As how, pray?
ORGILUS. Bassanes,
The man that calls her wife, considers truly
What heaven of perfections he is lord of
By thinking fair Penthea his. This thought
Begets a kind of monster-love, which love
Is nurse unto a fear so strong and servile
As brands all dotage with a jealousy.
All eyes who gaze upon that shrine of beauty,
He doth resolve, do homage to the miracle.
Someone, he is assur'd, may now or then,
If opportunity but sort, prevail.
So much out of a self-unworthiness
His fears transport him; not that he finds cause
In her obedience, but his own distrust.
CROTOLON. You spin out your discourse.
ORGILUS. My griefs are violent.
For knowing how the maid was heretofore
Courted by me, his jealousies grow wild
That I should steal again into her favours,
And undermine her virtues; which the gods
Know I nor dare nor dream of. Hence, from hence,
I undertake a voluntary exile.
First, by my absence to take off the cares
Of jealous Bassanes; but chiefly, sir,
To free Penthea from a hell on earth.

---

50 *insulting*: arrogant.
55 See Textual Notes, p. 339.
55 *savours not humanity*: has no trace of human nature.
65 *resolve*: conclude.
67 *sort*: occur.

Lastly, to lose the memory of something
Her presence makes to live in me afresh.
CROTOLON. Enough, my Orgilus, enough. To Athens.
I give a full consent. – Alas, good lady! –
We shall hear from thee often?
ORGILUS. Often.
CROTOLON. See,
Thy sister comes to give a farewell.

Enter EUPHRANIA.

EUPHRANIA. Brother!
ORGILUS. Euphrania, thus upon thy cheeks I print
A brother's kiss; more careful of thine honour,
Thy health, and thy well-doing, than my life.
Before we part, in presence of our father,
I must prefer a suit to ye.
EUPHRANIA. You may style it,
My brother, a command.
ORGILUS. That you will promise
To pass never to any man, however
Worthy, your faith, till, with our father's leave,
I give a free consent.
CROTOLON. An easy motion.
I'll promise for her, Orgilus.
ORGILUS. Your pardon;
Euphrania's oath must yield me satisfaction.
EUPHRANIA. By Vesta's sacred fires I swear.
CROTOLON. And I,
By great Apollo's beams, join in the vow,
Not without thy allowance to bestow her
On any living.
ORGILUS. Dear Euphrania,
Mistake me not. Far, far 'tis from my thought,

---

83 See Textual Notes, p. 339.
89 *well-doing*: prosperity.
91 *prefer*: present.
93–4 See Textual Notes, p. 339.
95 *motion*: proposal.
98 *Vesta's sacred fires*: Vesta was the Roman goddess of the hearth, served by Vestal Virgins. Here she represents chastity. See II.iii.27–33.
100 *allowance*: permission.

As far from any wish of mine, to hinder
Preferment to an honourable bed
Or fitting fortune. Thou art young and handsome;
And 'twere injustice – more, a tyranny –
Not to advance thy merit. Trust me, sister,
It shall be my first care to see thee match'd
As may become thy choice and our contents.
I have your oath.

EUPHRANIA. You have. But mean you, brother,
To leave us as you say?

CROTOLON. Ay, ay, Euphrania;
He has just grounds direct him. I will prove
A father and a brother to thee.

EUPHRANIA. Heaven
Does look into the secrets of all hearts.
Gods, you have mercy with ye, else –

CROTOLON. Doubt nothing;
Thy brother will return in safety to us.

ORGILUS. Souls sunk in sorrows never are without 'em;
They change fresh airs, but bear their griefs about 'em.

Exeunt all.

SCENE II

Flourish. Enter AMYCLAS *the king,* ARMOSTES, PROPHILUS, *and Attendants.*

AMYCLAS. The Spartan gods are gracious. Our humility
Shall bend before their altars, and perfume
Their temples with abundant sacrifice.
See, lords, Amyclas, your old king, is ent'ring
Into his youth again. I shall shake off
This silver badge of age, and change this snow

---

105 *fitting fortune*: socially appropriate match.
109 *contents*: satisfaction.
115 *Doubt*: fear.
118 *fresh airs*: new circumstances.

For hairs as gay as are Apollo's locks.
Our heart leaps in new vigour.
ARMOSTES. May old time
Run back to double your long life, great sir.
AMYCLAS. It will, it must, Armostes. Thy bold nephew,
Death-braving Ithocles, brings to our gates
Triumphs and peace upon his conquering sword.
Laconia is a monarchy at length,
Hath in this latter war trod underfoot
Messene's pride; Messene bows her neck
To Lacedemon's royalty. O, 'twas
A glorious victory, and doth deserve
More than a chronicle; a temple, lords,
A temple, to the name of Ithocles. –
Where didst thou leave him, Prophilus?
PROPHILUS. At Pephnon,
Most gracious sovereign. Twenty of the noblest
Of the Messenians there attend your pleasure
For such conditions as you shall propose,
In settling peace, and liberty of life.
AMYCLAS. When comes your friend the general?
PROPHILUS. He promis'd
To follow with all speed convenient.

Enter CROTOLON, CALANTHA, CHRYSTALLA, PHILEMA, *and* EUPHRANIA.

AMYCLAS. Our daughter! – Dear Calantha, the happy news,
The conquest of Messene, hath already
Enrich'd thy knowledge.
CALANTHA. With the circumstance
And manner of the fight, related faithfully
By Prophilus himself. But pray, sir, tell me,
How doth the youthful general demean
His actions in these fortunes?
PROPHILUS. Excellent princess,

---

7 *gay . . . locks*: Apollo had long golden hair.
13 *Laconia*: see Additional Notes, p. 348.
20 *Pephnon*: a town on the border between Sparta and Messenia. See Textual Notes, p. 339.
32 *demean*: conduct.

Your own fair eyes may soon report a truth
Unto your judgement, with what moderation,
Calmness of nature, measure, bounds and limits
Of thankfulness and joy, he doth digest
Such amplitude of his success as would
In others, moulded of a spirit less clear,
Advance 'em to comparison with heaven.
But Ithocles –

CALANTHA. Your friend –

PROPHILUS. He is so, madam,
In which the period of my fate consists.
He in this firmament of honour stands
Like a star fix'd, not mov'd with any thunder
Of popular applause, or sudden lightning
Of self-opinion. He hath serv'd his country,
And thinks 'twas but his duty.

CROTOLON. You describe
A miracle of man.

AMYCLAS. Such, Crotolon,
On forfeit of a king's word, thou wilt find
him. – [*Flourish.*]
Hark, warning of his coming! All attend him.

Enter ITHOCLES, LEMOPHIL, *and* GRONEAS; *and rest of the Lords ushering him in.*

AMYCLAS. Return into these arms, thy home, thy sanctuary,
Delight of Sparta, treasure of my bosom,
Mine own, own Ithocles!

ITHOCLES. Your humblest subject.

ARMOSTES. Proud of the blood I claim an interest in
As brother to thy mother, I embrace thee,
Right noble nephew.

ITHOCLES. Sir, your love's too partial.

CROTOLON. Our country speaks by me, who by thy valour,
Wisdom, and service, shares in this great action;

---

37 See Textual Notes, p. 339.
42 *period*: highest point.

Returning thee, in part of thy due merits,
A general welcome.
ITHOCLES. You exceed in bounty.
CALANTHA. Chrystalla, Philema, the chaplet! – Ithocles,
Upon the wings of fame the singular
And chosen fortune of an high attempt
Is borne so past the view of common sight
That I myself, with mine own hands, have wrought
To crown thy temples this provincial garland.
Accept, wear, and enjoy it, as our gift
Deserv'd, not purchas'd.
ITHOCLES. You're a royal maid.
AMYCLAS. She is in all our daughter.
ITHOCLES. Let me blush,
Acknowledging how poorly I have serv'd,
What nothings I have done, compar'd with th'honours
Heap'd on the issue of a willing mind.
In that lay mine ability, that only.
For who is he so sluggish from his birth,
So little worthy of a name, or country,
That owes not, out of gratitude for life,
A debt of service, in what kind soever
Safety or counsel of the commonwealth
Requires for payment?
CALANTHA. He speaks truth.
ITHOCLES. Whom heaven
Is pleas'd to style victorious, there, to such,
Applause runs madding, like the drunken priests
In Bacchus' sacrifices, without reason
Voicing the leader-on a demigod;
Whenas, indeed, each common soldier's blood

---

59 *in part*: in part payment.
61 *chaplet*: victor's garland; later described as *provincial* (66), that is, one intended to honour the acquisition by conquest of a new province.
72 *issue*: outcome.
73 *that*: i.e. a willing mind.
80 *style*: name.
82 See Textual Notes, p. 339.
83 *leader-on*: leading priest (coryphaeus) in the orgiastic rites of Bacchus (Dionysus).

Drops down as current coin in that hard
purchase
As his whose much more delicate condition
Hath suck'd the milk of ease. Judgement
commands,
But resolution executes. I use not,
Before this royal presence, these fit slights
As in contempt of such as can direct.
My speech hath other end: not to attribute
All praise to one man's fortune, which is
strength'd
By many hands. For instance, here is Prophilus,
A gentleman (I cannot flatter truth)
Of much desert; and, though in other rank,
Both Lemophil and Groneas were not missing
To wish their country's peace. For, in a word,
All there did strive their best, and 'twas our
duty.

AMYCLAS. Courtiers turn soldiers? We vouchsafe
our hand.
[LEMOPHIL *and* GRONEAS *kiss his hand.*]
Observe your great example.

LEMOPHIL. With all diligence.

GRONEAS. Obsequiously and hourly.

AMYCLAS. Some repose
After these toils are needful. We must think on
Conditions for the conquer'd; they expect 'em.
On! – Come, my Ithocles.

EUPHRANIA. [*to* PROPHILUS] Sir, with your
favour,
I need not a supporter.

PROPHILUS. Fate instructs me.

Exeunt all but LEMOPHIL, GRONEAS, CHRYSTALLA, *and* PHILEMA. LEMOPHIL *stays* CHRYSTALLA; GRONEAS, PHILEMA.

CHRYSTALLA. With me?

PHILEMA. Indeed I dare not stay.

---

89 *slights*: self-deprecations. See Textual Notes, p. 339.
92 *strength'd*: lent strength.
100 *Observe*: attend on.
103 *expect*: await.
105 *I . . . supporter*: Euphrania rejects Prophilus's offer of his arm to lead her off.

LEMOPHIL. Sweet lady,
Soldiers are blunt. – Your lip.
[*Kisses* CHRYSTALLA.]
CHRYSTALLA. Fie, this is rudeness!
You went not hence such creatures.
GRONEAS. Spirit of valour
Is of a mounting nature. [*Kisses* PHILEMA.]
PHILEMA. It appears so!
Pray, in earnest, how many men apiece
Have you two been the death of?
GRONEAS. Faith, not many;
We were compos'd of mercy.
LEMOPHIL. For our daring,
You heard the general's approbation
Before the king.
CHRYSTALLA. You wish'd your country's peace;
That show'd your charity. Where are your spoils,
Such as the soldier fights for?
LEMOPHIL. They are coming.
CHRYSTALLA. By the next carrier, are they not?
GRONEAS. Sweet Philema,
When I was in the thickest of mine enemies,
Slashing off one man's head, another's nose,
Another's arms and legs –
PHILEMA. And all together –
GRONEAS. Then would I with a sigh remember thee,
And cry, 'Dear Philema, 'tis for thy sake
I do these deeds of wonder!' Dost not love me
With all thy heart now?
PHILEMA. Now as heretofore.
I have not put my love to use; the principal
Will hardly yield an interest.
GRONEAS. By Mars,
I'll marry thee!

---

108 See Textual Notes, p. 339.
109 *mounting*: (1) aspiring, (2) sexually active.
111 See Textual Notes, p. 339.
113 See Textual Notes, p. 339.
116 See Textual Notes, p. 339.
120 See Textual Notes, p. 339.
125 *to use*: (1) out to interest, (2) into practice.

PHILEMA. By Vulcan, you're forsworn,
Except my mind do alter strangely.
GRONEAS. One word.
CHRYSTALLA. [*to* LEMOPHIL] You lie beyond all modesty. Forbear me.
LEMOPHIL. I'll make thee mistress of a city; 'tis
Mine own by conquest.
CHRYSTALLA. By petition; sue for't
In forma pauperis. City? Kennel! Gallants,
Off with your feathers; put on aprons, gallants.
Learn to reel, thrum, or trim a lady's dog,
And be good quiet souls of peace, hobgoblins.
LEMOPHIL. Chrystalla!
CHRYSTALLA. Practise to drill hogs, in hope
To share in the acorns. Soldiers? Corn-cutters,
But not so valiant; they ofttimes draw blood,
Which you durst never do. When you have practis'd
More wit, or more civility, we'll rank ye
I'th'list of men. Till then, brave things-at-arms,
Dare not to speak to us. Most potent Groneas –
PHILEMA. And Lemophil the hardy – at your services.
Exeunt CHRYSTALLA *and* PHILEMA.
GRONEAS. They scorn us as they did before we went.
LEMOPHIL. Hang 'em; let us scorn them and be reveng'd.
GRONEAS. Shall we?
LEMOPHIL. We will; and when we slight them thus,

---

127 *Vulcan*: the blacksmith-god cuckolded by Mars, god of war.
132 *In forma pauperis*: as a pauper.
Kennel: a dog-house is all you will conquer.
133 *feathers*: worn as soldiers' ornaments. See Textual Notes, p. 339.
aprons: workmen's clothing.
134 *reel, thrum*: wind wool or thread, weave.
137 *Corn-cutters*: members of a despised branch of the barber-surgeons. There may be a play on the idea of soldiers as reapers, harvesters.
143 See Textual Notes, p. 339.
146 See Textual Notes, p. 339.

Instead of following them, they'll follow us.
It is a woman's nature.
GRONEAS. 'Tis a scurvy one.
Exeunt all.

SCENE III

Enter TECNICUS, *a philosopher, and* ORGILUS *disguised like a scholar of his.*

TECNICUS. Tempt not the stars, young man; thou canst not play
With the severity of fate. This change
Of habit, and disguise in outward view,
Hides not the secrets of thy soul within thee
From their quick-piercing eyes, which dive at all times
Down to thy thoughts. In thy aspect I note
A consequence of danger.
ORGILUS. Give me leave,
Grave Tecnicus, without foredooming destiny,
Under thy roof to ease my silent griefs,
By applying to my hidden wounds the balm
Of thy oraculous lectures. If my fortune
Run such a crooked byway as to wrest
My steps to ruin, yet thy learned precepts
Shall call me back, and set my footings straight.
I will not court the world.
TECNICUS. Ah, Orgilus,
Neglects in young men of delights, and life,
Run often to extremities. They care not
For harms to others who contemn their own.
ORGILUS. But I, most learned artist, am not so much
At odds with nature that I grutch the thrift

---

3 *habit*: dress, clothing.
5 *their*: i.e. the gods'.
7 *consequence*: augury.
8 *foredooming*: prejudging.
18 *contemn*: scorn, despise.
19 *artist*: scholar.
20 *grutch the thrift*: grudge the success.

Of any true deserver. Nor doth malice
Of present hopes so check them with despair
As that I yield to thought of more affliction
Than what is incident to frailty. Wherefore,
Impute not this retired course of living
Some little time to any other cause
Than what I justly render: the information
Of an unsettled mind, as the effect
Must clearly witness.

TECNICUS. Spirit of truth inspire thee!
On these conditions I conceal thy change,
And willingly admit thee for an auditor.
I'll to my study.

ORGILUS. I to contemplations
In these delightful walks. [*Exit* TECNICUS.]
– Thus metamorphos'd,
I may without suspicion hearken after
Penthea's usage and Euphrania's faith.
Love, thou art full of mystery! The deities
Themselves are not secure. In searching out
The secrets of those flames which, hidden, waste
A breast made tributary to the laws
Of beauty, physic yet hath never found
A remedy to cure a lover's wound.
Ha! Who are those that cross yon private walk
Into the shadowing grove, in amorous foldings?

PROPHILUS *passeth over, supporting* EUPHRANIA, *and whispering*.

My sister! O, my sister! 'Tis Euphrania
With Prophilus; supported too. I would
It were an apparition. Prophilus
Is Ithocles his friend. It strangely puzzles me.

---

21 *malice*: discouragement.
24 *frailty*: natural human imperfection.
27 *information*: disorder.
31 *auditor*: student.
34 *hearken after*: inquire into.
37 *secure*: immune from love. See Textual Notes, p. 339.
40 *physic*: medical science.
43 *foldings*: embraces; Euphrania has actually only taken Prophilus's arm, as the stage direction indicates.
43 s.d. *passeth over*: walks across the stage and exits on the other side.

Again? Help me, my book; this scholar's habit
Must stand my privilege. My mind is busy,
Mine eyes and ears are open. *Walks by, reading.*

Enter again PROPHILUS *and* EUPHRANIA.

PROPHILUS. Do not waste
The span of this stol'n time (lent by the gods
For precious use) in niceness! Bright Euphrania,
Should I repeat old vows, or study new,
For purchase of belief to my desires –
ORGILUS. [*aside*] Desires?
PROPHILUS. My service, my integrity –
ORGILUS. [*aside*] That's better.
PROPHILUS. I should but repeat a lesson
Oft conn'd without a prompter – but thine eyes.
My love is honourable –
ORGILUS. [*aside*] So was mine
To my Penthea; chastely honourable.
PROPHILUS. Nor wants there more addition to my wish
Of happiness than having thee a wife;
Already sure of Ithocles, a friend
Firm and unalterable.
ORGILUS. [*aside*] But a brother
More cruel than the grave.
EUPHRANIA. What can you look for,
In answer to your noble protestations,
From an unskilful maid, but language suited
To a divided mind?
ORGILUS. [*aside*] Hold out, Euphrania!
EUPHRANIA. Know, Prophilus, I never undervalu'd,
From the first time you mention'd worthy love,
Your merit, means, or person. It had been
A fault of judgement in me, and a dullness
In my affections, not to weigh and thank
My better stars, that offer'd me the grace
Of so much blissfulness. For, to speak truth,

49 *stand my privilege*: supply my right (to be here).
50 See Textual Notes, p. 339.
52 *niceness*: excessive coyness.
66 *unskilful*: inexperienced.

The law of my desires kept equal pace
With yours, nor have I left that resolution;
But only, in a word, whatever choice
Lives nearest in my heart must first procure
Consent both from my father, and my brother,
Ere he can own me his.

ORGILUS. [*aside*] She is forsworn else.

PROPHILUS. Leave me that task.

EUPHRANIA. My brother, ere he parted
To Athens, had my oath.

ORGILUS. [*aside*] Yes, yes, he had sure.

PROPHILUS. I doubt not, with the means the court supplies,
But to prevail at pleasure.

ORGILUS. [*aside*] Very likely.

PROPHILUS. Meantime, best, dearest, I may build my hopes
On the foundation of thy constant suff'rance
In any opposition.

EUPHRANIA. Death shall sooner
Divorce life and the joys I have in living,
Than my chaste vows from truth.

PROPHILUS. On thy fair hand
I seal the like.

ORGILUS. [*aside*] There is no faith in woman.
Passion, O, be contain'd! My very heartstrings
Are on the tenters.

EUPHRANIA. Sir, we are overheard.
Cupid protect us! 'Twas a stirring, sir,
Of someone near.

PROPHILUS. Your fears are needless, lady.
None have access into these private pleasures,
Except some near in court, or bosom student
From Tecnicus his oratory, granted
By special favour lately from the king

---

75 *law*: controlling power.
77 *choice*: chosen lover.
86–7 *constant . . . opposition*: steadfast endurance in the event of any opposition to our marriage.
90 *seal the like*: confirm a similar vow (with a kiss).
92 *tenters*: hooks used for stretching cloth. Orgilus means that he is almost heartbroken; cf. V.iii.75.
95 *pleasures*: pleasure-grounds.
97 *oratory*: school for studying the arts of expression.

Unto the grave philosopher.
EUPHRANIA. Methinks
I hear one talking to himself. I see him.
PROPHILUS. 'Tis a poor scholar, as I told you, lady.
ORGILUS. [*aside*] I am discover'd. – [*Aloud*] Say it. Is it possible
With a smooth tongue, a leering countenance,
Flattery, or force of reason – I come t'ye, sir –
To turn or to appease the raging sea?
Answer to that. Your art? What art to catch
And hold fast in a net the sun's small atoms?
No, no; they'll out, they'll out. Ye may as easily
Outrun a cloud driven by a northern blast
As fiddle faddle so. Peace, or speak sense.
EUPHRANIA. Call you this thing a scholar? 'Las, he's lunatic.
PROPHILUS. Observe him, sweet; 'tis but his recreation.
ORGILUS. But will you hear a little? You are so tetchy,
You keep no rule in argument. Philosophy
Works not upon impossibilities,
But natural conclusions. – Mew! – Absurd!
The metaphysics are but speculations
Of the celestial bodies, or such accidents
As, not mix'd perfectly, in the air engender'd,
Appear to us unnatural; that's all.
Prove it. Yet, with a reverence to your gravity,
I'll balk illiterate sauciness, submitting
My sole opinion to the touch of writers.
PROPHILUS. Now let us fall in with him.

---

100 See Additional Notes, p. 348.
103 *leering*: grimacing, grinning.
107 *atoms*: motes in a sunbeam.
110 *fiddle faddle*: trifle.
116 *Mew*: an expression of contempt.
118 *Of*: about.
accidents: technical term in Aristotelian philosophy for non-substances, lacking essential being.
119 *mix'd perfectly*: composed of the four humours in perfect balance.
122 *balk illiterate sauciness*: avoid unlearned arrogance.
123 *touch of writers*: test of written authority.

ORGILUS. Ha, ha, ha!
These apish boys, when they but taste the grammates
And principles of theory, imagine
They can oppose their teachers. Confidence
Leads many into errors.
PROPHILUS. By your leave, sir.
EUPHRANIA. Are you a scholar, friend?
ORGILUS. I am, gay creature,
With pardon of your deities, a mushroom
On whom the dew of heaven drops now and then.
The sun shines on me too, I thank his beams.
Sometime I feel their warmth, and eat, and sleep.
PROPHILUS. Does Tecnicus read to thee?
ORGILUS. Yes, forsooth,
He is my master surely. Yonder door
Opens upon his study.
PROPHILUS. Happy creatures!
Such people toil not, sweet, in heats of state,
Nor sink in thaws of greatness. Their affections
Keep order with the limits of their modesty.
Their love is love of virtue. – What's thy name?
ORGILUS. Aplotes, sumptuous master; a poor wretch.
EUPHRANIA. Dost thou want anything?
ORGILUS. Books, Venus, books.
PROPHILUS. Lady, a new conceit comes in my thought,
And most available for both our comforts.
EUPHRANIA. My lord?
PROPHILUS. Whiles I endeavour to deserve
Your father's blessing to our loves, this scholar

---

125 *taste the grammates*: acquire the rudiments.
134 *read*: instruct through lectures.
137 *state*: matters of state.
138–9 *affections . . . modesty*: desires remain within the bounds set by their moderation.
141 *sumptuous*: richly dressed, and therefore wealthy. Aplotes plays on the meaning of his own name, 'Simplicity'.
143 *conceit*: idea.
144 *available*: helpful.

May daily at some certain hours attend
What notice I can write of my success,
Here in this grove, and give it to your hands.
The like from you to me. So can we never,
Barr'd of our mutual speech, want sure intelligence;
And thus our hearts may talk when our tongues cannot.

EUPHRANIA. Occasion is most favourable; use it.

PROPHILUS. Aplotes, wilt thou wait us twice a day,
At nine i'th'morning, and at four at night,
Here in this bower, to convey such letters
As each shall send to other? Do it willingly,
Safely, and secretly, and I will furnish
Thy study, or what else thou canst desire.

ORGILUS. Jove, make me thankful, thankful, I beseech thee,
Propitious Jove! I will prove sure and trusty.
You will not fail me books?

PROPHILUS. Nor aught besides
Thy heart can wish. This lady's name's Euphrania;
Mine Prophilus.

ORGILUS. I have a pretty memory;
It must prove my best friend. I will not miss
One minute of the hours appointed.

PROPHILUS. Write
The books thou wouldst have bought thee in a note,
Or take thyself some money.

ORGILUS. No, no money.
Money to scholars is a spirit invisible;
We dare not finger it. Or books, or nothing.

PROPHILUS. Books of what sort thou wilt. Do not forget
Our names.

---

147 *attend*: wait for.
151 *want sure intelligence*: lack reliable information.
162 *fail me books*: fail to provide me with books.
164 *pretty*: fine.

ORGILUS. I warrant ye, I warrant ye.
PROPHILUS. Smile, Hymen, on the growth of our desires;
We'll feed thy torches with eternal fires.
Exeunt [EUPHRANIA *and* PROPHILUS].
ORGILUS. Put out thy torches, Hymen, or their light
Shall meet a darkness of eternal night.
Inspire me, Mercury, with swift deceits;
Ingenious fate has leapt into mine arms,
Beyond the compass of my brain. Mortality
Creeps on the dung of earth, and cannot reach
The riddles which are purpos'd by the gods.
Great acts best write themselves in their own stories.
They die too basely who outlive their glories.
Exit.

ACT II

SCENE I

Enter BASSANES *and* PHULAS.

BASSANES. I'll have that window next the street damm'd up;
It gives too full a prospect to temptation,
And courts a gazer's glances. There's a lust
Committed by the eye, that sweats and travails,

173–4 *Smile . . . fires*: Hymen, god of marriage, was usually represented as carrying a lighted torch symbolising the establishment of a new family.
177 *Mercury*: the god associated with cunning tricks.
180 *reach*: plumb.
182 See Textual Notes, p. 339.
1 *damm'd*: blocked.
4 *sweats*: toils; but sweating was also associated with sexual desire and activity, and with jealousy (cf. II.i.127).

Plots, wakes, contrives, till the deform'd bear-whelp,
Adultery, be lick'd into the act,
The very act. That light shall be damm'd up.
D'ye hear, sir?
PHULAS. I do hear, my lord; a mason
Shall be provided suddenly.
BASSANES. Some rogue,
Some rogue of your confederacy – factor
For slaves and strumpets – to convey close packets
From this spruce springal, and the tother youngster;
That gaudy earwig, or my lord your patron,
Whose pensioner you are. I'll tear thy throat out,
Son of a cat, ill-looking hound's-head; rip up
Thy ulcerous maw, if I but scent a paper,
A scroll, but half as big as what can cover
A wart upon thy nose, a spot, a pimple,
Directed to my lady. It may prove
A mystical preparative to lewdness.
PHULAS. Care shall be had. I will turn every thread
About me to an eye. – [*Aside*] Here's a sweet life!
BASSANES. The city housewives, cunning in the traffic

5–6 *deform'd . . . act*: there was an ancient belief, derived from the Roman writer Pliny, that mother bears licked the bodies of their cubs, unformed at birth, into shape.
7 *light*: window.
9 *suddenly*: at once.
10 *factor*: agent, pander.
11 *close packets*: secret letters.
12 *springal*: youth.
tother: other.
13 *earwig*: flatterer; as the Quarto form *Eare-wrig* suggests, the insects were thought capable of wriggling into the brain through the ear.
14 *pensioner*: hired servant.
16 *maw*: stomach.
20 *mystical*: with a secret meaning.
21–2 See Additional Notes, p. 348.

Of chamber-merchandise, set all at price
By wholesale, yet they wipe their mouths and simper,
Cull, kiss, and cry 'sweetheart', and stroke the head
Which they have branch'd, and all is well again.
Dull clods of dirt, who dare not feel the rubs
Stuck on their foreheads!

PHULAS. 'Tis a villainous world;
One cannot hold his own in't.

BASSANES. Dames at court,
Who flaunt in riots, run another bias.
Their pleasure heaves the patient ass that suffers
Up on the stilts of office, titles, incomes.
Promotion justifies the shame, and sues for't.
Poor honour! Thou art stabb'd, and bleed'st to death
By such unlawful hire. The country mistress
Is yet more wary, and in blushes hides
Whatever trespass draws her troth to guilt.
But all are false. On this truth I am bold:
No woman but can fall, and doth, or would.
Now for the newest news about the city;
What blab the voices, sirrah?

PHULAS. O my lord,
The rarest, quaintest, strangest, tickling news
That ever –

BASSANES. Heyday! Up and ride me, rascal!
What is't?

---

24 *chamber-merchandise*: bedroom-goods.
26 *Cull*: embrace.
27 *branch'd*: furnished with cuckold's horns.
28 *rubs*: (1) impediments, unevennesses (a bowling term), (2) reproofs.
29 See Textual Notes, p. 339.
31 *riots*: extravagant living.
bias: crooked course (another bowling term).
32 *ass that suffers*: foolish husband who allows it.
36 *unlawful hire*: (1) prostitution of the wife to gain the husband's advancement, (2) hired assassin.
38 *troth*: plighted marriage vow; with a play on 'truth' (honesty) caught up in the following line.
39 *bold*: confident.
44 *Up and ride me*: an expression of impatience; Bassanes wants Phulas to 'get on' with his news.

PHULAS. Forsooth, they say, the king has mew'd
All his grey beard instead of which is budded
Another of a pure carnation colour,
Speckled with green and russet.
BASSANES. Ignorant block!
PHULAS. Yes, truly, and 'tis talk'd about the streets
That since Lord Ithocles came home the lions
Never left roaring, at which noise the bears
Have danc'd their very hearts out.
BASSANES. Dance out thine too.
PHULAS. Besides, Lord Orgilus is fled to Athens
Upon a fiery dragon, and 'tis thought
He never can return.
BASSANES. Grant it, Apollo!
PHULAS. Moreover, please your lordship, 'tis reported
For certain that whoever is found jealous
Without apparent proof that's wife is wanton
Shall be divorc'd. But this is but she-news;
I had it from a midwife. I have more yet.
BASSANES. Antic, no more! Idiots and stupid fools
Grate my calamities. Why, to be fair
Should yield presumption of a faulty soul!
Look to the doors.
PHULAS. [*aside*] The horn of plenty crest him.
Exit PHULAS.
BASSANES. Swarms of confusion huddle in my thoughts
In rare distemper. Beauty! O, it is
An unmatch'd blessing, or a horrid curse.

Enter PENTHEA *and* GRAUSIS, *an old lady.*

---

45 *mew'd*: shed (used of a bird moulting).
47 *carnation*: pink.
50–2 See Additional Notes, p. 348.
53–4 *fled . . . dragon*: perhaps suggested by Medea's flight to Athens in a chariot drawn by winged dragons.
61 *Antic*: clown.
62 *Grate*: exacerbate.
62–3 See Textual Notes, p. 339, and Additional Notes, p. 348.
64 *horn . . . him*: may he be frequently cuckolded; with a reference to the cornucopia, or horn of plenty.

She comes, she comes! So shoots the morning forth,
Spangled with pearls of transparent dew.
The way to poverty is to be rich;
As I in her am wealthy, but for her
In all contents a bankrupt. – Lov'd Penthea,
How fares my heart's best joy?
GRAUSIS. In sooth not well,
She is so oversad.
BASSANES. Leave chattering, magpie. –
Thy brother is return'd, sweet, safe, and honour'd
With a triumphant victory. Thou shalt visit him.
We will to court, where, if it be thy pleasure,
Thou shalt appear in such a ravishing lustre
Of jewels above value, that the dames
Who brave it there, in rage to be outshin'd,
Shall hide them in their closets, and unseen
Fret in their tears; whiles every wond'ring eye
Shall crave none other brightness but thy presence.
Choose thine own recreations. Be a queen
Of what delights thou fanciest best; what company,
What place, what times. Do anything, do all things
Youth can command; so thou wilt chase these clouds
From the pure firmament of thy fair looks.
GRAUSIS. Now 'tis well said, my lord. – What, lady? Laugh,
Be merry. Time is precious.
BASSANES. [*aside*] Furies whip thee!
PENTHEA. Alas, my lord, this language to your handmaid
Sounds as would music to the deaf. I need

---

69 *pearls*: two syllables, derived from the author's west-country pronunciation.
72 *contents*: contentments.
80 *brave it*: flaunt themselves.
90 *Furies whip thee*: in Roman mythology, the three Furies punished wrongdoers with whips of snakes or scorpions.

No braveries nor cost of art to draw
The whiteness of my name into offence.
Let such, if any such there are, who covet
A curiosity of admiration,
By laying out their plenty to full view,
Appear in gaudy outsides. My attires
Shall suit the inward fashion of my mind;
From which, if your opinion, nobly plac'd,
Change not the livery your words bestow,
My fortunes with my hopes are at the highest.

BASSANES. This house, methinks, stands somewhat too much inward.
It is too melancholy. We'll remove
Nearer the court. Or what thinks my Penthea
Of the delightful island we command?
Rule me as thou canst wish.

PENTHEA. I am no mistress.
Whither you please, I must attend; all ways
Are alike pleasant to me.

GRAUSIS. Island? Prison!
A prison is as gaysome. We'll no islands.
Marry, out upon 'em! Whom shall we see there?
Seagulls, and porpoises, and water rats,
And crabs, and mews, and dogfish? Goodly gear
For a young lady's dealing, or an old one's.
On no terms islands; I'll be stew'd first!

BASSANES. [*aside to* GRAUSIS] Grausis,
You are a juggling bawd. – This sadness, sweetest,
Becomes not youthful blood. – [*Aside to* GRAUSIS] I'll have you pounded. –
For my sake put on a more cheerful mirth.
Thou'lt mar thy cheeks, and make me old in griefs. –
[*Aside to* GRAUSIS] Damnable bitch-fox!

GRAUSIS. I am thick of hearing

---

93 *braveries*: finery.
101 *livery*: servant's uniform and badge of service. Penthea plays on ideas of rich clothing and acceptance of her faithful and wifely service.
113 *mews*: gulls.
115 *stew'd*: sent to a brothel.
116 *juggling*: cheating.
117 *pounded*: shut up, impounded (like an animal).

Still when the wind blows southerly. What think ye
If your fresh lady breed young bones, my lord?
Would not a chopping boy d'ye good at heart?
But as you said –

BASSANES. [*aside to* GRAUSIS] I'll spit thee on a stake,
Or chop thee into collops.

GRAUSIS. Pray speak louder.
Sure, sure, the wind blows south still.

PENTHEA. Thou prat'st madly.

BASSANES. 'Tis very hot; I sweat extremely.

Enter PHULAS.

– Now?

PHULAS. A herd of lords, sir.

BASSANES. Ha?

PHULAS. A flock of ladies.

BASSANES. Where?

PHULAS. Shoals of horses.

BASSANES. Peasant, how?

PHULAS. Caroches
In drifts. Th'one enter, th'other stand without, sir.
And now I vanish. *Exit* PHULAS.

Enter PROPHILUS, LEMOPHIL, GRONEAS, CHRYSTALLA, *and* PHILEMA.

PROPHILUS. Noble Bassanes!

BASSANES. Most welcome, Prophilus, ladies, gentlemen;
To all my heart is open. You all honour me, –
[*Aside*] A tympany swells in my head already –

---

121 *Still*: always; the normal meaning of this word in this and the following texts.
123 *chopping*: healthy.
125 *collops*: slices of meat.
127 See Textual Notes, p. 339.
129 *Caroches*: luxurious coaches.
130 *drifts*: droves (like cattle).
134 *tympany*: tumour; Bassanes can feel the cuckold's horn growing.

Honour me bountifully. – [*Aside*] How they flutter,
Wagtails and jays together!
PROPHILUS. From your brother,
By virtue of your love to him, I require
Your instant presence, fairest.
PENTHEA. He is well, sir?
PROPHILUS. The gods preserve him ever. Yet, dear beauty,
I find some alteration in him lately,
Since his return to Sparta. – My good lord,
I pray use no delay.
BASSANES. We had not needed
An invitation if his sister's health
Had not fallen into question. – Haste, Penthea,
Slack not a minute. – Lead the way, good Prophilus;
I'll follow step by step.
PROPHILUS. Your arm, fair madam.
Exeunt all but BASSANES *and* GRAUSIS.

BASSANES. One word with your old bawdship. Th'hadst been better
Rail'd at the sins thou worshipp'st than have thwarted
My will. I'll use thee cursedly.
GRAUSIS. You dote,
You are beside yourself. A politician
In jealousy? No, you're too gross, too vulgar.
Pish, teach not me my trade; I know my cue.
My crossing you sinks me into her trust,
By which I shall know all. My trade's a sure one.
BASSANES. Forgive me, Grausis; 'twas consideration
I relish'd not. But have a care now.
GRAUSIS. Fear not;

---

136 *Wagtails and jays*: bird names applied to licentious and chattering women.
149 *cursedly*: cruelly.
150 *politician*: cunning schemer.
156 *relish'd not*: did not appreciate.

I am no new-come-to't.
BASSANES. Thy life's upon it,
And so is mine. My agonies are infinite.
Exeunt all.

SCENE II

Enter ITHOCLES, *alone.*

ITHOCLES. Ambition! 'Tis of viper's breed; it gnaws
A passage through the womb that gave it motion.
Ambition, like a seeled dove, mounts upward,
Higher and higher still, to perch on clouds,
But tumbles headlong down with heavier ruin.
So squibs and crackers fly into the air;
Then, only breaking with a noise, they vanish
In stench and smoke. Morality applied
To timely practice keeps the soul in tune,
At whose sweet music all our actions dance.
But this is form of books and school tradition;
It physics not the sickness of a mind
Broken with griefs. Strong fevers are not eas'd
With counsel, but with best receipts and means.
Means, speedy means and certain; that's the cure.

Enter ARMOSTES *and* CROTOLON.

ARMOSTES. You stick, Lord Crotolon, upon a point
Too nice, and too unnecessary. Prophilus
Is every way desertful. I am confident
Your wisdom is too ripe to need instruction

1–2 *'Tis . . . motion*: young vipers were thought to eat their way out of their mother at birth.
3–5 See Additional Notes, p. 348.
7 *only . . . noise*: exploding with a mere bang.
9 *timely*: (1) keeping correct time, (2) opportune.
11 *form of books*: textbook behaviour.
school tradition: scholastic philosophy.
14 *receipts*: prescriptions.
17 *nice*: over-subtle.

From your son's tutelage.
CROTOLON. Yet not so ripe,
My Lord Armostes, that it dares to dote
Upon the painted meat of smooth persuasion
Which tempts me to a breach of faith.
ITHOCLES. Not yet
Resolv'd, my lord? Why, if your son's consent
Be so available, we'll write to Athens
For his repair to Sparta. The king's hand
Will join with our desires; he has been mov'd to't.
ARMOSTES. Yes, and the king himself importun'd Crotolon
For a dispatch.
CROTOLON. Kings may command; their wills
Are laws not to be question'd.
ITHOCLES. By this marriage
You knit an union so devout, so hearty,
Between your loves to me, and mine to yours,
As if mine own blood had an interest in it;
For Prophilus is mine, and I am his.
CROTOLON. My lord, my lord!
ITHOCLES. What, good sir? Speak your thought.
CROTOLON. Had this sincerity been real once,
My Orgilus had not been now unwiv'd,
Nor your lost sister buried in a bride-bed.
Your uncle here, Armostes, knows this truth,
For had your father Thrasus liv'd – but peace
Dwell in his grave. I have done.
ARMOSTES. You're bold and bitter.
ITHOCLES. [*aside*] He presses home the injury; it smarts. –
No reprehensions, uncle; I deserve 'em.
Yet, gentle sir, consider what the heat
Of an unsteady youth, a giddy brain,
Green indiscretion, flattery of greatness,
Rawness of judgement, wilfulness in folly,
Thoughts vagrant as the wind, and as uncertain,

---

22 *painted meat*: false food; Ford may be thinking of the thick cosmetic colouring worn by fashionable women.
25 *available*: capable of producing the desired result.
26 *repair*: return.

Might lead a boy in years to. 'Twas a fault,
A capital fault, for then I could not dive
Into the secrets of commanding love;
Since when, experience by the extremities – in others –
Hath forc'd me to collect. And trust me, Crotolon,
I will redeem those wrongs with any service
Your satisfaction can require for current.

ARMOSTES. Thy acknowledgement is satisfaction. –
What would you more?

CROTOLON. I'm conquer'd. If Euphrania
Herself admit the motion, let it be so.
I doubt not my son's liking.

ITHOCLES. Use my fortunes,
Life, power, sword, and heart; all are your own.

Enter BASSANES, PROPHILUS, CALANTHA, PENTHEA, EUPHRANIA, CHRYSTALLA, PHILEMA, *and* GRAUSIS.

ARMOSTES. The princess, with your sister.

CALANTHA. I present ye
A stranger here in court, my lord, for did not
Desire of seeing you draw her abroad,
We had not been made happy in her company.

ITHOCLES. You are a gracious princess. – Sister, wedlock
Holds too severe a passion in your nature,
Which can engross all duty to your husband
Without attendance on so dear a mistress. –
'Tis not my brother's pleasure, I presume,
T'immure her in a chamber.

BASSANES. 'Tis her will;
She governs her own hours. Noble Ithocles,

---

50 *capital*: deadly.
53 *collect*: draw (more correct) conclusions.
55 *for current*: as valid, acceptable (metaphor from coinage).
58 *admit the motion*: accept the proposal.
64 See Textual Notes, p. 339.
68 *mistress*: i.e. Calantha.
69 *brother's*: brother-in-law's.

We thank the gods for your success and welfare.
Our lady has of late been indispos'd,
Else we had waited on you with the first.
ITHOCLES. How does Penthea now?
PENTHEA. You best know, brother,
From whom my health and comforts are deriv'd.
BASSANES. [*aside*] I like the answer well; 'tis sad and modest.
There may be tricks yet, tricks. – Have an eye, Grausis.
CALANTHA. Now, Crotolon, the suit we join'd in must not
Fall by too long demur.
CROTOLON. 'Tis granted, princess,
For my part.
ARMOSTES. With condition, that his son
Favour the contract.
CALANTHA. Such delay is easy. –
The joys of marriage make thee, Prophilus,
A proud deserver of Euphrania's love,
And her of thy desert.
PROPHILUS. Most sweetly gracious!
BASSANES. The joys of marriage are the heaven on earth,
Life's paradise, great princess, the soul's quiet,
Sinews of concord, earthly immortality,
Eternity of pleasures; no restoratives
Like to a constant woman. – [*Aside*] But where is she?
'Twould puzzle all the gods but to create
Such a new monster. – I can speak by proof,
For I rest in Elysium; 'tis my happiness.
CROTOLON. Euphrania, how are you resolv'd – speak freely –
In your affections to this gentleman?
EUPHRANIA. Nor more nor less than as his love assures me,
Which (if your liking, with my brother's, warrants)
I cannot but approve in all points worthy.

---

77 *sad*: sober, serious.
93 *Elysium*: the paradise of marriage.
97 *warrants*: sanctions.

CROTOLON. So, so. – [*To* PROPHILUS] I know your answer.
ITHOCLES. 'T had been pity
To sunder hearts so equally consented.

Enter LEMOPHIL.

LEMOPHIL. The king, Lord Ithocles, commands your presence;
And, fairest princess, yours.
CALANTHA. We will attend him.

Enter GRONEAS.

GRONEAS. Where are the lords? All must unto the king
Without delay. The Prince of Argos –
CALANTHA. Well, sir?
GRONEAS. Is coming to the court, sweet lady.
CALANTHA. How!
The Prince of Argos?
GRONEAS. 'Twas my fortune, madam,
T'enjoy the honour of these happy tidings.
ITHOCLES. Penthea.
PENTHEA. Brother?
ITHOCLES. Let me an hour hence
Meet you alone, within the palace grove.
I have some secret with you. – [*To* PROPHILUS] Prithee, friend,
Conduct her thither, and have special care
The walks be clear'd of any to disturb us.
PROPHILUS. I shall.
BASSANES. [*aside*] How's that?
ITHOCLES. Alone, pray be alone. –
I am your creature, princess. – On, my lords!
Exeunt [*all but* BASSANES].
BASSANES. Alone, alone? What means that word 'alone'?
Why might not I be there? Hum! He's her brother;
Brothers and sisters are but flesh and blood,
And this same whoreson court-ease is temptation

100 *equally consented*: mutual in feeling.
104 *Argos*: a Peleponnesian city-state north-east of Sparta.

To a rebellion in the veins. Besides,
His fine friend Prophilus must be her guardian.
Why may not he dispatch a business nimbly
Before the other come? Or, pand'ring; pand'ring
For one another? Be't to sister, mother,
Wife, cousin, anything, 'mongst youths of
mettle,
Is in request. It is so. Stubborn fate.
But if I be a cuckold, and can know it,
I will be fell, and fell.

Enter GRONEAS.

GRONEAS. My lord, you're call'd for.
BASSANES. Most heartily I thank ye. Where's my
wife, pray?
GRONEAS. Retir'd amongst the ladies.
BASSANES. Still I thank ye.
There's an old waiter with her; saw you her too?
GRONEAS. She sits i'th'presence lobby fast asleep,
sir.
BASSANES. Asleep? Sleep, sir?
GRONEAS. Is your lordship troubled?
You will not to the king?
BASSANES. Your humblest vassal.
GRONEAS. Your servant, my good lord.
BASSANES. I wait your footsteps.
Exeunt.

SCENE III

[*Enter*] PROPHILUS, PENTHEA.

PROPHILUS. In this walk, lady, will your brother
find you.
And with your favour, give me leave a little
To work a preparation. In his fashion

---

126 *know*: be sure of.
127 *fell*: ruthless, cruel.
130 *waiter*: attendant.
131 *presence lobby*: anteroom of a reception chamber.
134 *wait*: follow.
3 *fashion*: mode of conduct.

I have observ'd of late some kind of slackness
To such alacrity as nature once
And custom took delight in. Sadness grows
Upon his recreations, which he hoards
In such a willing silence that to question
The grounds will argue little skill in friendship,
And less good manners.
PENTHEA. Sir, I'm not inquisitive
Of secrecies without an invitation.
PROPHILUS. With pardon, lady, not a syllable
Of mine implies so rude a sense. The drift –

Enter ORGILUS [*disguised as before*].

Do thy best
To make this lady merry for an hour.
ORGILUS. Your will shall be a law, sir.
Exit [PROPHILUS].
PENTHEA. Prithee leave me;
I have some private thoughts I would account with.
Use thou thine own.
ORGILUS. Speak on, fair nymph. Our souls
Can dance as well to music of the spheres
As any's who have feasted with the gods.
PENTHEA. Your school terms are too troublesome.
ORGILUS. What heaven
Refines mortality from dross of earth
But such as uncompounded beauty hallows
With glorified perfection?

---

5 See Textual Notes, p. 339.
8 *willing*: deliberate, obstinate.
9 See Textual Notes, p. 339.
14–16 *Do . . .* PROPHILUS: Prophilus's instruction to Orgilus and his own departure are so abrupt that they suggest a loss at this point.
16 See Textual Notes, p. 339.
17 *account*: occupy myself.
19 *music of the spheres*: see the Additional Note to *'Tis Pity She's a Whore*, II.v.55–6.
21 *school terms*: scholastic jargon.
21–4 *What . . . perfection*: whatever divine power works to purify human nature must sanctify such unalloyed beauty (as yours) with the glory belonging to perfection.
23 *uncompounded*: pure, therefore perfect.

PENTHEA. Set thy wits
In a less wild proportion.
ORGILUS. Time can never
On the white table of unguilty faith
Write counterfeit dishonour. Turn those eyes,
The arrows of pure love, upon that fire
Which once rose to a flame, perfum'd with vows
As sweetly scented as the incense smoking
On Vesta's altars; virgin tears, like
The holiest odours, sprinkled dews to feed 'em
And to increase their fervour.
PENTHEA. Be not frantic.
ORGILUS. All pleasures are but mere imagination,
Feeding the hungry appetite with steam
And sight of banquet, whilst the body pines,
Not relishing the real taste of food.
Such is the leanness of a heart divided
From intercourse of troth-contracted loves.
No horror should deface that precious figure
Seal'd with the lively stamp of equal souls.
PENTHEA. Away! Some Fury hath bewitch'd thy tongue.
The breath of ignorance that flies from thence
Ripens a knowledge in me of afflictions
Above all suff'rance. Thing of talk, be gone;
Be gone without reply.
ORGILUS. Be just, Penthea,
In thy commands. When thou send'st forth a doom
Of banishment, know first on whom it lights.
Thus I take off the shroud in which my cares
Are folded up from view of common eyes.
[*Throws off his disguise.*]
What is thy sentence next?
PENTHEA. Rash man, thou layest
A blemish on mine honour, with the hazard
Of thy too desperate life. Yet I profess,

---

25 *proportion*: order.
26 *table*: writing tablet.
31, 32 See Textual Notes, p. 339.
34 *mere*: pure.
37 *relishing*: tasting.
40 *figure*: image.
41 *equal*: in full agreement (cf. II.ii.100).

By all the laws of ceremonious wedlock,
I have not given admittance to one thought
Of female change, since cruelty enforc'd
Divorce betwixt my body and my heart.
Why would you fall from goodness thus?
ORGILUS. O, rather
Examine me how I could live to say
I have been much, much wrong'd. 'Tis for thy sake
I put on this imposture. Dear Penthea,
If thy soft bosom be not turn'd to marble,
Thou'lt pity our calamities. My interest
Confirms me thou art mine still.
PENTHEA. Lend your hand.
With both of mine I clasp it thus, thus kiss it,
Thus kneel before ye. [*Kneels.*]
ORGILUS. You instruct my duty. [*Kneels.*]
PENTHEA. We may stand up. Have you aught else to urge
Of new demand? As for the old, forget it;
'Tis buried in an everlasting silence,
And shall be, shall be ever. What more would ye?
ORGILUS. I would possess my wife; the equity
Of very reason bids me.
PENTHEA. Is that all?
ORGILUS. Why 'tis the all of me myself.
PENTHEA. Remove
Your steps some distance from me. At this space
A few words I dare change. But first put on
Your borrow'd shape.
[ORGILUS *resumes his disguise.*]
ORGILUS. You are obey'd, 'tis done.
PENTHEA. How, Orgilus, by promise I was thine,
The heavens do witness; they can witness, too,
A rape done on my truth. How I do love thee

---

56 *female change*: feminine inconstancy.
63 *interest*: right, title; the marriage contract broken by Ithocles.
64 *Confirms*: assures.
71–2 *equity . . . reason*: natural justice based on reason itself.
75 *change*: exchange.
76 *shape*: costume (a theatrical term).
79 *truth*: fidelity in love.

Yet, Orgilus, and yet, must best appear
In tendering thy freedom; for I find
The constant preservation of thy merit
By thy not daring to attempt my fame
With injury of any loose conceit,
Which might give deeper wounds to discontents.
Continue this fair race; then, though I cannot
Add to thy comfort, yet I shall more often
Remember from what fortune I am fallen,
And pity mine own ruin. Live, live happy,
Happy in thy next choice, that thou mayst people
This barren age with virtues in thy issue.
And O, when thou art married, think on me
With mercy, not contempt. I hope thy wife,
Hearing my story, will not scorn my fall.
Now let us part.

ORGILUS. Part! Yet advise thee better.
Penthea is the wife to Orgilus,
And ever shall be.

PENTHEA. Never shall nor will.

ORGILUS. How!

PENTHEA. Hear me; in a word I'll tell thee why.
The virgin dowry which my birth bestow'd
Is ravish'd by another. My true love
Abhors to think that Orgilus deserv'd
No better favours than a second bed.

ORGILUS. I must not take this reason.

PENTHEA. To confirm it,
Should I outlive my bondage let me meet
Another worse than this, and less desir'd,
If of all the men alive thou shouldst but touch
My lip or hand again.

ORGILUS. Penthea, now
I tell ye you grow wanton in my sufferance.
Come sweet, th'art mine.

PENTHEA. Uncivil sir, forbear,

---

81 *tendering*: cherishing.
83–4 *attempt . . . conceit*: attack my honour by damaging it through some indecent proposal.
86 *race*: course of action.
108 *grow . . . sufferance*: begin to abuse my patience.

Or I can turn affection into vengeance.
Your reputation, if you value any,
Lies bleeding at my feet. Unworthy man,
If ever henceforth thou appear in language,
Message, or letter to betray my frailty,
I'll call thy former protestations lust,
And curse my stars for forfeit of my judgement.
Go thou, fit only for disguise and walks
To hide thy shame. This once I spare thy life.
I laugh at mine own confidence; my sorrows
By thee are made inferior to my fortunes.
If ever thou didst harbour worthy love,
Dare not to answer. My good genius guide me,
That I may never see thee more. Go from me!

ORGILUS. I'll tear my veil of politic frenzy off,
And stand up like a man resolv'd to do.
Action, not words, shall show me. O, Penthea!
Exit ORGILUS.

PENTHEA. He sigh'd my name, sure, as he parted from me;
I fear I was too rough. Alas, poor gentleman,
He look'd not like the ruins of his youth,
But like the ruins of those ruins. Honour,
How much we fight with weakness to preserve thee.

Enter BASSANES *and* GRAUSIS.

BASSANES. Fie on thee! Damn thee, rotten maggot, damn thee!
Sleep? Sleep at court? And now? Aches, convulsions,
Impostumes, rheums, gouts, palsies clog thy bones

---

117 *walks*: cf. II.ii.108–12 and II.iii.1.
120 *inferior to*: less wretched than.
122 *good genius*: guardian spirit.
124 *politic frenzy*: cunning pretence of madness; that is, Orgilus's pose as a scholar deranged by excessive learning. Cf. Bassanes' similar declaration at IV.ii.66; see also Textual Notes, p. 339.
133 *Aches*: two syllables; pronounced 'aitches'.
134 *Impostumes*: abscesses.

A dozen years more yet!
GRAUSIS. Now you're in humours.
BASSANES. She's by herself; there's hope of that. She's sad, too;
She's in strong contemplation. Yes, and fix'd.
The signs are wholesome.
GRAUSIS. Very wholesome, truly.
BASSANES. Hold your chops, nightmare! – Lady, come. Your brother
Is carried to his closet; you must thither.
PENTHEA. Not well, my lord?
BASSANES. A sudden fit, 'twill off;
Some surfeit or disorder. How dost, dearest?
PENTHEA. Your news is none o'th'best.

Enter PROPHILUS.

PROPHILUS. The chief of men,
The excellentest Ithocles, desires
Your presence, madam.
BASSANES. We are hasting to him.
PENTHEA. In vain we labour in this course of life
To piece our journey out at length, or crave
Respite of breath. Our home is in the grave.
BASSANES. Perfect philosophy. Then let us care
To live so that our reckonings may fall even
When we're to make account.
PROPHILUS. He cannot fear
Who builds on noble grounds. Sickness or pain
Is the deserver's exercise, and such
Your virtuous brother to the world is known.
Speak comfort to him, lady; be all gentle.
Stars fall but in the grossness of our sight;
A good man dying, th'earth doth lose a light.
Exeunt all.

---

135 *in humours*: in a bad mood.
137 *fix'd*: composed.
139 *chops*: jaws; modern 'tongue'.
140 *closet*: private room.
149–51 See Additional Notes, p. 348.
150 *fall even*: come out square.
153 *exercise*: testing-ground.
156–7 *Stars . . . light*: the contrast is between the brief attention given to the sight of a shooting star, and the major loss of 'light' noticed on the death of a good man.

ACT III

SCENE I

Enter TECNICUS, *and* ORGILUS *in his own shape.*

TECNICUS. Be well advis'd. Let not a resolution
Of giddy rashness choke the breath of reason.
ORGILUS. It shall not, most sage master.
TECNICUS. I am jealous.
For if the borrow'd shape so late put on
Inferr'd a consequence, we must conclude
Some violent design of sudden nature
Hath shook that shadow off, to fly upon
A new-hatch'd execution. Orgilus,
Take heed thou hast not, under our integrity,
Shrouded unlawful plots. Our mortal eyes
Pierce not the secrets of your heart; the gods
Are only privy to them.
ORGILUS. Learned Tecnicus,
Such doubts are causeless; and to clear the truth
From misconceit, the present state commands me.
The Prince of Argos comes himself in person
In quest of great Calantha for his bride,
Our kingdom's heir; besides, mine only sister,
Euphrania, is dispos'd to Prophilus.
Lastly, the king is sending letters for me

0 s.d. *shape*: clothing; Orgilus is no longer dressed as a student.
3 *jealous*: suspicious.
7 *shadow*: disguise.
8 *execution*: undertaking; the ironic sense of 'punishment' is also available.
11 See Textual Notes, p. 339.
12 *only*: alone.
14 *misconceit*: misunderstanding.
state: state business.
18 *dispos'd*: betrothed.

To Athens, for my quick repair to court.
Please to accept these reasons.
TECNICUS. Just ones, Orgilus,
Not to be contradicted. Yet beware
Of an unsure foundation; no fair colours
Can fortify a building faintly jointed.
I have observ'd a growth in thy aspect
Of dangerous extent, sudden, and (look to't)
I might add, certain –
ORGILUS. My aspect? Could art
Run through mine inmost thoughts, it should not sift
An inclination there, more than what suited
With justice, of mine honour.
TECNICUS. I believe it.
But know then, Orgilus, what honour is.
Honour consists not in a bare opinion
By doing any act that feeds content,
Brave in appearance 'cause we think it brave.
Such honour comes by accident, not nature;
Proceeding from the vices of our passion,
Which makes our reason drunk. But real honour
Is the reward of virtue, and acquir'd
By justice, or by valour which for basis
Hath justice to uphold it. He then fails
In honour who for lucre or revenge
Commits thefts, murders, treasons and adulteries,
With suchlike, by intrenching on just laws,
Whose sov'reignty is best preserv'd by justice.
Thus, as you see how honour must be grounded
On knowledge, not opinion – for opinion
Relies on probability and accident,
But knowledge on necessity and truth –
I leave thee to the fit consideration
Of what becomes the grace of real honour,

---

24 *faintly*: weakly.
27 *art*: professional knowledge.
33 *By*: derived from.
content: self-conceit.
35 See Textual Notes, p. 339.
39 See Textual Notes, p. 339.
40–50 See Additional Notes, p. 348.
41 *lucre*: monetary reward. See Textual Notes, p. 339.

Wishing success to all thy virtuous meanings.
ORGILUS. The gods increase thy wisdom, reverend oracle,
And in thy precepts make me ever thrifty.
TECNICUS. I thank thy wish. – *Exit* ORGILUS.
Much mystery of fate
Lies hid in that man's fortunes. Curiosity
May lead his actions into rare attempts.
But let the gods be moderators still;
No human power can prevent their will.

Enter ARMOSTES.

From whence come ye?
ARMOSTES. From King Amyclas. (Pardon
My interruption of your studies.) Here
In this seal'd box he sends a treasure dear
To him as his crown. He prays your gravity
You would examine, ponder, sift, and bolt
The pith and circumstance of every tittle
The scroll within contains.
TECNICUS. What is't, Armostes?
ARMOSTES. It is the health of Sparta, the king's life,
Sinews and safety of the commonwealth:
The sum of what the oracle deliver'd,
When last he visited the prophetic temple
At Delphos. What his reasons are, for which
After so long a silence he requires
Your counsel now, grave man, his majesty
Will soon himself acquaint you with.
TECNICUS. Apollo
Inspire my intellect! The Prince of Argos
Is entertain'd?

---

51 *meanings*: intentions.
53 *thrifty*: successful.
54 See Textual Notes, p. 340.
55 *Curiosity*: a spirit of intellectual inquiry.
57 *moderators*: arbiters.
58 *power*: two syllables.
prevent: anticipate and forestall.
63 *bolt*: sieve.
64 *circumstance*: incidental details.
70 *Delphos*: a common contemporary spelling of Delphi, site of the Delphic oracle on Mount Parnassus.
72 See Textual Notes, p. 340.
75 *entertain'd*: received as a guest.

ARMOSTES. He is, and has demanded
Our princess for his wife; which I conceive
One special cause the king importunes you
For resolution of the oracle.
TECNICUS. My duty to the king, good peace to Sparta,
And fair day to Armostes!
ARMOSTES. Like to Tecnicus!
Exeunt.

SCENE II

Soft Music. A song.

Can you paint a thought? or number
Every fancy in a slumber?
Can you count soft minutes roving
From a dial's point by moving?
Can you grasp a sigh? or lastly,
Rob a virgin's honour chastely?
No, O no! Yet you may
Sooner do both that and this,
This and that, and never miss,
Than by any praise display
Beauty's beauty; such a glory
As beyond all fate, all story,
All arms, all arts,
All loves, all hearts,
Greater than those or they,
Do, shall, and must obey.

During which time, enter PROPHILUS, BASSANES, PENTHEA, GRAUSIS, *passing over the stage.* BASSANES *and* GRAUSIS *enter again softly, stealing to several stands, and listen.*

---

78 *resolution*: interpretation.
16 s.d. *passing . . . stage*: see note to I.iii.43 s.d. *several stands*: separate positions.

BASSANES. All silent, calm, secure. – Grausis, no creaking?
No noise? Dost hear nothing?
GRAUSIS. Not a mouse,
Or whisper of the wind.
BASSANES. The floor is matted,
The bedposts, sure, are steel or marble. Soldiers
Should not affect, methinks, strains so effeminate;
Sounds of such delicacy are but fawnings
Upon the sloth of luxury. They heighten
Cinders of covert lust up to a flame.
GRAUSIS. What do you mean, my lord? Speak low. That gabbling
Of yours will but undo us.
BASSANES. Chamber-combats
Are felt, not heard.
PROPHILUS. [*within*] He wakes.
BASSANES. What's that?
ITHOCLES. [*within*] Who's there?
Sister? – All quit the room else!
BASSANES. 'Tis consented.

Enter PROPHILUS.

PROPHILUS. Lord Bassanes, your brother would be private;
We must forbear. His sleep hath newly left him.
Please ye withdraw?
BASSANES. By any means; 'tis fit.
PROPHILUS. Pray, gentlewoman, walk too.
GRAUSIS. Yes, I will, sir.
Exeunt [BASSANES, PROPHILUS, *and* GRAUSIS].

ITHOCLES *discovered in a chair, and* PENTHEA.

20–1 See Additional Notes, p. 348.
21 *affect*: like.
strains: melodies.
23 *luxury*: lechery.
26 *Chamber-combats*: amorous encounters in bedrooms.
29 *brother*: brother-in-law.
32 s.d. *discovered*: revealed. Probably done in Ford's theatre by drawing aside a curtain at the back of the stage.

ITHOCLES. Sit nearer, sister, to me; nearer yet.
We had one father, in one womb took life,
Were brought up twins together, yet have liv'd
At distance like two strangers. I could wish
That the first pillow whereon I was cradl'd
Had prov'd to me a grave.
PENTHEA. You had been happy.
Then had you never known that sin of life
Which blots all following glories with a vengeance
For forfeiting the last will of the dead,
From whom you had your being.
ITHOCLES. Sad Penthea,
Thou canst not be too cruel. My rash spleen
Hath with a violent hand pluck'd from thy bosom
A lover-bless'd heart, to grind it into dust,
For which mine's now a-breaking.
PENTHEA. Not yet, heaven,
I do beseech thee! First let some wild fires
Scorch, not consume it. May the heat be cherish'd
With desires infinite, but hopes impossible.
ITHOCLES. Wrong'd soul, thy prayers are heard.
PENTHEA. Here, lo, I breathe,
A miserable creature led to ruin
By an unnatural brother.
ITHOCLES. I consume
In languishing affections for that trespass,
Yet cannot die.
PENTHEA. The handmaid to the wages
Of country toil drinks the untroubl'd streams
With leaping kids and with the bleating lambs,
And so allays her thirst secure, whiles I
Quench my hot sighs with fleetings of my tears.
ITHOCLES. The labourer doth eat his coarsest bread,
Earn'd with his sweat, and lies him down to sleep,

---

53 *languishing affections*: emotions of grief.
55 See Textual Notes, p. 340.
57 *secure*: free from cares.
58 *fleetings*: downpourings.

Whiles every bit I touch turns in digestion
To gall, as bitter as Penthea's curse.
Put me to any penance for my tyranny,
And I will call thee merciful.
PENTHEA. Pray kill me;
Rid me from living with a jealous husband.
Then we will join in friendship, be again
Brother and sister. Kill me, pray. Nay, will ye?
ITHOCLES. How does thy lord esteem thee?
PENTHEA. Such an one
As only you have made me: a faith-breaker,
A spotted whore. Forgive me. I am one
In act, not in desires, the gods must witness.
ITHOCLES. Thou dost belie thy friend.
PENTHEA. I do not, Ithocles;
For she that's wife to Orgilus, and lives
In known adultery with Bassanes
Is at best a whore. Wilt kill me now?
The ashes of our parents will assume
Some dreadful figure and appear to charge
Thy bloody guilt, that hast betray'd their name
To infamy in this reproachful match.
ITHOCLES. After my victories abroad, at home
I meet despair; ingratitude of nature
Hath made my actions monstrous. Thou shalt
stand
A deity, my sister, and be worshipp'd
For thy resolved martyrdom. Wrong'd maids
And married wives shall to thy hallow'd shrine
Offer their orisons, and sacrifice
Pure turtles crown'd with myrtle, if thy pity
Unto a yielding brother's pressure lend
One finger but to ease it.
PENTHEA. O, no more!

---

61 See Textual Notes, p. 340.
71 *act*: (imposed) behaviour. See Textual Notes, p. 340.
72 *belie thy friend*: misrepresent me, your friend.
85 *wives*: women.
87 *turtles*: turtle-doves; emblems of faithful love.
88 *yielding brother's pressure*: brother succumbing to his afflictions.

ITHOCLES. Death waits to waft me to the Stygian banks,
And free me from this chaos of my bondage;
And till thou wilt forgive, I must endure.
PENTHEA. Who is the saint you serve?
ITHOCLES. Friendship, or nearness
Of birth to any but my sister, durst not
Have mov'd that question. 'Tis a secret, sister,
I dare not murmur to myself.
PENTHEA. Let me –
By your new protestations I conjure ye –
Partake her name.
ITHOCLES. Her name – 'tis – 'tis – I dare not.
PENTHEA. All your respects are forg'd.
ITHOCLES. They are not. – Peace!
Calantha is the princess; the king's daughter,
Sole heir of Sparta. Me most miserable!
Do I now love thee? For my injuries
Revenge thyself with bravery, and gossip
My treasons to the king's ears; do. Calantha
Knows it not yet, nor Prophilus my nearest.
PENTHEA. Suppose you were contracted to her, would it not
Split even your very soul to see her father
Snatch her out of your arms against her will,
And force her on the Prince of Argos?
ITHOCLES. Trouble not
The fountains of mine eyes with thine own story.
I sweat in blood for't.
PENTHEA. We are reconcil'd.
Alas, sir, being children, but two branches
Of one stock, 'tis not fit we should divide.
Have comfort; you may find it.

---

90 *Stygian banks*: the shores of the river Styx, crossed by the souls of the dead on their way to the land of shades.
93 *saint*: adored mistress. See Textual Notes, p. 340.
95 See Textual Notes, p. 340.
99 *respects*: considerations.
102 *my injuries*: the injuries I have done you.
104 *treasons*: to attempt to marry the heiress to the throne might be regarded as treasonable in a subject.

ITHOCLES. Yes, in thee.
Only in thee, Penthea mine.
PENTHEA. If sorrows
Have not too much dull'd my infected brain,
I'll cheer invention for an active strain.
ITHOCLES. Mad man! Why have I wrong'd a maid so excellent?

Enter BASSANES *with a poniard;* PROPHILUS, GRONEAS, LEMOPHIL, *and* GRAUSIS.

BASSANES. I can forbear no longer. More, I will not.
Keep off your hands, or fall upon my point.
Patience is tir'd, for like a slow-pac'd ass
Ye ride my easy nature, and proclaim
My sloth to vengeance a reproach and property.
ITHOCLES. The meaning of this rudeness?
PROPHILUS. He's distracted.
PENTHEA. O my griev'd lord!
GRAUSIS. Sweet lady, come not near him;
He holds his perilous weapon in his hand
To prick he cares not whom nor where. – See, see, see!
BASSANES. [*to* ITHOCLES] My birth is noble. Though the popular blast
Of vanity, as giddy as thy youth,
Hath rear'd thy name up to bestride a cloud
Or progress in the chariot of the sun,
I am no clod of trade, to lackey pride,

---

117 *cheer . . . strain*: try to think of a plan of action.
118 s.d. *poniard*: dagger.
123 *property*: personal characteristic.
125–7 *Sweet . . . where*: unconscious bawdy talk by Grausis. As Penthea moves towards Bassanes, he flourishes his dagger wildly.
128 See Textual Notes, p. 340.
128–9 *popular . . . vanity*: pride induced by the winds of public adulation.
130–1 *bestride . . . sun*: the behaviour of Ixion and Phaethon, both types of outrageous ambition leading to disaster (cf. IV.i.69–71 and IV.iv.25–6).
132 *lackey pride*: meanly serve (your) haughtiness.

Nor, like your slave of expectation, wait
The bawdy hinges of your doors, or whistle
For mystical conveyance to your bed-sports.
GRONEAS. Fine humours! They become him.
LEMOPHIL. How he stares,
Struts, puffs, and sweats. Most admirable
lunacy!
ITHOCLES. But that I may conceive the spirit of
wine
Has took possession of your soberer custom,
I'd say you were unmannerly.
PENTHEA. Dear brother –
BASSANES. Unmannerly! Mew, kitling! Smooth
formality
Is usher to the rankness of the blood,
But impudence bears up the train. Indeed, sir,
Your fiery mettle, or your springal blaze
Of huge renown, is no sufficient royalty
To print upon my forehead the scorn 'cuckold'.
ITHOCLES. His jealousy has robb'd him of his
wits;
He talks he knows not what.
BASSANES. Yes, and he knows
To whom he talks: to one that franks his lust
In swine-security of bestial incest.
ITHOCLES. Ha, devil!
BASSANES. I will halloo't, though I
blush more
To name the filthiness than thou to act it.
ITHOCLES. Monster!

133–5 *wait . . . bed-sports*: wait for the door of the room where you make love to open, or for your summons to be taken secretly to a place for love-making.
137 *admirable*: amazing.
141 *kitling*: kitten.
144 *springal*: youthful.
145 *royalty*: royal warrant.
149 *franks*: feeds; a frank was an enclosure in which a boar (symbol of animal lust) was fattened for slaughter.
151 *halloo't*: shout it aloud (as a hunter might).
153 *Monster*: Ithocles threatens to attack Bassanes, provoking Prophilus and Penthea to restrain him.

PROPHILUS. Sir, by our friendship –
PENTHEA. By our bloods,
Will you quite both undo us, brother?
GRAUSIS. Out on him!
These are his megrims, firks, and melancholies.
LEMOPHIL. Well said, old touchhole.
GRONEAS. Kick him out at doors.
PENTHEA. With favour, let me speak. – My lord, what slackness
In my obedience hath deserv'd this rage?
Except humility and silent duty
Have drawn on your unquiet, my simplicity
Ne'er studied your vexation.
BASSANES. Light of beauty,
Deal not ungently with a desperate wound!
No breach of reason dares make war with her
Whose looks are sovereignty, whose breath is balm.
O that I could preserve thee in fruition
As in devotion!
PENTHEA. Sir, may every evil
Lock'd in Pandora's box show'r, in your presence,
On my unhappy head, if since you made me
A partner in your bed, I have been faulty
In one unseemly thought against your honour.
ITHOCLES. Purge not his griefs, Penthea.
BASSANES. Yes, say on,
Excellent creature. – Good, be not a hindrance
To peace and praise of virtue. – O, my senses
Are charm'd with sounds celestial! – On, dear, on.

---

155 *megrims, firks*: whims, pranks.
156 *touchhole*: term of sexual abuse; literally, the ignition hole in the breech of a gun.
159 See Textual Notes, p. 340.
161 *studied*: deliberately sought.
165 *fruition*: the pleasures of possession.
166–7 *every . . . box*: Jupiter gave Pandora a box in which was confined every human ill. They were released into the world when the box was mistakenly opened.
172 *Good*: good sir (Ithocles).

I never gave you one ill word; say, did I?
Indeed I did not.
PENTHEA. Nor, by Juno's forehead,
Was I e'er guilty of a wanton error.
BASSANES. A goddess; let me kneel!
GRAUSIS. Alas, kind animal.
ITHOCLES. No; but for penance –
BASSANES. Noble sir, what is it?
With gladness I embrace it; yet pray let not
My rashness teach you to be too unmerciful.
ITHOCLES. When you shall show good proof that manly wisdom,
Not oversway'd by passion or opinion,
Knows how to lead your judgement, then this lady,
Your wife, my sister, shall return in safety
Home, to be guided by you. But till first
I can out of clear evidence approve it,
She shall be my care.
BASSANES. Rip my bosom up,
I'll stand the execution with a constancy.
This torture is unsufferable.
ITHOCLES. Well, sir,
I dare not trust her to your fury.
BASSANES. But
Penthea says not so.
PENTHEA. She needs no tongue
To plead excuse, who never purpos'd wrong.
[*They begin to leave.*]
LEMOPHIL. [*to* GRAUSIS] Virgin of reverence and antiquity,
Stay you behind.
GRONEAS. [*to* GRAUSIS] The court wants not your diligence.
Exeunt all but BASSANES *and* GRAUSIS.
GRAUSIS. What will you do, my lord? My lady's gone;

---

176 *Juno's forehead*: the modesty of Juno, Roman goddess of marriage, who punished erring wives.
178 *kind*: foolish.
184 See Textual Notes, p. 340.
187 *approve*: certify.

I am denied to follow.
BASSANES. I may see her,
Or speak to her once more?
GRAUSIS. And feel her too, man.
Be of good cheer; she's your own flesh and bone.
BASSANES. Diseases desperate must find cures alike.
She swore she has been true.
GRAUSIS. True, on my modesty.
BASSANES. Let him want truth who credits not her vows.
Much wrong I did her, but her brother infinite.
Rumour will voice me the contempt of manhood
Should I run on thus. Some way I must try
To outdo art and cry a' jealousy.
Exeunt all.

SCENE III

Flourish. Enter AMYCLAS, NEARCHUS *leading* CALANTHA, ARMOSTES, CROTOLON, EUPHRANIA, CHRYSTALLA, PHILEMA, *and* AMELUS.

AMYCLAS. Cousin of Argos, what the heavens have pleas'd
In their unchanging counsels to conclude
For both our kingdoms' weal, we must submit to.
Nor can we be unthankful to their bounties,
Who when we were even creeping to our grave,
Sent us a daughter, in whose birth our hope
Continues of succession. As you are
In title next, being grandchild to our aunt,

---

197 *denied*: refused permission.
202 *want truth*: lack honesty.
206 *outdo . . . jealousy*: exceed human skill and denounce jealousy. See Textual Notes, p. 340.
3 *weal*: welfare, prosperity.
5 See Textual Notes, p. 340.

So we in heart desire you may sit nearest
Calantha's love – since we have ever vow'd
Not to enforce affection by our will,
But by her own choice to confirm it gladly.
NEARCHUS. You speak the nature of a right just father.
I come not hither roughly to demand
My cousin's thraldom, but to free mine own.
Report of great Calantha's beauty, virtue,
Sweetness, and singular perfections, courted
All ears to credit what I find was publish'd
By constant truth; from which, if any service
Of my desert can purchase fair construction,
This lady must command it.
CALANTHA. Princely sir,
So well you know how to profess observance
That you instruct your hearers to become
Practitioners in duty; of which number
I'll study to be chief.
NEARCHUS. Chief, glorious virgin,
In my devotions, as in all men's wonder.
AMYCLAS. Excellent cousin, we deny no liberty;
Use thine own opportunities. – Armostes,
We must consult with the philosophers;
The business is of weight.
ARMOSTES. Sir, at your pleasure.
AMYCLAS. You told me, Crotolon, your son's return'd
From Athens. Wherefore comes he not to court
As we commanded?
CROTOLON. He shall soon attend
Your royal will, great sir.
AMYCLAS. The marriage
Between young Prophilus and Euphrania
Tastes of too much delay.
CROTOLON. My lord.
AMYCLAS. Some pleasures
At celebration of it would give life

19–20 *service . . . desert*: meritorious service on my part.
22 *observance*: dutiful service, courtship.
28 *Armostes*: while Amyclas talks to Armostes, Nearchus and Calantha continue a private conversation.
34 *marriage*: three syllables.

To th'entertainment of the prince our kinsman.
Our court wears gravity more than we relish.
ARMOSTES. Yet the heavens smile on all your high attempts,
Without a cloud.
CROTOLON. So may the gods protect us.
CALANTHA. [*to* NEARCHUS] A prince a subject?
NEARCHUS. Yes, to beauty's sceptre.
As all hearts kneel, so mine.
CALANTHA. You are too courtly.

[*Enter*] *to them,* ITHOCLES, ORGILUS, PROPHILUS.

ITHOCLES. [*to* ORGILUS] Your safe return to Sparta is most welcome.
I joy to meet you here, and as occasion
Shall grant us privacy, will yield you reasons
Why I should covet to deserve the title
Of your respected friend. For, without compliment,
Believe it, Orgilus, 'tis my ambition.
ORGILUS. Your lordship may command me your poor servant.
ITHOCLES. [*aside*] So amorously close? So soon? My heart!
PROPHILUS. What sudden change is next?
ITHOCLES. Life to the king,
To whom I here present this noble gentleman,
New come from Athens. Royal sir, vouchsafe
Your gracious hand in favour of his merit.
CROTOLON. [*aside*] My son preferr'd by Ithocles!
AMYCLAS. Our bounties
Shall open to thee, Orgilus. For instance –
Hark in thine ear – if out of those inventions
Which flow in Athens thou hast there engross'd
Some rarity of wit to grace the nuptials
Of thy fair sister, and renown our court

---

40 *high attempts*: noble enterprises.
48 *compliment*: courtly flattery.
51 *So amorously . . . heart*: spoken as Ithocles notices Nearchus and Calantha standing close together.
56 *preferr'd*: put forward.
59 *engross'd*: acquired.

In th'eyes of this young prince, we shall be debtor
To thy conceit. Think on't.
ORGILUS. Your highness honours me.
NEARCHUS. [*to* CALANTHA] My tongue and heart are twins.
CALANTHA. A noble birth,
Becoming such a father. – Worthy Orgilus,
You are a guest most wish'd for.
ORGILUS. May my duty
Still rise in your opinion, sacred princess.
ITHOCLES. [*to* NEARCHUS] Euphrania's brother, sir; a gentleman
Well worthy of your knowledge.
NEARCHUS. We embrace him,
Proud of so dear acquaintance.
AMYCLAS. All prepare
For revels and disport. The joys of Hymen,
Like Phoebus in his lustre, puts to flight
All mists of dullness. Crown the hours with gladness.
No sounds but music; no discourse but mirth.
CALANTHA. Thine arm, I prithee, Ithocles. [*To* NEARCHUS] Nay, good
My lord, keep on your way; I am provided.
NEARCHUS. I dare not disobey.
ITHOCLES. Most heavenly lady!
Exeunt.

SCENE IV

Enter CROTOLON, ORGILUS.

CROTOLON. The king hath spoke his mind.
ORGILUS. His will he hath;
But were it lawful to hold plea against

---

63 *conceit*: inventive imagination.
72 *Phoebus*: the sun god, Phoebus Apollo. Apollo was also the god of reason and the patron of music and poetry; cf. IV.i.132, V.i.43 and the note to *Perkin Warbeck*, Commendatory Verse II, 2.
2 *hold plea*: try a legal action.

The power of greatness, not the reason, haply
Such undershrubs as subjects sometimes might
Borrow of nature justice, to inform
That licence sovereignty holds without check
Over a meek obedience.

CROTOLON. How resolve you
Touching your sister's marriage? Prophilus
Is a deserving and a hopeful youth.

ORGILUS. I envy not his merit, but applaud it;
Could wish him thrift in all his best desires,
And with a willingness inleague our blood
With his, for purchase of full growth in friendship.
He never touch'd on any wrong that malic'd
The honour of our house, nor stirr'd our peace;
Yet, with your favour, let me not forget
Under whose wing he gathers warmth and comfort;
Whose creature he is bound, made, and must live so.

CROTOLON. Son, son, I find in thee a harsh condition.
No courtesy can win it; 'tis too rancorous.

ORGILUS. Good sir, be not severe in your construction.
I am no stranger to such easy calms
As sit in tender bosoms. Lordly Ithocles
Hath grac'd my entertainment in abundance;
Too humbly hath descended from that height
Of arrogance and spleen which wrought the rape
On griev'd Penthea's purity. His scorn
Of my untoward fortunes is reclaim'd
Unto a courtship, almost to a fawning.
I'll kiss his foot, since you will have it so.

CROTOLON. Since I will have it so? Friend, I will have it so,

---

5 *Borrow . . . inform*: draw on natural justice to give formative principle to.
6 *licence*: authority.
11 *thrift*: success. See Textual Notes, p. 340.
14 *malic'd*: threatened to harm.
19 *condition*: disposition.
24 *entertainment*: reception.
28 *untoward*: failing.
reclaim'd: changed for the better.

Without our ruin by your politic plots,
Or wolf of hatred snarling in your breast.
You have a spirit, sir, have ye? A familiar
That posts i'th'air for your intelligence?
Some such hobgoblin hurried you from Athens,
For yet you come unsent for.
ORGILUS. If unwelcome,
I might have found a grave there.
CROTOLON. Sure your business
Was soon dispatch'd, or your mind alter'd quickly.
ORGILUS. 'Twas care, sir, of my health cut short my journey;
For there a general infection
Threatens a desolation.
CROTOLON. And I fear
Thou hast brought back a worse infection with thee:
Infection of thy mind, which, as thou say'st,
Threatens the desolation of our family.
ORGILUS. Forbid it, our dear genius! I will rather
Be made a sacrifice on Thrasus' monument,
Or kneel to Ithocles his son in dust,
Than woo a father's curse. My sister's marriage
With Prophilus is from my heart confirm'd.
May I live hated, may I die despis'd,
If I omit to further it in all
That can concern me.
CROTOLON. I have been too rough.
My duty to my king made me so earnest;
Excuse it, Orgilus.
ORGILUS. Dear sir!

Enter to them, PROPHILUS, EUPHRANIA, ITHOCLES, GRONEAS, LEMOPHIL.

CROTOLON. Here comes
Euphrania, with Prophilus and Ithocles.

---

32 *politic*: cunning.
34 *familiar*: witch's personal attendant spirit.
35 *posts . . . intelligence*: speeds through the air to bring you news.
41 *general infection*: scan as seven syllables.
46 *genius*: family guardian spirit.

ORGILUS. Most honour'd, ever famous!
ITHOCLES. Your true friend;
On earth not any truer. With smooth eyes
Look on this worthy couple. Your consent
Can only make them one.
ORGILUS. They have it. – Sister,
Thou pawn'dst to me an oath, of which engagement
I never will release thee, if thou aim'st
At any other choice than this.
EUPHRANIA. Dear brother,
At him or none.
CROTOLON. To which my blessing's added.
ORGILUS. Which till a greater ceremony perfect,
Euphrania, lend thy hand. – Here, take her, Prophilus.
Live long a happy man and wife; and further,
That these in presence may conclude an omen,
Thus for a bridal song I close my wishes:
Comforts lasting, loves increasing,
Like soft hours never ceasing;
Plenty's pleasure, peace complying
Without jars or tongues envying;
Hearts by holy union wedded,
More than theirs by custom bedded;
Fruitful issues; life so graced,
Not by age to be defaced,
Budding, as the year ensu'th,
Every spring another youth:
All what thought can add beside,
Crown this bridegroom and this bride.
PROPHILUS. You have seal'd joy close to my soul. – Euphrania,
Now I may call thee mine.
ITHOCLES. I but exchange
One good friend for another.
ORGILUS. If these gallants

---

58 *smooth*: kindly.
60 *only*: alone.
61 *pawn'dst*: pledged.
65 See Additional Notes, p. 348.
68 *That*: in a way that.
71 *hours*: two syllables.
73 *jars*: domestic quarrels.

Will please to grace a poor invention,
By joining with me in some slight device,
I'll venture on a strain my younger days
Have studied for delight.

LEMOPHIL. With thankful willingness
I offer my attendance.

GRONEAS. No endeavour
Of mine shall fail to show itself.

ITHOCLES. We will
All join to wait on thy directions, Orgilus.

ORGILUS. O my good lord, your favours flow towards
A too unworthy worm. But as you please;
I am what you will shape me.

ITHOCLES. A fast friend.

CROTOLON. I thank thee, son, for this acknowledgement;
It is a sight of gladness.

ORGILUS. But my duty.

Exeunt all.

SCENE V

Enter CALANTHA, PENTHEA, CHRYSTALLA, PHILEMA.

CALANTHA. Whoe'er would speak with us, deny his entrance.
Be careful of our charge.

CHRYSTALLA. We shall, madam.

CALANTHA. Except the king himself, give none admittance;
Not any.

PHILEMA. Madam, it shall be our care.

[*Exeunt* CHRYSTALLA *and* PHILEMA.]

CALANTHA. Being alone, Penthea, you have granted
The opportunity you sought, and might

---

86 *device*: (1) dramatic presentation, (2) cunning stratagem.
96 *But*: only.
1 *deny*: refuse.

At all times have commanded.
PENTHEA. 'Tis a benefit
Which I shall owe your goodness even in death for.
My glass of life, sweet princess, hath few minutes
Remaining to run down; the sands are spent;
For by an inward messenger I feel
The summons of departure short and certain.
CALANTHA. You feed too much your melancholy.
PENTHEA. Glories
Of human greatness are but pleasing dreams,
And shadows soon decaying. On the stage
Of my mortality, my youth hath acted
Some scenes of vanity, drawn out at length
By varied pleasures, sweeten'd in the mixture,
But tragical in issue. Beauty, pomp,
With every sensuality our giddiness
Doth frame an idol, are unconstant friends
When any troubl'd passion makes assault
On the unguarded castle of the mind.
CALANTHA. Contemn not your condition for the proof
Of bare opinion only. To what end
Reach all these moral texts?
PENTHEA. To place before ye
A perfect mirror, wherein you may see
How weary I am of a ling'ring life,
Who count the best a misery.
CALANTHA. Indeed
You have no little cause; yet none so great
As to distrust a remedy.
PENTHEA. That remedy
Must be a winding-sheet, a fold of lead,
And some untrod-on corner in the earth.
Not to detain your expectation, princess,

---

9 *My glass of life*: the hourglass measuring my life.
12 *short*: soon to come.
20 *sensuality*: pleasure of the senses.
giddiness: changeableness.
24 *Contemn*: despise.
condition: situation in life.
25 *opinion*: worldly wisdom; cf. III.i.46–8.
31 *distrust*: despair of.

I have an humble suit.
CALANTHA. Speak; I enjoin it.
PENTHEA. Vouchsafe, then, to be my executrix,
And take that trouble on ye, to dispose
Such legacies as I bequeath impartially.
I have not much to give; the pains are easy.
Heaven will reward your piety, and thank it
When I am dead. For sure I must not live;
I hope I cannot.
CALANTHA. Now beshrew thy sadness;
Thou turn'st me too much woman. [*Weeps.*]
PENTHEA. [*aside*] Her fair eyes
Melt into passion. Then I have assurance
Encouraging my boldness. – In this paper
My will was character'd, which you, with pardon,
Shall now know from mine own mouth.
CALANTHA. Talk on, prithee;
It is a pretty earnest.
PENTHEA. I have left me
But three poor jewels to bequeath. The first is
My youth; for though I am much old in griefs,
In years I am a child.
CALANTHA. To whom that?
PENTHEA. To virgin wives, such as abuse not wedlock
By freedom of desires, but covet chiefly
The pledges of chaste beds for ties of love,
Rather than ranging of their blood. And next
To married maids, such as prefer the number
Of honourable issue in their virtues
Before the flattery of delights by marriage.
May those be ever young.
CALANTHA. A second jewel
You mean to part with.
PENTHEA. 'Tis my fame, I trust

35, 36 See Textual Notes, p. 340.
46 *character'd*: written.
48 *earnest*: foretaste, introduction.
49 *jewels*: two syllables, here and at 59 and 68.
54 *pledges*: children (as tokens of mutual love).
55 *ranging of their blood*: sexual desire given freedom to stray beyond the marriage relationship.
56 See Additional Notes, p. 348.

By scandal yet untouch'd. This I bequeath
To Memory, and Time's old daughter, Truth.
If ever my unhappy name find mention
When I am fall'n to dust, may it deserve
Beseeming charity without dishonour.
CALANTHA. How handsomely thou play'st with harmless sport
Of mere imagination. Speak the last:
I strangely like thy will.
PENTHEA. This jewel, madam,
Is dearly precious to me. You must use
The best of your discretion to employ
This gift as I intend it.
CALANTHA. Do not doubt me.
PENTHEA. 'Tis long agone since first I lost my heart.
Long I have liv'd without it, else for certain
I should have given that too. But instead
Of it, to great Calantha, Sparta's heir,
By service bound, and by affection vow'd,
I do bequeath in holiest rites of love
Mine only brother, Ithocles.
CALANTHA. What saidst thou?
PENTHEA. Impute not, heaven-blest lady, to ambition
A faith as humbly perfect as the prayers
Of a devoted suppliant can endow it.
Look on him, princess, with an eye of pity;
How like the ghost of what he late appear'd
He moves before you.
CALANTHA. [*aside*] Shall I answer here,
Or lend my ear too grossly?
PENTHEA. First his heart
Shall fall in cinders, scorch'd by your disdain,
Ere he will dare, poor man, to ope an eye
On these divine looks, but with low-bent thoughts
Accusing such presumption. As for words,
He dares not utter any but of service.
Yet this lost creature loves ye. Be a princess

---

67 *mere*: pure.
85 *grossly*: indecorously.

In sweetness as in blood; give him his doom,
Or raise him up to comfort.
CALANTHA. What new change
Appears in my behaviour, that thou dar'st
Tempt my displeasure?
PENTHEA. I must leave the world
To revel in Elysium, and 'tis just
To wish my brother some advantage here.
Yet, by my best hopes, Ithocles is ignorant
Of this pursuit. But if you please to kill him,
Lend him one angry look, or one harsh word,
And you shall soon conclude how strong a power
Your absolute authority holds over
His life and end.
CALANTHA. You have forgot, Penthea,
How still I have a father.
PENTHEA. But remember
I am a sister, though to me this brother
Hath been, you know, unkind. O, most unkind!
CALANTHA. Chrystalla, Philema, where are ye? – Lady,
Your check lies in my silence.

Enter CHRYSTALLA *and* PHILEMA.

BOTH. Madam, here.
CALANTHA. I think ye sleep, ye drones! Wait on Penthea
Unto her lodging. – [*Aside*] Ithocles? Wrong'd lady!
PENTHEA. My reckonings are made even. Death or fate
Can now nor strike too soon, nor force too late.
Exeunt.

---

96 *revel in Elysium*: experience the joys of paradise. See Textual Notes, p. 340.
99 *pursuit*: petition.
108 *check*: reproof.
111 *My . . . even*: the account of my life (to be made at the final judgement) is now balanced; cf. II.iii.149–51.

ACT IV

SCENE I

Enter ITHOCLES *and* ARMOSTES.

ITHOCLES. Forbear your inquisition. Curiosity
Is of too subtle and too searching nature;
In fears of love too quick, too slow of credit.
I am not what you doubt me.
ARMOSTES. Nephew, be then
As I would wish. – [*Aside*] All is not right. – Good heaven
Confirm your resolutions for dependence
On worthy ends which may advance your quiet.
ITHOCLES. I did the noble Orgilus much injury,
But griev'd Penthea more. I now repent it;
Now, uncle, now. This 'now' is now too late.
So provident is folly in sad issue
That after-wit, like bankrupts' debts, stand tallied
Without all possibilities of payment.
Sure he's an honest, very honest gentleman;
A man of single meaning.
ARMOSTES. I believe it.
Yet nephew, 'tis the tongue informs our ears;
Our eyes can never pierce into the thoughts,
For they are lodg'd too inward. But I question
No truth in Orgilus. The princess, sir!
ITHOCLES. The princess? Ha!
ARMOSTES. With her, the Prince of Argos.

4 *doubt me*: fear me to be.
11 *provident*: fertile.
12 *after-wit . . . tallied*: wisdom after the event remains with its tally of disasters. As frequently in Elizabethan English, the verb *stand* is attracted in number to the preceding noun *debts* rather than to its grammatical subject *after-wit*.
13 *Without*: beyond.

Enter NEARCHUS, *leading* CALANTHA; AMELUS, CHRYSTALLA, PHILEMA.

NEARCHUS. Great fair one, grace my hopes with any instance
Of livery, from the allowance of your favour.
This little spark –
[*Indicating* CALANTHA'*s ring.*]
CALANTHA. A toy.
NEARCHUS. Love feasts on toys,
For Cupid is a child. Vouchsafe this bounty;
It cannot be denied.
CALANTHA. You shall not value,
Sweet cousin, at a price, what I count cheap;
So cheap, that let him take it who dares stoop for't,
And give it at next meeting to a mistress.
She'll thank him for't, perhaps.
Casts it to ITHOCLES.
AMELUS. The ring, sir, is
The princess's. I could have took it up.
ITHOCLES. Learn manners, prithee. – To the blessed owner,
Upon my knees. [*Offers the ring to* CALANTHA.]
NEARCHUS. You're saucy!
CALANTHA. This is pretty.
I am, belike, a mistress! Wondrous pretty.
Let the man keep his fortune, since he found it;
He's worthy on't. – On, cousin.
ITHOCLES. [*to* AMELUS]. Follow, spaniel.
I'll force ye to a fawning else.
AMELUS. You dare not.
Exeunt all but ITHOCLES *and* ARMOSTES.
ARMOSTES. My lord, you were too forward.
ITHOCLES. Look ye, uncle,
Some such there are whose liberal contents
Swarm without care in every sort of plenty;

21–2 *instance Of livery*: badge of service.
23 *spark*: ruby or diamond.
toy: (1) trifle, (2) child's toy; Nearchus picks up the second meaning.
25 See Textual Notes, p. 340.
38 *liberal contents*: easy satisfactions.

Who, after full repasts, can lay them down
To sleep. And they sleep, uncle; in which silence
Their very dreams present 'em choice of pleasures;
Pleasures (observe me, uncle) of rare object:
Here heaps of gold, there increments of honours;
Now change of garments, then the votes of people;
Anon varieties of beauties, courting
In flatteries of the night, exchange of dalliance.
Yet these are still but dreams. Give me felicity
Of which my senses waking are partakers,
A real, visible, material happiness;
And then, too, when I stagger in expectance
Of the least comfort that can cherish life.
I saw it, sir, I saw it; for it came
From her own hand.

ARMOSTES. The princess threw it t'ye.

ITHOCLES. True, and she said – well I remember what.
Her cousin prince would beg it.

ARMOSTES. Yes, and parted
In anger at your taking on't.

ITHOCLES. Penthea!
O, thou hast pleaded with a powerful language!
I want a fee to gratify thy merit.
But I will do –

ARMOSTES. What is't you say?

ITHOCLES. In anger,
In anger let him part; for could his breath,
Like whirlwinds, toss such servile slaves as lick
The dust his footsteps print into a vapour,
It durst not stir a hair of mine. It should not;
I'd rend it up by th'roots first. To be anything
Calantha smiles on is to be a blessing
More sacred than a petty-prince of Argos

---

43 *object*: appearance.
46 *beauties*: lovely women.
51 *stagger in*: am doubtful about.
59 *want . . . merit*: lack the means to reward your excellence (as an advocate).
65 *it*: Ithocles' hair.

Can wish to equal, or in worth or title.
ARMOSTES. Contain yourself, my lord. Ixion, aiming
To embrace Juno, bosom'd but a cloud,
And begat centaurs. 'Tis an useful moral:
Ambition, hatch'd in clouds of mere opinion,
Proves but in birth a prodigy.
ITHOCLES. I thank ye;
Yet, with your licence, I should seem uncharitable
To gentler fate, if, relishing the dainties
Of a soul's settled peace, I were so feeble
Not to digest it.
ARMOSTES. He deserves small trust
Who is not privy counsellor to himself.

Enter NEARCHUS, ORGILUS, *and* AMELUS.

NEARCHUS. Brave me?
ORGILUS. Your excellence mistakes his temper,
For Ithocles in fashion of his mind
Is beautiful, soft, gentle, the clear mirror
Of absolute perfection.
AMELUS. Was't your modesty
Term'd any of the prince his servants 'spaniel'?
Your nurse, sure, taught you other language.
ITHOCLES. Language!
NEARCHUS. A gallant man at arms is here. A doctor
In feats of chivalry; blunt and rough-spoken,
Vouchsafing not the fustian of civility,
Which less rash spirits style good manners.
ITHOCLES. Manners!

---

69 *Ixion*: cf. III.ii.130.
70 *bosom'd*: sexually embraced.
72 *mere opinion*: pure fantasy; cf. III.i.46–7.
73 *prodigy*: monster.
75 *relishing the dainties*: tasting the delicacies or pleasures.
79 *temper*: disposition.
85 *doctor*: one qualified by experience to teach.
87 *Vouchsafing not the fustian*: intolerant of the bombast.
88 See Textual Notes, p. 340.

ORGILUS. No more, illustrious sir; 'tis matchless Ithocles.
NEARCHUS. You might have understood who I am.
ITHOCLES. Yes,
I did; else – but the presence calm'd th'affront.
You're cousin to the princess.
NEARCHUS. To the king too;
A certain instrument that lent supportance
To your colossic greatness. To that king too,
You might have added.
ITHOCLES. There is more divinity
In beauty than in majesty.
ARMOSTES. O fie, fie!
NEARCHUS. This odd youth's pride turns heretic in loyalty.
Sirrah, low mushrooms never rival cedars.
Exeunt NEARCHUS *and* AMELUS.
ITHOCLES. Come back! What pitiful dull thing am I
So to be tamely scolded at? Come back!
Let him come back and echo once again
That scornful sound of 'mushroom'; painted colts,
Like heralds' coats gilt o'er with crowns and sceptres,
May bait a muzzl'd lion.
ARMOSTES. Cousin, cousin,
Thy tongue is not thy friend.
ORGILUS. In point of honour
Discretion knows no bounds. Amelus told me
'Twas all about a little ring.
ITHOCLES. A ring
The princess threw away, and I took up.
Admit she threw't to me, what arm of brass
Can snatch it hence? No, could he grind the hoop
To powder, he might sooner reach my heart

---

91 *presence . . . affront*: presence of royalty prevented a violent response to the insult.

98 *mushrooms*: base upstarts.
cedars: symbols of greatness and royalty.

102–4 See Additional Notes, p. 349.

Than steal and wear one dust on't. Orgilus,
I am extremely wrong'd.
ORGILUS. A lady's favour
Is not to be so slighted.
ITHOCLES. Slighted!
ARMOSTES. Quiet
These vain unruly passions, which will render ye
Into a madness.
ORGILUS. Griefs will have their vent.

Enter TECNICUS.

ARMOSTES. Welcome. Thou com'st in season, reverend man,
To pour the balsam of a supplying patience
Into the festering wound of ill-spent fury.
ORGILUS. [*aside*] What makes he here?
TECNICUS. The hurts are yet but mortal,
Which shortly will prove deadly. To the king,
Armostes, see in safety thou deliver
This seal'd up counsel; bid him with a constancy
Peruse the secrets of the gods. – O Sparta,
O Lacedemon! Double-nam'd, but one
In fate. When kingdoms reel (mark well my saw)
Their heads must needs be giddy. – Tell the king
That henceforth he no more must inquire after
My aged head; Apollo wills it so.
I am for Delphos.
ARMOSTES. Not without some conference
With our great master?
TECNICUS. Never more to see him.
A greater prince commands me. – Ithocles,
When youth is ripe, and age from time doth part,

---

112 *dust*: particle.
118 *supplying*: relieving.
120 *makes he*: is his business.
mortal: grievous.
123 *counsel*: Tecnicus's interpretation of the oracle; cf. III.i.59–80.
126 *saw*: wise saying.
132 *prince*: Apollo, the god Tecnicus serves.
133 *time*: i.e. life.

The lifeless trunk shall wed the broken heart.
ITHOCLES. What's this, if understood?
TECNICUS. List, Orgilus.
Remember what I told thee long before;
These tears shall be my witness.
ARMOSTES. 'Las, good man.
TECNICUS. *Let craft with courtesy a while confer,*
Revenge proves its own executioner.
ORGILUS. Dark sentences are for Apollo's priests.
I am not Oedipus.
TECNICUS. My hour is come.
Cheer up the king. Farewell to all. – O Sparta,
O Lacedemon! *Exit* TECNICUS.
ARMOSTES. If prophetic fire
Have warm'd this old man's bosom, we might construe
His words to fatal sense.
ITHOCLES. Leave to the powers
Above us the effects of their decrees;
My burden lies within me. Servile fears
Prevent no great effects. – Divine Calantha!
ARMOSTES. The gods be still propitious!
Exeunt [ITHOCLES *and* ARMOSTES].
ORGILUS. Something oddly
The book-man prated, yet he talk'd it weeping:
Let craft with courtesy a while confer,
Revenge proves its own executioner.
Con it again. For what? It shall not puzzle me;
'Tis dotage of a wither'd brain. Penthea
Forbade me not her presence; I may see her,
And gaze my fill. Why see her then I may;
When if I faint to speak, I must be silent.
Exit ORGILUS.

---

140 *sentences*: sayings.
141 *Oedipus*: solver of riddles, like Oedipus, who saved the city of Thebes by solving the riddle proposed by the Sphinx.
148 *Prevent*: anticipate.
153 *Con*: read over.
157 *faint*: lack courage.

SCENE II

Enter BASSANES, GRAUSIS, *and* PHULAS.

BASSANES. Pray use your recreations; all the service
I will expect is quietness amongst ye.
Take liberty at home, abroad, at all times,
And in your charities appease the gods
Whom I with my distractions have offended.
GRAUSIS. Fair blessings on thy heart!
PHULAS. [*aside*] Here's a rare change.
My lord, to cure the itch, is surely gelded;
The cuckold in conceit hath cast his horns.
BASSANES. Betake ye to your several occasions,
And wherein I have heretofore been faulty,
Let your constructions mildly pass it over.
Henceforth I'll study reformation. More
I have not for employment.
GRAUSIS. O sweet man!
Thou art the very honeycomb of honesty.
PHULAS. The garland of good will. – Old lady, hold up
Thy reverend snout, and trot behind me softly,
As it becomes a moil of ancient carriage.
Exeunt [GRAUSIS *and* PHULAS].
BASSANES. Beasts, only capable of sense, enjoy
The benefit of food and ease with thankfulness.
Such silly creatures with a grudging kick not
Against the portion nature hath bestow'd.
But men, endow'd with reason and the use
Of reason to distinguish from the chaff
Of abject scarcity the quintessence,
Soul, and elixir of the earth's abundance,
The treasures of the sea, the air, nay, heaven,
Repining at these glories of creation,

---

8 *conceit*: his own imagination.
9 *several occasions*: various activities.
17 *moil . . . carriage*: old pack-mule.
18 *capable of sense*: possessing (only) sensory faculties (and lacking the power of reason).
25 *elixir*: essence.

Are verier beasts than beasts. And of those beasts
The worst am I. I, who was made a monarch
Of what a heart could wish for, a chaste wife,
Endeavour'd what in me lay to pull down
That temple built for adoration only,
And level't in the dust of causeless scandal.
But, to redeem a sacrilege so impious,
Humility shall pour before the deities
I have incens'd a largeness of more patience
Than their displeased altars can require.
No tempests of commotion shall disquiet
The calms of my composure.

Enter ORGILUS.

ORGILUS. I have found thee,
Thou patron of more horrors than the bulk
Of manhood, hoop'd about with ribs of iron,
Can cram within thy breast. Penthea, Bassanes,
Curs'd by thy jealousies – more, by thy dotage –
Is left a prey to madness.

BASSANES. Exercise
Your trials for addition to my penance;
I am resolv'd.

ORGILUS. Play not with misery
Past cure. Some angry minister of fate hath
Depos'd the empress of her soul, her reason,
From its most proper throne; but what's the miracle
More new, I, I have seen it, and yet live.

BASSANES. You may delude my senses, not my judgement.
'Tis anchor'd into a firm resolution.
Dalliance of mirth or wit can ne'er unfix it.
Practise yet further.

ORGILUS. May thy dearth of love to her
Damn all thy comforts to a lasting fast

---

35 See Textual Notes, p. 340.
36 *largeness*: lavish gift-offering.
40 *bulk*: huge body; the image is of a barrel-man.
44 See Textual Notes, p. 340.
44–5 *Exercise Your trials*: go on testing my powers of endurance.
54 See Textual Notes, p. 340.

From every joy of life! Thou barren rock,
By thee we have been split in ken of harbour.

Enter ITHOCLES, PENTHEA, *her hair about her ears,* PHILEMA, CHRYSTALLA, [*and* ARMOSTES].

ITHOCLES. Sister, look up; your Ithocles, your brother,
Speaks t'ye. Why do you weep? Dear, turn not from me. –
Here is a killing sight; lo, Bassanes,
A lamentable object.

ORGILUS. Man, dost see't?
Sports are more gamesome; am I yet in merriment?
Why dost not laugh?

BASSANES. Divine, and best of ladies,
Please to forget my outrage! Mercy ever
Cannot but lodge under a roof so excellent.
I have cast off that cruelty of frenzy
Which once appear'd, impost'rous, and then juggl'd
To cheat my sleeps of rest.

ORGILUS. Was I in earnest?

PENTHEA. Sure, if we were all sirens we should sing pitifully;
And 'twere a comely music when in parts
One sung another's knell. The turtle sighs
When he hath lost his mate, and yet some say
He must be dead first. 'Tis a fine deceit
To pass away in a dream. Indeed, I've slept
With mine eyes open a great while. No falsehood
Equals a broken faith. There's not a hair

---

57 *ken*: sight. See Textual Notes, p. 340.
62 *gamesome*: full of fun.
65 See Textual Notes, p. 340.
67 *impost'rous*: as a deceiver; the metaphorical implication is that he has been beguiled by an evil spirit. See Textual Notes, p. 340.
juggl'd: played tricks.
69 *if . . . pitifully*: sirens, creatures part-bird, part-woman, normally sang to lure human beings to destruction.
71 *turtle*: turtle-dove.
73 *deceit*: Penthea confuses 'deceit' and 'conceit' (idea).

Sticks on my head but like a leaden plummet
It sinks me to the grave. I must creep thither;
The journey is not long.
ITHOCLES. But thou, Penthea,
Hast many years, I hope, to number yet
Ere thou canst travel that way.
BASSANES. Let the sun first
Be wrapp'd up in an everlasting darkness,
Before the light of nature, chiefly form'd
For the whole world's delight, feel an eclipse
So universal.
ORGILUS. Wisdom, look ye, begins
To rave. Art thou mad too, antiquity?
PENTHEA. Since I was first a wife, I might have been
Mother to many pretty prattling babes.
They would have smil'd when I smil'd; and, for certain,
I should have cried when they cried. Truly, brother,
My father would have pick'd me out a husband,
And then my little ones had been no bastards.
But 'tis too late for me to marry now,
I am past child-bearing; 'tis not my fault.
BASSANES. Fall on me, if there be a burning Aetna,
And bury me in flames! Sweats hot as sulphur
Boil through my pores! Affliction hath in store
No torture like to this.
ORGILUS. Behold a patience!
Lay by thy whining, grey dissimulation;
Do something worth a chronicle. Show justice
Upon the author of this mischief; dig out
The jealousies that hatch'd this thraldom first
With thine own poniard. Every antic rapture

81 See Textual Notes, p. 340.
85–6 See Textual Notes, p. 340.
86 *antiquity*: old man.
95 *Aetna*: a famous volcano in north-east Sicily.
103 *antic rapture*: fool's frenzy; *antic* also suggests a clown or ham actor, and Bassanes picks this up in *talking motion* (105), a puppet that talks.

Can roar as thine does.
ITHOCLES. Orgilus, forbear.
BASSANES. Disturb him not, it is a talking motion
Provided for my torment. What a fool am I
To bandy passion. Ere I'll speak a word
I will look on and burst.
PENTHEA. [*to* ORGILUS] I lov'd you once.
ORGILUS. Thou didst, wrong'd creature, in despite of malice.
For it I love thee ever.
PENTHEA. Spare your hand;
Believe me, I'll not hurt it.
ORGILUS. Pain my heart too.
PENTHEA. Complain not though I wring it hard. I'll kiss it;
O, 'tis a fine soft palm. Hark in thine ear,
Like whom do I look, prithee? – Nay, no whispering. –
Goodness! we had been happy. Too much happiness
Will make folk proud, they say. – But that is he; *Points at* ITHOCLES.
And yet he paid for't home. Alas, his heart
Is crept into the cabinet of the princess;
We shall have points and bride-laces. Remember,
When we last gather'd roses in the garden
I found my wits, but truly you lost yours.
That's he, and still 'tis he.
[*Points at* ITHOCLES *again.*]
ITHOCLES. Poor soul, how idly
Her fancies guide her tongue.
BASSANES. [*aside*] Keep in vexation,

---

107 See Textual Notes, p. 340.
109 *malice*: the wrong done to Penthea and Orgilus.
110 See Additional Notes, p. 349.
111 See Textual Notes, p. 340.
112 See Textual Notes, p. 340.
117 *home*: fully.
118 *cabinet*: jewel box.
119 *points and bride-laces*: tagged laces used to tie dresses, and ribbons used to bind sprigs of rosemary worn at a wedding; given away to members of the bridal party.
122 *idly*: irrationally.
123 *Keep in vexation*: suppress your grief.

And break not into clamour.
ORGILUS. [*aside*] She has tutor'd me;
Some powerful inspiration checks my laziness. –
Now let me kiss your hand, griev'd beauty.
PENTHEA. Kiss it. –
Alack, alack, his lips be wondrous cold;
Dear soul, he's lost his colour. Have ye seen
A straying heart? All crannies, every drop
Of blood is turned to an amethyst,
Which married bachelors hang in their ears.
ORGILUS. Peace usher her into Elysium!
If this be madness, madness is an oracle.
Exit ORGILUS.
ITHOCLES. Chrystalla, Philema, when slept my sister?
Her ravings are so wild.
CHRYSTALLA. Sir, not these ten days.
PHILEMA. We watch by her continually; besides,
We cannot any way pray her to eat.
BASSANES. O, misery of miseries!
PENTHEA. Take comfort;
You may live well and die a good old man.
By yea and nay, an oath not to be broken,
If you had join'd our hands once in the temple –
'Twas since my father died, for had he liv'd
He would have done't – I must have call'd you father.
O, my wrack'd honour, ruin'd by those tyrants,
A cruel brother, and a desperate dotage!
There is no peace left for a ravish'd wife
Widow'd by lawless marriage; to all memory
Penthea's, poor Penthea's name is strumpeted.
But since her blood was season'd, by the forfeit
Of noble shame, with mixtures of pollution,
Her blood – 'tis just – be henceforth never heighten'd

---

125 *checks my laziness*: reproves my dilatoriness.
129–31 See Additional Notes, p. 349.
140 *By yea and nay*: a mild oath (derived from James 5.12); the only one English Puritans allowed themselves.
141 *you*: i.e. Crotolon.

With taste of sustenance. Starve! Let that fullness
Whose plurisy hath fever'd faith and modesty –
Forgive me. O, I faint!
[CHRYSTALLA *and* PHILEMA *support* PENTHEA.]

ARMOSTES. Be not so wilful,
Sweet niece, to work thine own destruction.

ITHOCLES. Nature
Will call her daughter monster. What? Not eat?
Refuse the only ordinary means
Which are ordain'd for life? Be not, my sister,
A murd'ress to thyself. – Hear'st thou this, Bassanes?

BASSANES. Foh! I am busy; for I have not thoughts
Enow to think. All shall be well anon;
'Tis tumbling in my head. There is a mastery
In art to fatten and keep smooth the outside;
Yes, and to comfort up the vital spirits
Without the help of food, fumes or perfumes,
Perfumes or fumes. Let her alone; I'll search out
The trick on't.

PENTHEA. Lead me gently; heavens reward ye.
Griefs are sure friends; they leave, without control,
Nor cure nor comforts for a leprous soul.
Exeunt the Maids, supporting PENTHEA.

BASSANES. I grant t'ye and will put in practice instantly
What you shall still admire. 'Tis wonderful,
'Tis super-singular, not to be match'd.
Yet when I've done't, I've done't; ye shall all thank me. *Exit* BASSANES.

ARMOSTES. The sight is full of terror.

ITHOCLES. On my soul

---

153 *plurisy*: excess.
161 See Textual Notes, p. 340.
162–3 *mastery In art*: expert skill.
164–6 See Additional Notes, p. 349.
168 *control*: diminution.
171 *admire*: wonder at.

Lies such an infinite clog of massy dullness
As that I have not sense enough to feel it.
See, uncle, th'angry thing returns again;
Shall's welcome him with thunder? We are haunted,
And must use exorcism to conjure down
This spirit of malevolence.

ARMOSTES. Mildly, nephew.

Enter NEARCHUS *and* AMELUS.

NEARCHUS. I come not, sir, to chide your late disorder,
Admitting that th'inurement to a roughness
In soldiers of your years and fortunes, chiefly
So lately prosperous, hath not yet shook off
The custom of the war in hours of leisure.
Nor shall you need excuse, since you're to render
Account to that fair excellence, the princess,
Who in her private gallery expects it
From your own mouth alone. I am a messenger
But to her pleasure.

ITHOCLES. Excellent Nearchus,
Be prince still of my services, and conquer
Without the combat of dispute. I honour ye.

NEARCHUS. The king is on a sudden indispos'd;
Physicians are call'd for. 'Twere fit, Armostes,
You should be near him.

ARMOSTES. Sir, I kiss your hands.

Exeunt all but NEARCHUS *and* AMELUS.

NEARCHUS. Amelus, I perceive Calantha's bosom
Is warm'd with other fires than such as can
Take strength from any fuel of the love
I might address to her. Young Ithocles,
Or ever I mistake, is lord ascendant

---

177 See Textual Notes, p. 340.
181 *disorder*: unmannerly conduct.
192 *honour*: Ithocles may kneel to Nearchus here.
200 *Or ever*: unless.
lord ascendant: an astrological as well as a princely term: the planet with a dominant influence in the 'house' or part of the Zodiac rising above the eastern horizon at the time of any particular event.

Of her devotions; one, to speak him truly,
In every disposition nobly fashion'd.

AMELUS. But can your Highness brook to be so rivall'd,
Considering th'inequality of the persons?

NEARCHUS. I can, Amelus; for affections injur'd
By tyranny, or rigour of compulsion,
Like tempest-threaten'd trees unfirmly rooted,
Ne'er spring to timely growth. Observe, for instance,
Life-spent Penthea and unhappy Orgilus.

AMELUS. How does your grace determine?

NEARCHUS. To be jealous
In public of what privately I'll further;
And though they shall not know, yet they shall find it.

Exeunt all.

SCENE III

Enter LEMOPHIL *and* GRONEAS, *leading* AMYCLAS *and placing him in a chair, followed by* ARMOSTES, CROTOLON, *and* PROPHILUS.

AMYCLAS. Our daughter is not near?

ARMOSTES. She is retir'd, sir,
Into her gallery.

AMYCLAS. Where's the prince our cousin?

PROPHILUS. New walk'd into the grove, my lord.

AMYCLAS. All leave us
Except Armostes, and you, Crotolon.
We would be private.

PROPHILUS. Health unto your majesty!

Exeunt PROPHILUS, LEMOPHIL, *and* GRONEAS.

AMYCLAS. What, Tecnicus is gone?

ARMOSTES. He is, to Delphos;
And to your royal hands presents this box.

---

0 s.d. ARMOSTES: he carries a box which is given to Amyclas at 7.

AMYCLAS. Unseal it, good Armostes; therein lies
The secrets of the oracle. Out with it.
Apollo live our patron! Read, Armostes.
ARMOSTES. *The plot in which the vine takes root*
Begins to dry, from head to foot;
The stock soon withering, want of sap
Doth cause to quail the budding grape.
But from the neighbouring elm a dew
Shall drop and feed the plot anew.

AMYCLAS. That is the oracle; what exposition
Makes the philosopher?
ARMOSTES. This brief one only:
The plot is Sparta, the dried vine the king,
The quailing grape his daughter; but the thing
Of most importance, not to be reveal'd,
Is a near prince, the elm; the rest conceal'd.
Tecnicus.
AMYCLAS. Enough. Although the opening of this riddle
Be but itself a riddle, yet we construe
How near our labouring age draws to a rest.
But must Calantha quail too, that young grape
Untimely budded? I could mourn for her.
Her tenderness hath yet deserv'd no rigour
So to be cross'd by fate.
ARMOSTES. You misapply, sir –
With favour let me speak it – what Apollo
Hath clouded in hid sense. I here conjecture
Her marriage with some neighbouring prince, the dew
Of which befriending elm shall ever strengthen
Your subjects with a sovereignty of power.
CROTOLON. Besides, most gracious lord, the pith of oracles
Is to be then digested when th'events
Expound their truth, not brought as soon to light
As utter'd. Truth is child of Time, and herein

---

14 *quail*: wither, fail.
24 *opening*: expounding.
27, 30 See Textual Notes, p. 340.
37 *events*: outcomes.

I find no scruple; rather cause of comfort,
With unity of kingdoms.
AMYCLAS. May it prove so
For weal of this dear nation. – Where is Ithocles?
Armostes, Crotolon, when this wither'd vine
Of my frail carcass on the funeral pile
Is fir'd into its ashes, let that young man
Be hedg'd about still with your cares and loves.
Much owe I to his worth, much to his service. –
Let such as wait come in now.
ARMOSTES. All attend here!

Enter ITHOCLES, CALANTHA, PROPHILUS, ORGILUS, EUPHRANIA, LEMOPHIL *and* GRONEAS.

CALANTHA. Dear sir, king, father!
ITHOCLES. O my royal master!
AMYCLAS. Cleave not my heart, sweet twins of my life's solace,
With your forejudging fears. There is no physic
So cunningly restorative to cherish
The fall of age, or call back youth and vigour,
As your consents in duty. I will shake off
This languishing disease of time, to quicken
Fresh pleasures in these drooping hours of sadness.
Is fair Euphrania married yet to Prophilus?
CROTOLON. This morning, gracious lord.
ORGILUS. This very morning;
Which, with your Highness' leave, you may observe too.
Our sister looks, methinks, mirthful and sprightly;
As if her chaster fancy could already
Expound the riddle of her gain in losing
A trifle maids know only that they know not.
Pish! prithee blush not; 'tis but honest change

---

40 *scruple*: disturbing thought.
51 *physic*: medicine.
63 *know not*: (1) do not know, (2) have no sexual experience. See Textual Notes, p. 340.

Of fashion in the garment, loose for strait,
And so the modest maid is made a wife.
Shrewd business, is't not, sister?
EUPHRANIA. You are pleasant.
AMYCLAS. We thank thee, Orgilus; this mirth becomes thee.
But wherefore sits the court in such a silence?
A wedding without revels is not seemly.
CALANTHA. Your late indisposition, sir, forbade it.
AMYCLAS. Be it thy charge, Calantha, to set forward
The bridal sports, to which I will be present;
If not, at least consenting. – Mine own Ithocles,
I have done little for thee yet.
ITHOCLES. Y'have built me
To the full height I stand in.
CALANTHA. [*aside*] Now or never! –
May I propose a suit?
AMYCLAS. Demand and have it.
CALANTHA. Pray, sir, give me this young man, and no further
Account him yours than he deserves in all things
To be thought worthy mine. I will esteem him
According to his merit.
AMYCLAS. Still th'art my daughter,
Still grow'st upon my heart. – [*To* ITHOCLES] Give me thine hand. –
Calantha, take thine own. In noble actions
Thou'lt find him firm and absolute. – I would not
Have parted with thee, Ithocles, to any
But to a mistress who is all what I am.
ITHOCLES. A change, great king, most wish'd for, 'cause the same.

---

65 See Additional Notes, p. 349.
67 *Shrewd*: (1) wicked, (2) painful.
75, 76 See Textual Notes, p. 340.
87 See Textual Notes, p. 340.

CALANTHA. Th'art mine. – [*Aside to* ITHOCLES] Have I now kept my word?
ITHOCLES. [*aside to* CALANTHA] Divinely.
ORGILUS. Rich fortunes, guard to favour of a princess,
Rock thee, brave man, in ever-crowned plenty.
You're minion of the time; be thankful for it. –
[*Aside*] Ho, here's a swinge in destiny! Apparent,
The youth is up on tiptoe, yet may stumble.
AMYCLAS. On to your recreations. – Now convey me
Unto my bedchamber. None on his forehead
Wear a distemper'd look.
ALL. The gods preserve ye!
CALANTHA. [*aside to* ITHOCLES] Sweet, be not from my sight.
ITHOCLES. [*aside to* CALANTHA] My whole felicity!

Exeunt, carrying out of the king. ORGILUS *stays* ITHOCLES.

ORGILUS. Shall I be bold, my lord?
ITHOCLES. Thou canst not, Orgilus.
Call me thine own, for Prophilus must henceforth
Be all thy sister's; friendship, though it cease not
In marriage, yet is oft at less command
Than when a single freedom can dispose it.
ORGILUS. Most right, my most good lord, my most great lord,
My gracious princely lord – I might add, royal.
ITHOCLES. Royal? A subject royal?
ORGILUS. Why not, pray, sir?
The sovereignty of kingdoms in their nonage
Stoop'd to desert, not birth. There's as much merit

88 See Additional Notes, p. 349.
89 See Textual Notes, p. 340.
91 *minion of the time*: favourite for the moment.
92 *swinge*: violent swing.
96 See Textual Notes, p. 340.
98 *bold*: presumptuous.
106 *nonage*: early stages.

In clearness of affection as in puddle
Of generation. You have conquer'd love
Even in the loveliest; if I greatly err not,
The son of Venus hath bequeath'd his quiver
To Ithocles his manage, by whose arrows
Calantha's breast is open'd.

ITHOCLES. Can't be possible?

ORGILUS. I was myself a piece of suitor once,
And forward in preferment too; so forward,
That, speaking truth, I may without offence, sir,
Presume to whisper that my hopes and, hark ye,
My certainty of marriage, stood assur'd
With as firm footing, by your leave, as any's
Now at this very instant – but –

ITHOCLES. 'Tis granted.
And for a league of privacy between us,
Read o'er my bosom and partake a secret.
The princess is contracted mine.

ORGILUS. Still, why not?
I now applaud her wisdom. When your kingdom
Stands seated in your will, secure and settl'd,
I dare pronounce you will be a just monarch.
Greece must admire, and tremble.

ITHOCLES. Then the sweetness
Of so imparadis'd a comfort, Orgilus!
It is to banquet with the gods.

ORGILUS. The glory
Of numerous children, potency of nobles,
Bent knees, hearts pav'd to tread on.

ITHOCLES. With a friendship
So dear, so fast as thine.

ORGILUS. I am unfitting
For office; but for service –

ITHOCLES. We'll distinguish
Our fortunes merely in the title; partners
In all respects else but the bed.

ORGILUS. The bed?
Forfend it, Jove's own jealousy, till lastly

---

108 *clearness of affection*: purity of love.
puddle: murkiness, uncertainty.
112 *Ithocles his manage*: the control of Ithocles.
127 *admire*: wonder.

We slip down in the common earth together;
And there our beds are equal, save some monument
To show this was the king, and this the subject.
Soft sad music.
List, what sad sounds are these? Extremely sad ones.

ITHOCLES. Sure from Penthea's lodgings.
ORGILUS. Hark, a voice too.

A Song [*within*].

O no more, no more; too late
Sighs are spent. The burning tapers
Of a life as chaste as fate,
Pure as are unwritten papers,
Are burnt out. No heat, no light
Now remains; 'tis ever night.
Love is dead; let lovers' eyes,
Lock'd in endless dreams,
Th'extremes of all extremes,
Ope no more, for now love dies,
Now love dies, implying
Love's martyrs must be ever, ever dying.

ITHOCLES. O my misgiving heart!
ORGILUS. A horrid stillness
Succeeds this deathful air; let's know the reason.
Tread softly; there is mystery in mourning.
Exeunt.

SCENE IV

Enter CHRYSTALLA *and* PHILEMA, *bringing in* PENTHEA *in a chair, veil'd; two other* SERVANTS *placing two chairs, one on the one side, and the other with an engine on the other. The Maids sit down at her feet, mourning. The* SERVANTS *go out; meet them* ITHOCLES *and* ORGILUS.

---

139 See Textual Notes, p. 340.
155 *air*: song.
0 s.d. See Additional Notes, p. 349.

SERVANT. [*aside to* ORGILUS]
'Tis done; that on her right hand.
ORGILUS. Good, begone.
[*Exeunt* SERVANTS.]
ITHOCLES. Soft peace enrich this room.
ORGILUS. How fares the lady?
PHILEMA. Dead.
CHRYSTALLA. Dead!
PHILEMA. Starv'd.
CHRYSTALLA. Starv'd!
ITHOCLES. Me miserable!
ORGILUS. Tell us,
How parted she from life?
PHILEMA. She call'd for music,
And begg'd some gentle voice to tune a farewell
To life and griefs. Chrystalla touch'd the lute;
I wept the funeral song.
CHRYSTALLA. Which scarce was ended,
But her last breath seal'd up these hollow sounds,
'O cruel Ithocles, and injur'd Orgilus!'
So down she drew her veil; so died.
ITHOCLES. So died!
ORGILUS. Up! You are messengers of death, go from us.
Here's woe enough to court without a prompter.
Away; and hark ye, till you see us next,
No syllable that she is dead. Away;
Keep a smooth brow.
Exeunt PHILEMA *and* CHRYSTALLA.
– My lord.
ITHOCLES. Mine only sister;
Another is not left me.
ORGILUS. Take that chair;
I'll seat me here in this. Between us sits
The object of our sorrows. Some few tears
We'll part among us; I perhaps can mix
One lamentable story to prepare 'em.
There, there, sit there, my lord.

3 *Me miserable*: unhappy man that I am.

ITHOCLES. Yes, as you please.
ITHOCLES *sits down, and is catch'd in the engine.*
What means this treachery?
ORGILUS. Caught, you are caught,
Young master! 'Tis thy throne of coronation,
Thou fool of greatness. See, I take this veil off;
Survey a beauty wither'd by the flames
Of an insulting Phaethon, her brother.
ITHOCLES. Thou mean'st to kill me basely.
ORGILUS. I foreknew
The last act of her life, and train'd thee hither
To sacrifice a tyrant to a turtle.
You dreamt of kingdoms, did ye? How to bosom
The delicacies of a youngling princess,
How with this nod to grace that subtle courtier,
How with that frown to make this noble tremble,
And so forth; whiles Penthea's groans, and tortures,
Her agonies, her miseries, afflictions,
Ne'er touch'd upon your thought. As for my injuries,
Alas, they were beneath your royal pity,
But yet they liv'd, thou proud man, to confound thee.
Behold thy fate, this steel. [*Draws a dagger.*]
ITHOCLES. Strike home; a courage
As keen as thy revenge shall give it welcome.
But prithee faint not; if the wound close up,
Tent it with double force, and search it deeply.
Thou look'st that I should whine and beg compassion,
As loth to leave the vainness of my glories.
A statelier resolution arms my confidence,

---

26 *insulting Phaethon*: arrogant Phaethon (three syllables). Son of Helios, the sun, Phaethon attempted to drive his father's chariot but lost control of it and almost burned up the earth. Zeus destroyed him with a thunderbolt.
28 *train'd*: lured.
29 *turtle*: dove; Orgilus's image for Penthea.
30–1 *bosom The delicacies*: embrace the physical charms.
38 *confound*: ruin, destroy.
42 *Tent it*: open it out, probe it (a medical metaphor).

To cozen thee of honour. Neither could I,
With equal trial of unequal fortune,
By hazard of a duel; 'twere a bravery
Too mighty for a slave intending murder.
On to the execution, and inherit
A conflict with thy horrors.

ORGILUS. By Apollo,
Thou talk'st a goodly language. For requital,
I will report thee to thy mistress richly.
And take this peace along: some few short minutes
Determin'd, my resolves shall quickly follow
Thy wrathful ghost. Then, if we tug for mastery,
Penthea's sacred eyes shall lend new courage.
Give me thy hand; be healthful in thy parting
From lost mortality. Thus, thus, I free it.
[*Stabs*] *him.*

ITHOCLES. Yet, yet, I scorn to shrink.

ORGILUS. Keep up thy spirit.
I will be gentle even in blood; to linger
Pain, which I strive to cure, were to be cruel.
[*Stabs him again.*]

ITHOCLES. Nimble in vengeance, I forgive thee. Follow
Safety, with best success. O, may it prosper! –
Penthea, by thy side thy brother bleeds,
The earnest of his wrongs to thy forc'd faith.
Thoughts of ambition, or delicious banquet,
With beauty, youth, and love, together perish
In my last breath, which on the sacred altar
Of a long-look'd-for peace – now – moves – to heaven. *Dies.*

ORGILUS. Farewell, fair spring of manhood; henceforth welcome
Best expectation of a noble suff'rance.

---

46 *cozen*: cheat.
48 *bravery*: distinction; it was considered dishonourable for a man of superior rank to duel with a social inferior.
55 *Determin'd*: ended.
59 See Textual Notes, p. 340.
61 *linger*: prolong.
64 See Textual Notes, p. 340.
66 *earnest*: payment.

I'll lock the bodies safe, till what must follow
Shall be approv'd. Sweet twins, shine stars forever.
In vain they build their hopes, whose life is shame;
No monument lasts but a happy name.
Exit ORGILUS.

ACT V

SCENE I

Enter BASSANES, *alone.*

BASSANES. Athens, to Athens I have sent, the nursery
Of Greece for learning, and the fount of knowledge.
For here in Sparta there's not left amongst us
One wise man to direct; we're all turn'd madcaps.
'Tis said Apollo is the god of herbs;
Then certainly he knows the virtue of 'em.
To Delphos I have sent too; if there can be
A help for nature, we are sure yet.

Enter ORGILUS.

ORGILUS. Honour
Attend thy counsels ever.
BASSANES. I beseech thee
With all my heart, let me go from thee quietly;
I will not aught to do with thee of all men.
The doubles of a hare, or, in a morning,

---

74 *approv'd*: confirmed by experience.

1–8 *Athens . . . yet*: not aware of Penthea's death, Bassanes is still looking for a means to cure her.

7 See Textual Notes, p. 340.

12 *doubles*: a hare's sharp turns in running. It was regarded as a bad omen for a hare to cross one's path. See Textual Notes, p. 341.

Salutes from a splay-footed witch, to drop
Three drops of blood at th'nose, just and no
more,
Croaking of ravens, or the screech of owls,
Are not so boding mischief as thy crossing
My private meditations. Shun me, prithee;
And if I cannot love thee heartily,
I'll love thee as well as I can.

ORGILUS. Noble Bassanes,
Mistake me not.

BASSANES. Phew, then we shall be troubl'd.
Thou wert ordain'd my plague; heaven make me
thankful,
And give me patience too, heaven, I beseech
thee.

ORGILUS. Accept a league of amity; for
henceforth,
I vow by my best genius, in a syllable
Never to speak vexation. I will study
Service and friendship with a zealous sorrow
For my past incivility towards ye.

BASSANES. Heyday, good words, good words! I
must believe 'em,
And be a coxcomb for my labour.

ORGILUS. Use not
So hard a language; your misdoubt is causeless.
For instance, if you promise to put on
A constancy of patience – such a patience
As chronicle or history ne'er mention'd,
As follows not example, but shall stand
A wonder and a theme for imitation,
The first, the index pointing to a second –
I will acquaint ye with an unmatch'd secret,

---

13 *Salutes*: greetings.
splay-footed: splayed feet were taken to be the sign of a witch.

14–15 *Three . . . owls*: all superstitious omens of evil.

24 *by my best genius*: cf. II.iii.122.

29 *coxcomb*: fool.

34 *follows not example*: has no precedent.

36 *index*: pointer; from the pointing hand used in printed books to mark a noteworthy passage.

Whose knowledge to your griefs shall set a period.
BASSANES. Thou canst not, Orgilus; 'tis in the power
Of the gods only. Yet, for satisfaction,
Because I note an earnest in thine utterance,
Unforc'd and naturally free, be resolute
The virgin bays shall not withstand the lightning
With a more careless danger than my constancy
The full of thy relation. Could it move
Distraction in a senseless marble statue,
It should find me a rock. I do expect now
Some truth of unheard moment.
ORGILUS. To your patience
You must add privacy, as strong in silence
As mysteries lock'd up in Jove's own bosom.
BASSANES. A skull hid in the earth a treble age
Shall sooner prate.
ORGILUS. Lastly, to such direction
As the severity of a glorious action
Deserves to lead your wisdom and your judgement,
You ought to yield obedience.
BASSANES. With assurance
Of will and thankfulness.
ORGILUS. With manly courage
Please then to follow me.
BASSANES. Where'er, I fear not.
Exeunt all.

---

38 *period*: end.
41 *earnest*: seriousness.
42 *resolute*: assured.
43 *withstand the lightning*: it was a classical belief that lightning would not strike the laurel (bay) tree, which was sacred to Apollo.
44 *careless danger*: contempt of danger.
48 *unheard moment*: unprecedented importance.
52 *prate*: prattle, tell tales.

SCENE II

Loud music. Enter GRONEAS *and* LEMOPHIL, *leading* EUPHRANIA; CHRYSTALLA *and* PHILEMA, *leading* PROPHILUS; NEARCHUS *supporting* CALANTHA; CROTOLON *and* AMELUS. *Cease loud music; all make a stand.*

CALANTHA. We miss our servant Ithocles and Orgilus;
On whom attend they?
CROTOLON. My son, gracious princess,
Whisper'd some new device, to which these revels
Should be but usher, wherein I conceive
Lord Ithocles and he himself are actors.
CALANTHA. A fair excuse for absence. As for Bassanes,
Delights to him are troublesome. Armostes
Is with the king?
CROTOLON. He is.
CALANTHA. On to the dance. –
Dear cousin, hand you the bride; the bridegroom must be
Intrusted to my courtship. – Be not jealous,
Euphrania; I shall scarcely prove a temptress. –
Fall to our dance.

Music.

NEARCHUS *dance with* EUPHRANIA, PROPHILUS *with* CALANTHA, CHRYSTALLA *with* LEMOPHIL, PHILEMA *with* GRONEAS. *Dance the first change, during which enter* ARMOSTES.

ARMOSTES. (*in* CALANTHA*'s ear*) The king your father's dead.

---

0 s.d. *supporting*: escorting on his arm.
3 *device*: dramatic performance.
9 *hand*: lead by the hand. See Textual Notes, p. 341.
12 s.d. *change*: completed figure or round of a dance.

CALANTHA. To the other change.
ARMOSTES. Is't possible?

Dance again. Enter BASSANES.

BASSANES. [*in* CALANTHA*'s ear*] O, madam!
Penthea, poor Penthea's starv'd.
CALANTHA. Beshrew thee. –
Lead to the next.
BASSANES. Amazement dulls my senses.

Dance again. Enter ORGILUS.

ORGILUS. (*in* CALANTHA*'s ear*) Brave Ithocles is murder'd, murder'd cruelly.
CALANTHA. How dull this music sounds! Strike up more sprightly;
Our footings are not active like our heart,
Which treads the nimbler measure.
ORGILUS. I am thunderstruck.
Last change. Cease music.
CALANTHA. So, let us breathe awhile. Hath not this motion
Rais'd fresher colour on your cheeks?
NEARCHUS. Sweet princess,
A perfect purity of blood enamels
The beauty of your white.
CALANTHA. We all look cheerfully.
And cousin, 'tis, methinks, a rare presumption
In any who prefers our lawful pleasures
Before their own sour censure, to interrupt
The custom of this ceremony bluntly.
NEARCHUS. None dares, lady.
CALANTHA. Yes, yes; some hollow voice deliver'd to me
How that the king was dead.
ARMOSTES. The king is dead.
That fatal news was mine; for in mine arms
He breath'd his last, and with his crown bequeath'd ye

---

19 *measure*: dance; a measure was a slow, solemn dance.
22 *enamels*: colours. The ideal beauty displayed a blush of colour on a perfectly white cheek.
25 *prefers*: sets first.

Your mother's wedding ring, which here I tender.
CROTOLON. Most strange!
CALANTHA. Peace crown his ashes.
We are queen, then.
NEARCHUS. Long live Calantha, Sparta's sovereign queen!
ALL. Long live the queen!
CALANTHA. What whisper'd Bassanes?
BASSANES. That my Penthea, miserable soul,
Was starv'd to death.
CALANTHA. She's happy; she hath finish'd
A long and painful progress. A third murmur
Pierc'd mine unwilling ears.
ORGILUS. That Ithocles
Was murder'd; rather butcher'd, had not bravery
Of an undaunted spirit, conquering terror,
Proclaim'd his last act triumph over ruin.
ARMOSTES. How? Murder'd!
CALANTHA. By whose hand?
ORGILUS. [*draws his dagger*] By mine. This weapon
Was instrument to my revenge. The reasons
Are just and known; quit him of these, and then
Never liv'd gentleman of greater merit,
Hope, or abiliment to steer a kingdom.
CROTOLON. Fie, Orgilus!
EUPHRANIA. Fie, brother!
CALANTHA. You have done it?
BASSANES. How it was done let him report, the forfeit
Of whose allegiance to our laws doth covet
Rigour of justice; but that done it is,
Mine eyes have been an evidence of credit
Too sure to be convinc'd. – Armostes, rend not
Thine arteries with hearing the bare circumstances
Of these calamities. Thou'st lost a nephew,
A niece, and I a wife. Continue man still;

---

43 *last act*: probably a theatrical metaphor.
46 *quit*: acquit.
48 *abiliment*: ability, capacity.
54 *convinc'd*: confuted. See Textual Notes, p. 341.
55 *circumstances*: details.

Make me the pattern of digesting evils,
Who can outlive my mighty ones, not shrinking
At such a pressure as would sink a soul
Into what's most of death, the worst of horrors.
But I have seal'd a covenant with sadness,
And enter'd into bonds without condition,
To stand these tempests calmly. – Mark me, nobles,
I do not shed a tear, not for Penthea.
Excellent misery!

CALANTHA. We begin our reign
With a first act of justice. – Thy confession,
Unhappy Orgilus, dooms thee a sentence.
But yet thy father's or thy sister's presence
Shall be excus'd. – Give, Crotolon, a blessing
To thy lost son. – Euphrania, take a farewell,
And both be gone.

CROTOLON. Confirm thee, noble sorrow,
In worthy resolution.

EUPHRANIA. Could my tears speak,
My griefs were slight.

ORGILUS. All goodness dwell amongst ye. –
Enjoy my sister, Prophilus; my vengeance
Aim'd never at thy prejudice.

CALANTHA. Now withdraw.

Exeunt CROTOLON, PROPHILUS, *and* EUPHRANIA.

Bloody relater of thy stains in blood,
For that thou hast reported him whose fortunes
And life by thee are both at once snatch'd from him
With honourable mention, make thy choice
Of what death likes thee best; there's all our bounty. –
But to excuse delays, let me, dear cousin,
Entreat you and these lords see execution
Instant, before ye part.

NEARCHUS. Your will commands us.

---

58 *digesting*: those who stomach, endure.
74 See Textual Notes, p. 341.
76 *prejudice*: harm.
81 *likes*: pleases.
82 *excuse*: obviate.

ORGILUS. One suit, just queen; my last. Vouchsafe your clemency
That by no commmon hand I be divided
From this my humble frailty.
CALANTHA. To their wisdoms
Who are to be spectators of thine end,
I make the reference. Those that are dead
Are dead. Had they not now died, of necessity
They must have paid the debt they ow'd to nature,
One time or other. Use dispatch, my lords;
We'll suddenly prepare our coronation.
Exeunt CALANTHA, PHILEMA, [*and*] CHRYSTALLA.
ARMOSTES. 'Tis strange these tragedies should never touch on
Her female pity.
BASSANES. She has a masculine spirit.
And wherefore should I pule, and like a girl
Put finger in the eye? Let's be all toughness,
Without distinction betwixt sex and sex.
NEARCHUS. Now Orgilus, thy choice.
ORGILUS. To bleed to death.
ARMOSTES. The executioner?
ORGILUS. Myself; no surgeon.
I am well skill'd in letting blood. Bind fast
This arm, that so the pipes may from their conduits
Convey a full stream. Here's a skilful instrument. [*Shows his dagger.*]
Only I am a beggar to some charity
To speed me in this execution,
By lending th'other prick to th'tother arm,
When this is bubbling life out.
BASSANES. I am for ye.
It most concerns my art, my care, my credit. –

---

87 *frailty*: fleshly existence.
93 *suddenly*: immediately.
96 *pule*: whine.
105 *speed*: assist.
108 *credit*: reputation.

Quick, fillet both these arms.
ORGILUS. Gramercy, friendship.
Such courtesies are real which flow cheerfully
Without an expectation of requital.
Reach me a staff in this hand. If a proneness
Or custom in my nature, from my cradle,
Had been inclin'd to fierce and eager bloodshed,
A coward guilt, hid in a coward quaking,
Would have betray'd fame to ignoble flight
And vagabond pursuit of dreadful safety.
But look upon my steadiness, and scorn not
The sickness of my fortune, which since Bassanes
Was husband to Penthea, had lain bedrid.
We trifle time in words. Thus I show cunning
In opening of a vein too full, too lively.
[*Opens a vein.*]
ARMOSTES. Desperate courage!
NEARCHUS. Honourable infamy!
LEMOPHIL. I tremble at the sight.
GRONEAS. Would I were loose!
BASSANES. It sparkles like a lusty wine new broach'd;
The vessel must be sound from which it issues.
Grasp hard this other stick. I'll be as nimble.
But prithee look not pale. Have at ye; stretch out
Thine arm with vigour and unshook virtue.
[*Opens another vein.*]
Good! O, I envy not a rival fitted
To conquer in extremities. This pastime
Appears majestical. Some high-tun'd poem
Hereafter shall deliver to posterity
The writer's glory and his subject's triumph.

---

109 *fillet*: bind, with a narrow strip of cloth. See Textual Notes, p. 341.
111 See Textual Notes, p. 341.
116 *fame*: reputation, honour.
117 *vagabond*: worthless.
dreadful: full of fear.
121 *cunning*: skill.
123 See Textual Notes, p. 341.
124 *loose*: free to leave.
125 *broach'd*: tapped (like a wine barrel).
129 *unshook*: unshaken.

How is't, man? Droop not yet.
ORGILUS. I feel no palsies.
On a pair-royal do I wait in death:
My sovereign, as his liegeman; on my mistress,
As a devoted servant; and on Ithocles,
As if no brave, yet no unworthy enemy.
Nor did I use an engine to entrap
His life out of a slavish fear to combat
Youth, strength, or cunning, but for that I durst not
Engage the goodness of a cause on fortune,
By which his name might have outfac'd my vengeance.
An Tecnicus, inspir'd with Phoebus' fire,
I call to mind thy augury; 'twas perfect:
Revenge proves its own executioner.
When feeble man is bending to his mother,
The dust he was first fram'd on, thus he totters.
BASSANES. Life's fountain is dried up.
ORGILUS. So falls the standards
Of my prerogative in being a creature.
A mist hangs o'er mine eyes; the sun's bright splendour
Is clouded in an everlasting shadow.
Welcome, thou ice that sitt'st about my heart;
No heat can ever thaw thee. *Dies.*
NEARCHUS. Speech hath left him.
BASSANES. He has shook hands with time. His funeral urn
Shall be my charge. Remove the bloodless body.
The coronation must require attendance.
That past, my few days can be but one mourning. *Exeunt.*

---

136 *pair-royal*: in cards, three of a kind; with an allusion to the royal nature of those who have died.
wait: attend.
143 *Engage*: stake.
149 *on*: of.
150 *falls the standards*: drop the ensigns. Orgilus drops the staves supporting him, or collapses himself.
151 *prerogative*: natural privilege.
156 *shook hands*: parted.
157 *charge*: responsibility.

SCENE III

An altar covered with white; two lights of virgin wax. Music of recorders, during which enter four bearing ITHOCLES *on a hearse, or in a chair, in a rich robe, and a crown on his head.* [*They*] *place him on one side of the altar. After him enter* CALANTHA *in a white robe and crown'd;* EUPHRANIA, PHILEMA, CHRYSTALLA, *in white;* NEARCHUS, ARMOSTES, CROTOLON, PROPHILUS, AMELUS, BASSANES, LEMOPHIL, *and* GRONEAS. CALANTHA *goes and kneels before the altar. The rest stand off, the women kneeling behind. Cease recorders during her devotions. Soft music.* CALANTHA *and the rest rise, doing obeisance to the altar.*

CALANTHA. Our orisons are heard; the gods are merciful.
Now tell me, you whose loyalties pays tribute
To us your lawful sovereign, how unskilful
Your duties or obedience is to render
Subjection to the sceptre of a virgin,
Who have been ever fortunate in princes
Of masculine and stirring composition.
A woman has enough to govern wisely
Her own demeanours, passions, and divisions.
A nation, warlike and inur'd to practice
Of policy and labour, cannot brook
A feminate authority. We therefore
Command your counsel, how you may advise us
In choosing of a husband whose abilities
Can better guide this kingdom.
NEARCHUS. Royal lady,

---

0 s.d. See Textual Notes, p. 341.
1 *orisons*: prayers.
3 *unskilful*: unwise.
9 *divisions*: inner strife.

Your law is in your will.
ARMOSTES. We have seen tokens
Of constancy too lately to mistrust it.
CROTOLON. Yet if your Highness settle on a choice
By your own judgement both allow'd and lik'd of,
Sparta may grow in power, and proceed
To an increasing height.
CALANTHA. [*to* BASSANES] Hold you the same mind?
BASSANES. Alas, great mistress, reason is so clouded
With the thick darkness of my infinite woes
That I forecast nor dangers, hopes, or safety.
Give me some corner of the world to wear out
The remnant of the minutes I must number,
Where I may hear no sounds but sad complaints
Of virgins who have lost contracted partners,
Of husbands howling that their wives were ravish'd
By some untimely fate, of friends divided
By churlish opposition, or of fathers
Weeping upon their children's slaughter'd carcasses,
Or daughters groaning o'er their fathers' hearses,
And I can dwell there, and with these keep consort
As musical as theirs. What can you look for
From an old, foolish, peevish, doting man,
But craziness of age?
CALANTHA. Cousin of Argos.
NEARCHUS. Madam?
CALANTHA. Were I presently
To choose you for my lord, I'll open freely
What articles I would propose to treat on
Before our marriage.
NEARCHUS. Name them, virtuous lady.
CALANTHA. I would presume you would retain the royalty
Of Sparta in her own bounds. Then in Argos

---

23 See Textual Notes, p. 341.
27 *complaints*: lamentations.
34 *consort*: (1) company, (2) harmony.
42 *royalty*: sovereign power.

Armostes might be viceroy; in Messene
Might Crotolon bear sway; and Bassanes –
BASSANES. I, queen? Alas, what I?
CALANTHA. Be Sparta's marshal.
The multitudes of high employments could not
But set a peace to private griefs. – [*To* NEARCHUS] These gentlemen,
Groneas and Lemophil, with worthy pensions,
Should wait upon your person in your chamber.
I would bestow Philema on Amelus;
She'll prove a constant wife. And Chrystalla
Should into Vesta's temple.
BASSANES. This is a testament;
It sounds not like conditions on a marriage.
NEARCHUS. All this should be perform'd.
CALANTHA. Lastly, for Prophilus,
He should be, cousin, solemnly invested
In all those honours, titles, and preferments
Which his dear friend, and my neglected husband,
Too short a time enjoy'd.
PROPHILUS. I am unworthy
To live in your remembrance.
EUPHRANIA. Excellent lady!
NEARCHUS. Madam, what means that word 'neglected husband'?
CALANTHA. Forgive me. Now I turn to thee, thou shadow
Of my contracted lord. – Bear witness all,
I put my mother's wedding ring upon
His finger; 'twas my father's last bequest.
Thus I new marry him whose wife I am;
Death shall not separate us. O my lords,
I but deceiv'd your eyes with antic gesture,
When one news straight came huddling on another,
Of death, and death, and death. Still I danc'd forward;

---

50 *wait . . . chamber*: act as your personal attendants.
51–3 See Textual Notes, p. 341, and Additional Notes, p. 349.
64 See Textual Notes, p. 341.
68 *antic gesture*: theatrical performance.

But it struck home, and here, and in an instant.
Be such mere women, who with shrieks and outcries
Can vow a present end to all their sorrows,
Yet live to vow new pleasures, and outlive them.
They are the silent griefs which cut the heartstrings.
Let me die smiling.

NEARCHUS. 'Tis a truth too ominous.

CALANTHA. One kiss on these cold lips; my last.
[*Kisses* ITHOCLES.]
Crack, crack! –
Argos now's Sparta's king. Command the voices
Which wait at th'altar now to sing the song
I fitted for my end.

NEARCHUS. Sirs, the song.

A Song.

ALL. *Glories, pleasures, pomps, delights, and ease*
Can but please
The outward senses, when the mind
Is not untroubl'd, or by peace refin'd.

1 [VOICE]. *Crowns may flourish and decay;*
Beauties shine, but fade away.

2 [VOICE]. *Youth may revel, yet it must*
Lie down in a bed of dust.

3 [VOICE]. *Earthly honours flow and waste;*
Time alone doth change and last.

ALL. *Sorrows mingl'd with contents prepare*
Rest for care;
Love only reigns in death; though art
Can find no comfort for a broken heart.

[CALANTHA *dies.*]

ARMOSTES. Look to the queen!

BASSANES. Her heart is broke indeed.

---

74 *vow new pleasures*: i.e. take new marriage partners.
75 See Additional Notes, p. 349.
83 See Textual Notes, p. 341.
91 *contents*: contentments.

O royal maid, would thou hadst miss'd this part;
Yet 'twas a brave one. I must weep to see
Her smile in death.

ARMOSTES. Wise Tecnicus! Thus said he:
When youth is ripe, and age from time doth part,
The lifeless trunk shall wed the broken heart.
'Tis here fulfill'd.

NEARCHUS. I am your king.

ALL. Long live
Nearchus, King of Sparta!

NEARCHUS. Her last will
Shall never be digress'd from. Wait in order
Upon these faithful lovers as becomes us.
The counsels of the gods are never known
Till men can call th'effects of them their own.
[*Exeunt*].

Finis

The Epilogue

Where noble judgements and clear eyes are fix'd
To grace endeavour, there sits truth not mix'd
With ignorance. Those censures may command
Belief which talk not till they understand.
Let some say, 'This was flat'; some, 'Here the scene
Fell from its height'; another, that the mean
Was 'ill observ'd' in such a growing passion
As it transcended either state or fashion.
Some few may cry, ''Twas pretty well', or 'So,
But –', and there shrug in silence. Yet we know

---

96 *part*: role.
97 *brave*: (1) courageous, (2) fine, rewarding (as an actor's part).
103 *Wait*: attend.
3 *censures*: critics' opinions.
6 *mean*: artistic moderation.
8 *state or fashion*: tragic dignity or social convention.

Our writer's aim was in the whole address'd
Well to deserve of all, but please the best.
Which granted, by th'allowance of this strain,
The Broken Heart may be piec'd up again.

Finis

---

13 *allowance*: approval; an invitation to applause from the audience.

14 *piec'd up*: put together.

'TIS
Pitty Shee's a Whore

Acted by the *Queenes* Maieſties Ser-
*uants, at The Phœnix in
Drury-Lane.*

LONDON.
Printed by *Nicholas Okes* for *Richard
Collins,* and are to be ſold at his ſhop
in *Pauls* Church-yard, at the ſigne
of the three Kings. 1633.

Title-page of the 1633 Quarto of *'Tis Pity She's a Whore*, reproduced by permission of the Bodleian Library, Oxford (shelfmark Mal. 238 (3)).

INTRODUCTORY NOTE

Sources

It is unlikely that Ford worked from any one source to create the multiple plots of *'Tis Pity She's a Whore*, and no single main source has been identified, though scholars have suggested a number of literary and historical analogues and influences, especially for the story of Giovanni and Annabella. They include Ovid's story of Canace (*Heroides*, xi) and Parthenius's fifth romance, the tale of Leucippus (both stories retold in Thomas Heywood's *Gunaikeion* (1624)), Beaumont and Fletcher's *A King and No King* (1611), and the notorious trial in 1631 of Sir Giles Alington for marrying the daughter of his half-sister.

François de Rosset's account of an incestuous love between the two beautiful children of a French country gentleman, the brother a brilliant young student who loses his sister to a wealthy old husband but sustains the affair after the marriage (*Les Histoires Tragiques de Nostre Temps* (Paris, 1615)), closely matches the central action of Ford's tragedy, Acts I–III, but the catastrophe has no parallel there and was perhaps suggested to the dramatist by Francis Quarles's *Argalus and Parthenia* (1629), a free retelling in verse of a story from Sidney's *Arcadia* (1590). Notably, Quarles's poem contains an original episode in which Death as bridegroom enters a wedding feast, carrying impaled on his dart the bleeding heart of his bride.

There are parallels between the scene in which Soranzo tries to force Annabella to reveal the name of her lover (IV.iii) and Chapman's *Bussy D'Ambois* (V.i), where Tamyra is treated even more brutally by her husband, and there are larger general debts to Shakespeare's *Romeo and Juliet*, particularly in the figures of Friar Bonaventura and the nurse Putana. The Bergetto sub-plot seems to owe something to the Ward's reluctant courtship of Isabella, in Middleton's *Women Beware Women*, and even to the historical episode of the attempted murder of Friar Serpi in Venice (1607) where the assassins took refuge in the house of the Papal Nuncio.

However, the weaving of the play's multiple plot structure and the development of the chief characters,

Giovanni, Annabella, Soranzo, and even Vasques and Bergetto, are achievements which source studies will not explain.

Stage history

Although the stage history of *'Tis Pity She's a Whore* begins in obscurity, since the date of composition has not been determined, there is a satisfying record of performances. The 1633 Quarto says that it was acted at the Phoenix theatre by the Queen's Men, one of the successive companies managed there by Christopher Beeston, but this may have been a revival rather than the original production. The apology at the end of the Quarto (possibly written by Ford himself) referring to the general commendation deserved by the actors in their presentation of the tragedy might mean that the play was well received by contemporary audiences; certainly, *'Tis Pity She's a Whore* remained in the Phoenix repertoire until the closing of all theatres by the Puritans in 1642.

Pepys saw the play at the Salisbury Court theatre, London, in 1661, and another diarist saw it at Norwich in 1663, both performances probably by George Jolly's troupe, but the tragedy then vanished from the stage until 1894, when Maeterlinck's cautious adaptation, *Annabella*, was given a Paris production at the Théâtre de l'Oeuvre.

The modern stage history of the play begins with private performances in London staged by the Phoenix Society at the Shaftesbury Theatre in 1923 and by the Arts Theatre Club in 1934, but it was not until 1940 that the first public performances of the play since the seventeenth century were mounted by Donald Wolfit, first at the Arts Theatre, Cambridge, then at the Strand Theatre in London. Productions by professional and amateur companies followed: at the Nottingham Playhouse in 1955, and again at the Arts Theatre, Cambridge, in 1958.

Since 1960 *'Tis Pity She's a Whore* has been regularly performed on the British stage. In 1961 David Thompson produced Bernard Miles's adaptation at the Mermaid Theatre, in an Elizabethan setting. The cast included Edward de Souza (Giovanni), Zena Walker

(Annabella), David Sumner (Soranzo), Barbara Barnett (Hippolita), John Woodvine (Vasques) and Patience Collier (Putana). In 1967 there was a RADA production at the Vanbrugh Theatre, in 1968 the Bristol Old Vic played the tragedy at the Little Theatre under the direction of John David, and in 1969 the Marlowe Society performed it at the Arts Theatre, Cambridge.

In 1972 Roland Joffé directed a production in period costume for the National Theatre at the Old Vic, with Nicholas Clay (Giovanni), Anna Carteret (Annabella), Diana Rigg (Hippolita), Gawn Grainger (Vasques), and James Hayes as a eunuch Putana. In the same year, the Actors Company took the play to Oxford and Cambridge after performances at the Edinburgh Festival; Ian McKellen played Giovanni, Paola Dionisotti Annabella, Edward Petherbridge Soranzo and John Bennett Vasques. An experimental Artaudian production took place at Vincennes in 1975, given by the Théâtre de la Tempête under the direction of Stuart Seide, and in 1976 boys from Alleyn's School, Dulwich, directed by Michael Lempriere and John Newton, played the tragedy as it might have been performed by Beeston's Boys on a reconstruction of the Cockpit stage. In the same year there were other productions at Bradford under the direction of John Howard, and (again) at Cambridge by the Amateur Dramatic Club.

1977 saw an important Royal Shakespeare Company studio production at The Other Place, Stratford-upon-Avon, followed by performances at Newcastle-upon-Tyne and the Donmar Warehouse, London. Roy Daniels directed Simon Rouse (Giovanni), Barbara Kellerman (Annabella), Nigel Terry (Soranzo), Anne Rait (Hippolita), Geoffrey Hutchings (Vasques), Tim Wylton (Bergetto), Ron Cook (Poggio) and Valerie Lush (Putana), giving the play a convincing turn-of-the-century, middle-class-Italian setting. It is described by J. M. Maguin, in *Cahiers Élisabéthains*, 12 (1977), 83–5. There were new productions in 1978 at the Northcott Theatre, Exeter, and the Citizens' Theatre, Glasgow, where *'Tis Pity She's a Whore* formed part of a four-hour compression of three Jacobean plays titled *Painter's Palace of Pleasure*, directed by Philip Prowse.

In 1979 the Great Eastern Stage Company toured the play in Lincolnshire and Humberside, and there were productions in the University Theatre, Manchester, and Theatre Gwynedd, Bangor. 1980 saw productions at London by RADA and by the New Theatre Company, at Oxford by the Magdalen Players and Merton Floats, and at Warwick by the Warwick Drama Society. In 1981 *'Tis Pity She's a Whore* was played at Cambridge by the Dryden Society, in 1983 at Cardiff by the Sherman Arena Theatre Company, and in 1984 at Edinburgh by the Oxford University College Players.

The place of Ford's tragedy on the contemporary stage now seems assured (Tom Stoppard quotes extensively from it in his tragi-comedy *The Real Thing* (1982)), and this is without taking into account performances in France, Germany and America. Radio versions of the play were broadcast by the BBC in 1962 and 1970, and in 1980 there was a BBC television production which gave it an effective nineteenth-century manor-house setting but radically altered Ford's plot (Soranzo survived to arrange the concealment of what had happened, and Bergetto eloped with Philotis). In 1971 a highly successful film of *'Tis Pity She's a Whore* was made by the Italian director Giuseppe Patroni Griffi, and released with English dialogue in 1973.

Further information about a number of these productions is to be found in Lucette Andrieu, 'Dommage qu'elle soit une p— (*'Tis Pity She's a Whore*) de John Ford: vitalité et devenir scénique de la tragédie', *Cahiers Élisabéthains*, 3 (1973), 16–40, and Michael Scott, *Renaissance Drama and a Modern Audience* (London: Macmillan (1982)), pp. 89–104 and 121–3.

Individual editions of the play

The only old-spelling, annotated edition of *'Tis Pity She's a Whore* is by Stuart P. Sherman (Boston, 1915); E.W. Schmitz's critical edition of the play for her Cambridge M.Litt. (1956–9), though often used by later editors, remains unpublished.

N.W. Bawcutt's 1966 edition for the Regents Renaissance Drama series (Nebraska and London: University of Nebraska Press and Edward Arnold) was the first founded on an extensive collation of copies of the 1633 Quarto (16 copies). It deals with matters of dating and sources, offers a brief stage history, and discusses questions of interpretation and characterisation. Like other editions in this series, it places Ford's work in its political and literary context. In the same year, Mark Stavig's less fully annotated edition was published by Appleton-Century-Crofts, New York.

Brian Morris's New Mermaid edition (London, 1968) deals briefly with Ford's life and the date of composition and sources of the play. It also contains a long, close and sensitive critical reading, and a stimulating section on the dramaturgy and language of the tragedy.

The fullest single edition of the play is Derek Roper's, in the Revels Plays series (London, 1975). The text is based on a collation of all the known copies of the 1633 Quarto and later scholarly editions. The fifty-three-page introduction deals with Ford's life and works, sources, date of composition, stage and textual history, and provides another important critical reading of the tragedy. The text is fully annotated and accompanied with substantial extracts (in translation) from de Rosset's incest story of Doralice and Lyzaran, an extended note on the Sannazaro poem mentioned in II.ii, and representative passages of criticism of *'Tis Pity She's a Whore* from Pepys to T.S. Eliot.

The play is also found in a number of annotated anthologies. These include: H.F. Rubenstein (ed.), *Great English Plays* (London, 1928), H.R. Walley and John H. Wilson (eds.), *Early Seventeenth Century Plays* (New York, 1930), Esther Cloudman Dunn (ed.), *Eight Famous Elizabethan Plays* (New York, 1932), G.B. Harrison (ed.), *Plays by John Webster and John Ford* (London, 1933), George Rylands (ed.), *Elizabethan Tragedy, Six Representative Plays* (London, 1933), E.W. Parks and R.C. Beatty (eds.), *The English Drama. An Anthology, 900–1642* (New York, 1935), G.E. Bentley (ed.), *The Development of English Drama* (New York, 1950), Mario Praz (ed.), *Il drama elisabettiano: Webster, Ford* (Rome, 1946), A.K. McIlwraith (ed.), *Five Stuart Tragedies* (Oxford, 1953), J. Dennis Huston and Alvin B. Kernan (eds.), *Classics of the Renaissance Theatre* (New York, 1969), and Russell A. Fraser and Norman Rabkin (eds.), *Drama of the English Renaissance* (London and New York, 1976).

[DEDICATORY EPISTLE]

To the truly noble John, Earl of Peterborough, Lord Mordaunt, Baron of Turvey.

My Lord,

Where a truth of merit hath a general warrant, there love is but a debt, acknowledgement a justice. Greatness cannot often claim virtue by inheritance; yet, in this, yours appears most eminent, for that you are not more rightly heir to your fortunes than glory shall be to your memory. Sweetness of disposition ennobles a freedom of birth; in both, your lawful interest adds honour to your own name, and mercy to my presumption. Your noble allowance of these first fruits of my leisure in the action, emboldens my confidence of your as noble construction in this presentment; especially since my service must ever owe particular duty to your favours, by a particular engagement. The gravity of the subject may easily excuse the lightness of the title; otherwise I had been a severe judge against mine own guilt. Princes have vouchsafed grace to trifles offered from a purity of devotion; your lordship may likewise please to admit into your good opinion, with these weak endeavours, the constancy of affection from the sincere lover of your deserts in honour,

John Ford.

Title *John . . . Turvey*: see Additional Notes, p. 350.

5 *Where . . . warrant*: where there is general proof of genuine merit.

12 *freedom*: gentility.
lawful interest: legitimate claim.

14 *allowance*: recognition, approval.

15 *in the action*: performed on stage.

17 *presentment*: dedication and presentation.

20 *lightness*: frivolity.

22–3 *Princes . . . devotion*: an idea also advanced by Ford's friend, Philip Massinger, in some of his dedications.

[COMMENDATORY VERSE]

To my Friend, the Author.

With admiration I beheld this Whore
Adorn'd with beauty, such as might restore
(If ever being as thy Muse hath fam'd)
Her Giovanni, in his love unblam'd.
The ready Graces lent their willing aid;
Pallas herself now play'd the chamber-maid
And help'd to put her dressings on. Secure
Rest thou, that thy name herein shall endure
To th'end of age; and Annabella be
Gloriously fair, even in her infamy.

Thomas Ellice.

This poem occurs on a single inserted leaf found in only a few copies of Q.

1 *admiration*: wonder.

5 *Graces*: three daughter of Zeus, whose gifts were beauty, grace and kindness.

6 *Pallas*: Greek goddess of wisdom, but also identified with poetic inspiration.

11 *Thomas Ellice*: see Additional Notes, p. 350.

The Scene,
PARMA

THE ACTORS' NAMES

BONAVENTURA A Friar
A Cardinal Nuncio to the Pope
SORANZO A nobleman
FLORIO A citizen of Parma
DONADO Another citizen
GRIMALDI A Roman gentleman
GIOVANNI Son to Florio
BERGETTO Nephew to Donado
RICHARDETTO A supposed physician
VASQUES Servant to Soranzo
POGGIO Servant to Bergetto
Banditti
[Officers, attendants]

WOMEN

ANNABELLA Daughter to Florio
HIPPOLITA Wife to Richardetto
PHILOTIS His niece
PUTANA Tutress to Annabella
[Ladies]

See Additional Notes, p. 350.
12 *supposed*: pretended.

'TIS PITY SHE'S A WHORE

ACT I

SCENE I

[*Enter*] FRIAR *and* GIOVANNI.

FRIAR. Dispute no more in this, for know, young man,
These are no school-points. Nice philosophy
May tolerate unlikely arguments,
But Heaven admits no jest: wits that presum'd
On wit too much, by striving how to prove
There was no God, with foolish grounds of art,
Discover'd first the nearest way to Hell,
And fill'd the world with devilish atheism.
Such questions, youth, are fond; for better 'tis
To bless the sun than reason why it shines;
Yet he thou talk'st of is above the sun –
No more! I may not hear it.
GIOVANNI. Gentle father,
To you I have unclasp'd my burden'd soul,
Emptied the storehouse of my thoughts and heart,
Made myself poor of secrets; have not left
Another word untold, which hath not spoke
All what I ever durst or think or know;
And yet is here the comfort I shall have?
Must I not do what all men else may – love?
FRIAR. Yes, you may love, fair son.
GIOVANNI. Must I not praise
That beauty which, if fram'd anew, the gods
Would make a god of, if they had it there,
And kneel to it, as I do kneel to them?

---

2 *school-points*: topics for academic debate.
Nice: (1) subtle, (2) dangerous.
4 *admits*: tolerates.
6 *art*: academic learning.
9 *fond*: foolish.

FRIAR. Why, foolish madman!
GIOVANNI. Shall a peevish sound,
A customary form, from man to man,
Of brother and of sister, be a bar
'Twixt my perpetual happiness and me?
Say that we had one father, say one womb
(Curse to my joys!) gave both us life, and birth;
Are we not therefore each to other bound
So much the more by nature? by the links
Of blood, of reason? nay, if you will have't,
Even of religion, to be ever one,
One soul, one flesh, one love, one heart, one all?
FRIAR. Have done, unhappy youth, for thou art lost.
GIOVANNI. Shall then, for that I am her brother born,
My joys be ever banish'd from her bed?
No, father; in your eyes I see the change
Of pity and compassion; from your age,
As from a sacred oracle, distils
The life of counsel. Tell me, holy man,
What cure shall give me ease in these extremes?
FRIAR. Repentance, son, and sorrow for this sin;
For thou hast mov'd a Majesty above
With thy unranged, almost, blasphemy.
GIOVANNI. O, do not speak of that, dear confessor.
FRIAR. Art thou, my son, that miracle of wit
Who once, within these three months, wert esteem'd
A wonder of thine age, throughout Bononia?
How did the university applaud
Thy government, behaviour, learning, speech,
Sweetness, and all that could make up a man!
I was proud of my tutelage, and chose

---

24 *peevish*: trifling.
32 *blood*: kinship; but the blood was also considered to be the physical location of sexual passion.
35 *unhappy*: ill-fated.
45 *unranged*: deranged, beyond all limits.
46 *confessor*: accented on the first syllable.
47 *wit*: intelligence.
49 *Bononia*: Bologna; the location of a famous university.
51 *government*: demeanour.

Rather to leave my books than part with thee.
I did so; but the fruits of all my hopes
Are lost in thee, as thou art in thyself.
O Giovanni! Hast thou left the schools
Of knowledge, to converse with lust and death?
For death waits on thy lust. Look through the world,
And thou shalt see a thousand faces shine
More glorious than this idol thou ador'st.
Leave her, and take thy choice; 'tis much less sin,
Though in such games as those they lose that win.

GIOVANNI. It were more ease to stop the ocean
From floats and ebbs, than to dissuade my vows.

FRIAR. Then I have done, and in thy wilful flames
Already see thy ruin; Heaven is just.
Yet hear my counsel.

GIOVANNI. As a voice of life.

FRIAR. Hie to thy father's house. There lock thee fast
Alone within thy chamber, then fall down
On both thy knees, and grovel on the ground;
Cry to thy heart, wash every word thou utter'st
In tears, and, if't be possible, of blood;
Beg Heaven to cleanse the leprosy of lust
That rots thy soul; acknowledge what thou art,
A wretch, a worm, a nothing; weep, sigh, pray
Three times a day, and three times every night.
For seven days' space do this, then if thou find'st
No change in thy desires, return to me:
I'll think on remedy. Pray for thyself
At home, whilst I pray for thee here. Away!
My blessing with thee; we have need to pray.

---

58 *death*: (1) spiritual death, (2) (an ironic sense) physical death.

59 *waits*: is in attendance.

64 *ocean*: three syllables.

65 *floats*: flowing.
vows: wishes.

73 *tears . . . blood*: tears expressing the profoundest sorrow were called 'tears of blood'.

GIOVANNI. All this I'll do, to free me from the rod
Of vengeance; else I'll swear my fate's my god.
Exeunt.

SCENE II

Enter GRIMALDI *and* VASQUES *ready to fight.*

VASQUES. Come, sir, stand to your tackling. If you prove craven I'll make you run quickly.

GRIMALDI. Thou art no equal match for me.

VASQUES. Indeed, I never went to the wars to bring home news, nor cannot play the mountebank for a meal's meat, and swear I got my wounds in the field. See you these grey hairs? They'll not flinch for a bloody nose. Wilt thou to this gear?

GRIMALDI. Why, slave, think'st thou I'll balance my reputation with a cast-suit? Call thy master; he shall know that I dare –

VASQUES. Scold like a cot-quean – that's your profession – thou poor shadow of a soldier. I will make thee know my master keeps servants thy betters in quality and performance. Com'st thou to fight, or prate?

GRIMALDI. Neither, with thee. I am a Roman and a gentleman; one that have got mine honour with expense of blood.

VASQUES. You are a lying coward, and a fool;

---

1 *tackling*: weapons.

3 *Thou . . . me*: it was legitimate to refuse to fight a social inferior; cf. *The Broken Heart*, IV.iv.48 and note.

5–6 *mountebank*: travelling salesman.
meat: food.

8–9 *Wilt . . . gear*: are you willing to fight?

11 *cast-suit*: servant (who might wear his master's cast-off clothing).

13 *cot-quean*: vulgar, abusive woman; literally, a cottage wife.

16 *quality*: birth and character.

fight, or by these hilts I'll kill thee. – Brave my
lord, – you'll fight.
GRIMALDI. Provoke me not, for if thou dost –
VASQUES. Have at you!
They fight; GRIMALDI *hath the worst.*

Enter FLORIO, DONADO, SORANZO.

FLORIO. What mean these sudden broils so near
my doors?
Have you not other places but my house
To vent the spleen of your disorder'd bloods?
Must I be haunted still with such unrest
As not to eat or sleep in peace at home?
Is this your love, Grimaldi? Fie, 'tis naught.
DONADO. And Vasques, I may tell thee 'tis not
well
To broach these quarrels; you are ever forward
In seconding contentions.

Enter above ANNABELLA *and* PUTANA.

FLORIO. What's the ground?
SORANZO. That, with your patience, signiors, I'll
resolve.
This gentleman, whom fame reports a soldier –
For else I know not – rivals me in love
To Signior Florio's daughter; to whose ears
He still prefers his suit, to my disgrace,
Thinking the way to recommend himself
Is to disparage me in his report.
But know, Grimaldi, though, may be, thou art
My equal in thy blood, yet this bewrays
A lowness in thy mind, which, wert thou noble,
Thou wouldst as much disdain as I do thee

22–3 See Additional Notes, p. 350.
26 *sudden*: violent. See Textual Notes, p. 341.
31 *naught*: worthless.
34 *seconding*: encouraging.
34 s.d. *above*: on the upper stage, from which they descend at 162.
35 *resolve*: answer.
39 *prefers*: advances.
43 *blood*: birth.
bewrays: reveals.

For this unworthiness; and on this ground
I will'd my servant to correct thy tongue,
Holding a man so base no match for me.

VASQUES. And had not your sudden coming prevented us, I had let my gentleman blood under the gills; I should have worm'd you, sir, for running mad.

GRIMALDI. I'll be reveng'd, Soranzo.

VASQUES. On a dish of warm broth to stay your stomach – do, honest innocence, do! Spoon-meat is a wholesomer diet than a Spanish blade.

GRIMALDI. Remember this!

SORANZO. I fear thee not, Grimaldi.

Exit GRIMALDI.

FLORIO. My lord Soranzo, this is strange to me,
Why you should storm, having my word
engag'd.
Owing her heart, what need you doubt her ear?
Losers may talk by law of any game.

VASQUES. Yet the villainy of words, Signior Florio, may be such as would make any unspleen'd dove choleric; blame not my lord in this.

FLORIO. Be you more silent.
I would not for my wealth my daughter's love
Should cause the spilling of one drop of blood.
Vasques, put up; let's end this fray in wine.

47, 49 See Textual Notes, p. 341.
50–1 *let . . . gills*: cut Grimaldi's throat; a doctor let blood to 'cool' his patient.
51 *worm'd*: worming consisted of cutting out a small ligament under a dog's tongue, to prevent rabies.
52 *mad*: (1) insane, (2) enraged.
54–5 *stay your stomach*: satisfy your appetite (for (1) food, (2) fighting).
55 *innocence*: harmless fool.
55–6 *Spoon-meat*: baby food (like broth).
59 *engag'd*: pledged.
60 *Owing*: possessing.
62 See Textual Notes, p. 341.
64 *unspleen'd dove*: the birds were thought to lack the physical capacity for anger, located in the spleen or gall-bladder.
69 *put up*: sheath your sword.

Exeunt [FLORIO, DONADO, SORANZO *and* VASQUES].

PUTANA. How like you this, child? Here's threat'ning, challenging, quarrelling, and fighting, on every side, and all is for your sake; you had need look to yourself, charge, you'll be stol'n away sleeping else shortly.

ANNABELLA. But tutress, such a life gives no content
To me; my thoughts are fix'd on other ends.
Would you would leave me.

PUTANA. Leave you? No marvel else; leave me no leaving, charge, this is love outright. Indeed I blame you not; you have choice fit for the best lady in Italy.

ANNABELLA. Pray do not talk so much.

PUTANA. Take the worst with the best, there's Grimaldi the soldier, a very well-timber'd fellow. They say he is a Roman, nephew to the Duke Mount Ferratto; they say he did good service in the wars against the Milanese, but faith, charge, I do not like him, and be for nothing but for being a soldier. One amongst twenty of your skirmishing captains but have some privy maim or other, that mars their standing upright. I like him the worse he crinkles so much in the hams; though he might serve, if there were no more men, yet he's not the man I would choose.

ANNABELLA. Fie, how thou prat'st.

PUTANA. As I am a very woman, I like Signior

---

76 *ends*: matters.
78 *else*: at all.
84 *well-timber'd*: physically well-built.
85–6 *Duke Mount Ferratto*: Monferrat became a duchy in 1575; from 1533 it had been under the rule of the Gonzaga dukes of Mantua.
88 *and be*: if it be.
90 *skirmishing*: weapon-waving.
privy: (1) secret, (2) in the privates; leading to the play on *standing upright* in 91.
92–3 *crinkles . . . hams*: (1) crumples (bows), (2) cringes away so much.
93 *serve*: (1) suffice, (2) give sexual satisfaction.
96 *very*: true, real.

Soranzo well. He is wise, and what is more, rich; and what is more than that, kind; and what is more than all this, a nobleman; such a one, were I the fair Annabella myself, I would wish and pray for. Then he is bountiful; besides he is handsome, and, by my troth, I think wholesome – and that's news in a gallant of three-and-twenty. Liberal, that I know; loving, that you know; and a man sure, else he could never ha' purchas'd such a good name with Hippolita the lusty widow, in her husband's lifetime: and 'twere but for that report, sweetheart, would he were thine! Commend a man for his qualities, but take a husband as he is a plain-sufficient, naked man. Such a one is for your bed, and such a one is Signior Soranzo, my life for't.

ANNABELLA. Sure the woman took her morning's draught too soon.

Enter BERGETTO *and* POGGIO.

PUTANA. But look, sweetheart, look what thing comes now; here's another of your ciphers to fill up the number. O, brave old ape in a silken coat! Observe.

BERGETTO. Didst thou think, Poggio, that I would spoil my new clothes, and leave my dinner to fight?

POGGIO. No, sir, I did not take you for so arrant a baby.

BERGETTO. I am wiser than so; for I hope, Poggio, thou never heard'st of an elder brother that was a coxcomb, didst, Poggio?

102–3 *wholesome*: free from sexual disease.

106 *good name*: favourable reputation; the first reference to Soranzo's liaison with Hippolita.

109 *qualities*: accomplishments.

113–14 *morning's draught*: drinks of ale and spirits were often taken early in the morning or at mid morning; cf. *Perkin Warbeck*, IV.ii.85–8.

116 *ciphers*: nonentities.

117 *brave*: richly dressed; there was a proverb, 'An ape is an ape though clad in scarlet.'

126 *coxcomb*: simpleton.

POGGIO. Never, indeed, sir, as long as they had either land or money left them to inherit.

BERGETTO. Is it possible, Poggio? O, monstruous! Why, I'll undertake, with a handful of silver, to buy a headful of wit at any time. But sirrah, I have another purchase in hand; I shall have the wench mine uncle says. I will but wash my face, and shift socks, and then have at her i'faith! – Mark my pace, Poggio.

[*Walks affectedly.*]

POGGIO. Sir, I have seen an ass and a mule trot the Spanish pavin with a better grace, I know not how often.

Exeunt [BERGETTO *and* POGGIO].

ANNABELLA. This idiot haunts me too.

PUTANA. Ay, ay, he needs no description. The rich magnifico that is below with your father, charge, Signior Donado his uncle, for that he means to make this his cousin a golden calf, thinks that you will be a right Israelite, and fall down to him presently: but I hope I have tutor'd you better. They say a fool's bauble is a lady's play-fellow; yet you having wealth enough, you need not cast upon the dearth of flesh at any rate. Hang him, innocent!

Enter GIOVANNI.

ANNABELLA. But see, Putana, see; what blessed shape
Of some celestial creature now appears?

136–8 *Sir . . . often*: some editors mark this as an aside, but Bergetto is capable of overlooking the plainest of insults.

137 *pavin*: stately dance, the pavane.

143–5 *he . . . presently*: see Exodus 32.

143 *cousin*: kinsman.

143–4 *golden calf*: (1) Biblical idol, (2) wealthy fool.

146–7 *They . . . play-fellow*: proverbially, 'Fools and little dogs are ladies' play-fellows.'

147 *bauble*: (1) fool's baton, (2) penis.

148–9 *you need . . . rate*: there is no need for you to take a reckless gamble and accept Bergetto as a husband for fear of lack of suitors.

149 *innocent*: simpleton.

149 s.d. Giovanni enters on the main stage below.

What man is he, that with such sad aspect
Walks careless of himself?
PUTANA. Where?
ANNABELLA. Look below.
PUTANA. O, 'tis your brother, sweet –
ANNABELLA. Ha!
PUTANA. 'Tis your brother.
ANNABELLA. Sure, 'tis not he; this is some woeful thing
Wrapp'd up in grief, some shadow of a man.
Alas, he beats his breast, and wipes his eyes
Drown'd all in tears. Methinks I hear him sigh.
Let's down, Putana, and partake the cause;
I know my brother, in the love he bears me,
Will not deny me partage in his sadness.
My soul is full of heaviness and fear.
Exeunt [ANNABELLA *and* PUTANA].
GIOVANNI. Lost! I am lost! My fates have doom'd my death.
The more I strive, I love; the more I love,
The less I hope. I see my ruin certain.
What judgement or endeavours could apply
To my incurable and restless wounds
I throughly have examin'd, but in vain.
O, that it were not in religion sin
To make our love a god, and worship it!
I have even wearied Heaven with prayers, dried up
The spring of my continual tears, even starv'd
My veins with daily fasts. What wit or art
Could counsel, I have practis'd; but alas,
I find all these but dreams, and old men's tales
To fright unsteady youth; I'm still the same.
Or I must speak, or burst; 'tis not, I know,
My lust, but 'tis my fate that leads me on.

---

159 *partake*: be informed of.
161 *partage*: share.
162 See Textual Notes, p. 341.
165 See Textual Notes, p. 341.
168 *throughly*: thoroughly.
171 *dried up*: exhausted, drained.
173 *wit or art*: intelligence or medical knowledge.

Keep fear and low faint-hearted shame with slaves!
I'll tell her that I love her, though my heart
Were rated at the price of that attempt.
Oh me! she comes.

Enter ANNABELLA *and* PUTANA.

ANNABELLA. Brother!
GIOVANNI. [*aside*] If such a thing
As courage dwell in men, ye heavenly powers,
Now double all that virtue in my tongue.
ANNABELLA. Why brother, will you not speak to me?
GIOVANNI. Yes;
How d'ye, sister?
ANNABELLA. Howsoever I am,
Methinks you are not well.
PUTANA. Bless us, why are you so sad, sir?
GIOVANNI. Let me entreat you leave us awhile, Putana, –
Sister, I would be private with you.
ANNABELLA. Withdraw, Putana.
PUTANA. I will. [*Aside*] If this were any other company for her, I should think my absence an office of some credit; but I will leave them together. *Exit.*
GIOVANNI. Come, sister, lend your hand; let's walk together.
I hope you need not blush to walk with me;
Here's none but you and I.
ANNABELLA. How's this?
GIOVANNI. Faith, I mean no harm.
ANNABELLA. Harm?
GIOVANNI. No, good faith. How is't with ye?
ANNABELLA. [*aside*] I trust he be not frantic.
– I am very well, brother.
GIOVANNI. Trust me, but I am sick; I fear so sick
'Twill cost my life.

---

179 *Keep fear*: let fear dwell.
185–7 See Textual Notes, p. 341.
194 *office of some credit*: (1) post of honour, (2) service deserving some reward.
203 *frantic*: lunatic.

ANNABELLA. Mercy forbid it! 'tis not so, I hope.
GIOVANNI. I think you love me, sister.
ANNABELLA. Yes, you know I do.
GIOVANNI. I know't, indeed. – You're very fair.
ANNABELLA. Nay, then I see you have a merry sickness.
GIOVANNI. That's as it proves. The poets feign, I read,
That Juno for her forehead did exceed
All other goddesses; but I durst swear
Your forehead exceeds hers, as hers did theirs.
ANNABELLA. Troth, this is pretty!
GIOVANNI. Such a pair of stars
As are thine eyes would, like Promethean fire,
If gently glanc'd, give life to senseless stones.
ANNABELLA. Fie upon ye!
GIOVANNI. The lily and the rose, most sweetly strange,
Upon your dimpled cheeks do strive for change.
Such lips would tempt a saint; such hands as those
Would make an anchorite lascivious.
ANNABELLA. D'ye mock me, or flatter me?
GIOVANNI. If you would see a beauty more exact
Than art can counterfeit, or nature frame,
Look in your glass, and there behold your own.
ANNABELLA. O, you are a trim youth.
GIOVANNI. Here! *Offers his dagger to her.*
ANNABELLA. What to do?
GIOVANNI. And here's my breast; strike home!
Rip up my bosom; there thou shalt behold

---

212 *feign*: invent the legend; see Homer's *Iliad*, xvi, and Ovid's *Fasti*, vi.29. See also Textual Notes, p. 341.
213 *Juno*: sister as well as wife of Jupiter.
217 *Promethean fire*: in Greek mythology, prometheus stole fire from heaven to give life to the man and woman he had created from clay.
220 *strange*: opposed.
221 *change*: interchange.
223 *anchorite*: hermit.
228 *trim*: fine (ironic).
229 See Textual Notes, p. 341.

A heart in which is writ the truth I speak.
Why stand ye?
ANNABELLA. Are you earnest?
GIOVANNI. Yes, most earnest.
You cannot love?
ANNABELLA. Whom?
GIOVANNI. Me. My tortur'd soul
Hath felt affliction in the heat of death.
O Annabella, I am quite undone;
The love of thee, my sister, and the view
Of thy immortal beauty hath untun'd
All harmony both of my rest and life.
Why d'ye not strike?
ANNABELLA. Forbid it, my just fears;
If this be true, 'twere fitter I were dead.
GIOVANNI. True, Annabella; 'tis no time to jest.
I have too long suppress'd the hidden flames
That almost have consum'd me. I have spent
Many a silent night in sighs and groans,
Ran over all my thoughts, despis'd my fate,
Reason'd against the reasons of my love,
Done all that smooth'd-cheek virtue could advise,
But found all bootless; 'tis my destiny
That you must either love, or I must die.
ANNABELLA. Comes this in sadness from you?
GIOVANNI. Let some mischief
Befall me soon, if I dissemble aught.
ANNABELLA. You are my brother, Giovanni.
GIOVANNI. You
My sister, Annabella. I know this,
And could afford you instance why to love
So much the more for this; to which intent

---

234 *affliction . . . death*: suffering of deadly intensity.
238 *rest*: peace.
245 *despis'd*: defied, scorned.
248 *bootless*: unavailing.
250 *sadness*: seriousness.
mischief: disaster.
251 *dissemble*: pretend.
252 See Textual Notes, p. 341.
253 See Textual Notes, p. 341.
254 *instance*: reason.

Wise Nature first in your creation meant
To make you mine: else't had been sin and foul
To share one beauty to a double soul.
Nearness in birth or blood doth but persuade
A nearer nearness in affection.
I have ask'd counsel of the holy Church,
Who tells me I may love you, and 'tis just
That since I may, I should; and will, yes, will.
Must I now live, or die?

ANNABELLA. Live. Thou hast won
The field, and never fought; what thou hast urg'd,
My captive heart had long ago resolv'd.
I blush to tell thee – but I'll tell thee now –
For every sigh that thou hast spent for me,
I have sigh'd ten; for every tear shed twenty.
And not so much for that I lov'd, as that
I durst not say I lov'd; nor scarcely think it.

GIOVANNI. Let not this music be a dream, ye gods,
For pity's sake I beg ye!

ANNABELLA. On my knees, *She kneels.*
Brother, even by our mother's dust I charge you,
Do not betray me to your mirth or hate;
Love me, or kill me, brother.

GIOVANNI. On my knees, *He kneels.*
Sister, even by my mother's dust I charge you,
Do not betray me to your mirth or hate;
Love me, or kill me, sister.

ANNABELLA. You mean good sooth then?

GIOVANNI. In good troth I do,
And so do you I hope. Say; I'm in earnest.

ANNABELLA. I'll swear't; and I.

GIOVANNI. And I; and by this kiss – *Kisses her.*
Once more, yet once more; now let's rise, by this – [*They rise.*]

---

259 *persuade*: encourage.
266 *resolv'd*: decided.
280 *sooth*: faith and truth.
282 See Textual Notes, p. 341.

I would not change this minute for Elysium.
What must we now do?
ANNABELLA. What you will.
GIOVANNI. Come then;
After so many tears as we have wept,
Let's learn to court in smiles, to kiss and sleep.
Exeunt.

SCENE III

Enter FLORIO *and* DONADO.

FLORIO. Signior Donado, you have said enough;
I understand you, but would have you know
I will not force my daughter 'gainst her will.
You see I have but two, a son and her;
And he is so devoted to his book,
As I must tell you true, I doubt his health.
Should he miscarry, all my hopes rely
Upon my girl. As for worldly fortune,
I am, I thank my stars, bless'd with enough.
My care is how to match her to her liking;
I would not have her marry wealth, but love,
And if she like your nephew, let him have her.
Here's all that I can say.
DONADO. Sir, you say well,
Like a true father, and for my part, I,
If the young folks can like ('twixt you and me)
Will promise to assure my nephew presently
Three thousand florins yearly during life,
And after I am dead, my whole estate.
FLORIO. 'Tis a fair proffer, sir. Meantime your nephew
Shall have free passage to commence his suit;
If he can thrive, he shall have my consent.
So, for this time I'll leave you, signior. *Exit.*

---

6 *doubt*: fear for.
7 *miscarry*: come to harm.
8 *girl*: two syllables ('girrel') and so throughout this text; cf. *The Broken Heart*, II.i.69 and note.
15 See Textual Notes, p. 341.
16 *presently*: immediately.

DONADO. Well,
Here's hope yet, if my nephew would have wit;
But he is such another dunce, I fear
He'll never win the wench. When I was young
I could have done't i'faith, and so shall he
If he will learn of me; and in good time
He comes himself.

Enter BERGETTO *and* POGGIO.

How now, Bergetto, whither away so fast?

BERGETTO. O uncle, I have heard the strangest news that ever came out of the mint – have I not, Poggio?

POGGIO. Yes indeed, sir.

DONADO. What news, Bergetto?

BERGETTO. Why, look ye, uncle, my barber told me just now that there is a fellow come to town, who undertakes to make a mill go without the mortal help of any water or wind, only with sandbags! And this fellow hath a strange horse, a most excellent beast, I'll assure you uncle (my barber says), whose head, to the wonder of all Christian people, stands just behind where his tail is – is't not true, Poggio?

POGGIO. So the barber swore, forsooth.

DONADO. And you are running thither?

BERGETTO. Ay forsooth, uncle.

DONADO. Wilt thou be a fool still? Come, sir, you shall not go; you have more mind of a puppet-play than on the business I told ye. Why, thou great baby, wilt never have wit? Wilt make thyself a may-game to all the world?

---

23 *wit*: some brains.
27 *in good time*: at the right moment.
29 See Textual Notes, p. 341.
31 *out of the mint*: fresh, new.
37–9 *undertakes . . . sandbags*: an early attempt at a perpetual-motion machine.
39–43 *horse . . . tail is*: a popular contemporary side-show at fairs; the horse's tail was tied to the manger.
45 See Textual Notes, p. 341.
48 *have more mind of*: show more interest in.
51 *may-game*: laughing-stock.

POGGIO. Answer for yourself, master.

BERGETTO. Why, uncle, should I sit at home still, and not go abroad to see fashions like other gallants?

DONADO. To see hobby-horses! What wise talk, I pray, and you with Annabella, when you were at Signior Florio's house?

BERGETTO. O, the wench? Ud's sa' me, uncle, I tickl'd her with a rare speech, that I made her almost burst her belly with laughing.

DONADO. Nay I think so, and what speech was't?

BERGETTO. What did I say, Poggio?

POGGIO. Forsooth, my master said that he lov'd her almost as well as he lov'd parmasent, and swore – I'll be sworn for him – that she wanted but such a nose as his was, to be as pretty a young woman as any was in Parma.

DONADO. O, gross!

BERGETTO. Nay, uncle, then she ask'd me whether my father had any more children than myself; and I said, 'No, 'twere better he should have had his brains knock'd out first.'

DONADO. This is intolerable!

BERGETTO. Then said she, 'Will Signior Donado, your uncle, leave you all his wealth?'

DONADO. Ha! that was good; did she harp upon that string?

BERGETTO. Did she harp upon that string? Ay, that she did. I answer'd, 'Leave me all his wealth? Why, woman, he hath no other wit; if he had he should hear on't to his everlasting glory and confusion. I know', quoth I, 'I am his

---

56 *hobby-horses*: performers dressed to appear as horse-riders took part in morris dances and other entertainments.
59 *Ud's sa' me*: God save me.
60 *tickl'd*: amused.
65 *parmasent*: Parmesan cheese.
67 *wanted*: lacked.
81 *wit*: thought.
83 *glory*: malapropism for 'shame'.

white boy, and will not be gull'd'; and with that she fell into a great smile, and went away. Nay, I did fit her.

DONADO. Ah sirrah, then I see there is no changing of nature. Well, Bergetto, I fear thou wilt be a very ass still.

BERGETTO. I should be sorry for that, uncle.

DONADO. Come, come you home with me. Since you are no better a speaker, I'll have you write to her after some courtly manner, and enclose some rich jewel in the letter.

BERGETTO. Ay, marry, that will be excellent.

DONADO. Peace, innocent!
Once in my time I'll set my wits to school;
If all fail, 'tis but the fortune of a fool.

BERGETTO. Poggio, 'twill do, Poggio!

Exeunt.

ACT II

SCENE I

Enter GIOVANNI *and* ANNABELLA, *as from their chamber.*

GIOVANNI. Come, Annabella, no more sister now,
But love, a name more gracious; do not blush,
Beauty's sweet wonder, but be proud to know
That yielding thou hast conquer'd, and inflam'd
A heart whose tribute is thy brother's life.

ANNABELLA. And mine is his. O, how these stol'n contents

84 *white boy*: favourite, darling.
gull'd: duped.
86 *fit*: answer aptly.
0 s.d. *chamber*: bedroom. The actors probably entered on the upper stage.
6 *contents*: pleasures.

Would print a modest crimson on my cheeks,
Had any but my heart's delight prevail'd!
GIOVANNI. I marvel why the chaster of your sex
Should think this pretty toy call'd maidenhead
So strange a loss, when being lost 'tis nothing,
And you are still the same.
ANNABELLA. 'Tis well for you;
Now you can talk.
GIOVANNI. Music as well consists
In th'ear, as in the playing.
ANNABELLA. O, you're wanton!
Tell on't, you're best, do.
GIOVANNI. Thou wilt chide me, then?
Kiss me, so; thus hung Jove on Leda's neck,
And suck'd divine ambrosia from her lips.
I envy not the mightiest man alive,
But hold myself, in being king of thee,
More great than were I king of all the world.
But I shall lose you, sweetheart.
ANNABELLA. But you shall not.
GIOVANNI. You must be married, mistress.
ANNABELLA. Yes, to whom?
GIOVANNI. Someone must have you.
ANNABELLA. You must.
GIOVANNI. Nay, some other.
ANNABELLA. Now prithee do not speak so, without jesting.
You'll make me weep in earnest.
GIOVANNI. What? You will not.
But tell me, sweet, canst thou be dar'd to swear

---

10 *toy*: trifle.

13–14 *Music . . . playing*: music is composed of the act of hearing as much as it is of the act of performance; but *music* is also a metaphor for love-making, and *ear* alludes to the female sex organ.

15 See Textual Notes, p. 341.

16 *thus . . . neck*: Giovanni images himself as the king of the gods, who took the form of a swan to seduce the maiden Leda.

17 *ambrosia*: the sweet and scented food of the gods, which gave immortality to those who ate it.

23 *have*: (1) possess in marriage, (2) have intercourse with.

24 See Textual Notes, p. 341.

26 *dar'd to*: so daring as to.

That thou wilt live to me, and to no other?

ANNABELLA. By both our loves I dare; for didst thou know,
My Giovanni, how all suitors seem
To my eyes hateful, thou wouldst trust me then.

GIOVANNI. Enough; I take thy word. Sweet, we must part:
Remember what thou vow'st; keep well my heart.

ANNABELLA. Will you begone?

GIOVANNI. I must.

ANNABELLA. When to return?

GIOVANNI. Soon.

ANNABELLA. Look you do.

GIOVANNI. Farewell. *Exit.*

ANNABELLA. Go where thou wilt, in mind I'il keep thee here,
And where thou art, I know I shall be there. – Guardian!

Enter PUTANA.

PUTANA. Child, how is't child? Well, thank Heaven, ha?

ANNABELLA. O guardian, what a paradise of joy
Have I pass'd over!

PUTANA. Nay, what a paradise of joy have you pass'd under? Why, now I commend thee, charge; fear nothing, sweetheart. What though he be your brother? Your brother's a man, I hope, and I say still, if a young wench feel the fit upon her, let her take anybody, father or brother, all is one.

ANNABELLA. I would not have it known for all the world.

PUTANA. Nor I indeed, for the speech of the people; else 'twere nothing.

FLORIO. (*within*) Daughter Annabella!

---

41 *over*: through.
47 *fit*: sexual impulse.
50–1 *for . . . people*: to avoid scandalous gossip.

ANNABELLA. O me, my father! – Here, sir! –
Reach my work.
FLORIO. (*within*) What are you doing?
ANNABELLA. So, let him come now.

Enter FLORIO, RICHARDETTO *like a Doctor of Physic, and* PHILOTIS *with a lute in her hand.*

FLORIO. So hard to work, that's well; you lose
no time.
Look, I have brought you company: here's one,
A learned doctor, lately come from Padua,
Much skill'd in physic; and for that I see
You have of late been sickly, I entreated
This reverend man to visit you some time.
ANNABELLA. You're very welcome, sir.
RICHARDETTO. I thank you, mistress.
Loud fame in large report hath spoke your
praise,
As well for virtue as perfection;
For which I have been bold to bring with me
A kinswoman of mine, a maid, for song
And music one perhaps will give content.
Please you to know her.
ANNABELLA. They are parts I love,
And she for them most welcome.
PHILOTIS. Thank you, lady.
FLORIO. Sir, now you know my house, pray make
not strange;
And if you find my daughter need your art,
I'll be your paymaster.
RICHARDETTO. Sir, what I am
She shall command.
FLORIO. You shall bind me to you. –
Daughter, I must have conference with you

---

53 *Reach my work*: hand me my needlework.
54 s.d. *Physic*: medicine.
55–60 See Textual Notes, p. 341.
57 *Padua*: famous for its university medical school.
63 See Textual Notes, p. 351.
67 *parts*: abilities.
69 *make not strange*: do not behave with formal reserve.
70 *art*: medical skill.
71–2 See Textual Notes, p. 341.

About some matters that concerns us both. –
Good master doctor, please you but walk in,
We'll crave a little of your cousin's cunning.
I think my girl hath not quite forgot
To touch an instrument; she could have done't;
We'll hear them both.

RICHARDETTO. I'll wait upon you, sir.

Exeunt.

SCENE II

Enter SORANZO *in his study, reading a book.*

SORANZO. 'Love's measure is extreme, the comfort pain,
The life unrest, and the reward disdain.'
What's here? Look't o'er again: 'tis so, so writes
This smooth licentious poet in his rhymes.
But Sannazar, thou liest, for had thy bosom
Felt such oppression as is laid on mine,
Thou wouldst have kiss'd the rod that made thee smart.
To work then, happy Muse, and contradict
What Sannazar hath in his envy writ. [*Writes.*]
'Love's measure is the mean, sweet his annoys,
His pleasures life, and his reward all joys.'
Had Annabella liv'd when Sannazar
Did in his brief encomium celebrate
Venice, that queen of cities, he had left
That verse which gain'd him such a sum of gold,
And for one only look from Annabell

---

76 *cousin's cunning*: niece's musical skill.
78 *touch*: play upon.
1 s.h. See Textual Notes, p. 341.
5 See Additional Notes, p. 351.
7 See Textual Notes, p. 341.
9 *envy*: ill will.
10 *the mean*: moderation, the golden mean.
12–15 *Had . . . gold*: see the Additional Note to 5.
13 *encomium*: eulogy.

Had writ of her, and her diviner cheeks.
O, how my thoughts are –
VASQUES. (*within*) Pray forbear; in rules of civility, let me give notice on't. I shall be tax'd of my neglect of duty and service.
SORANZO. What rude intrusion interrupts my peace?
Can I be nowhere private?
VASQUES. (*Within*) Troth, you wrong your modesty.
SORANZO. What's the matter, Vasques, who is't?

Enter HIPPOLITA *and* VASQUES.

HIPPOLITA. 'Tis I.
Do you know me now? Look, perjur'd man, on her
Whom thou and thy distracted lust have wrong'd.
Thy sensual rage of blood hath made my youth
A scorn to men and angels, and shall I
Be now a foil to thy unsated change?
Thou know'st, false wanton, when my modest fame
Stood free from stain or scandal, all the charms
Of Hell or sorcery could not prevail
Against the honour of my chaster bosom.
Thine eyes did plead in tears, thy tongue in oaths
Such and so many, that a heart of steel
Would have been wrought to pity, as was mine.
And shall the conquest of my lawful bed,
My husband's death urg'd on by his disgrace,
My loss of womanhood, be ill-rewarded
With hatred and contempt? No; know Soranzo,
I have a spirit doth as much distaste
The slavery of fearing thee, as thou

---

20 *tax'd of*: blamed for.
29 *distracted*: changeable, fickle.
30 *blood*: sexual passion.
32 *change*: promiscuity.
33 *modest fame*: reputation for modesty; cf. V.i.18.
42 *womanhood*: womanly modesty.
44 *distaste*: dislike.

Doth loathe the memory of what hath pass'd.
SORANZO. Nay, dear Hippolita –
HIPPOLITA. Call me not 'dear',
Nor think with supple words to smooth the grossness
Of my abuses. 'Tis not your new mistress,
Your goodly Madam Merchant, shall triumph
On my dejection; tell her thus from me,
My birth was nobler, and by much more free.
SORANZO. You are too violent.
HIPPOLITA. You are too double
In your dissimulation. Seest thou this,
This habit, these black mourning weeds of care?
'Tis thou art cause of this, and hast divorc'd
My husband from his life and me from him,
And made me widow in my widowhood.
SORANZO. Will you yet hear?
HIPPOLITA. More of thy perjuries?
Thy soul is drown'd too deeply in those sins;
Thou need'st not add to th'number.
SORANZO. Then I'll leave you;
You are past all rules of sense.
HIPPOLITA. And thou of grace.
VASQUES. Fie, mistress, you are not near the limits of reason: if my lord had a resolution as noble as virtue itself, you take the course to unedge it all. – Sir, I beseech you do not perplex her; griefs, alas, will have a vent. I dare undertake Madam Hippolita will now freely hear you.
SORANZO. Talk to a woman frantic! Are these the fruits of your love?
HIPPOLITA. They are the fruits of thy untruth, false man!
Didst thou not swear, whilst yet my husband liv'd,
That thou wouldst wish no happiness on earth

50–1 *triumph On my dejection*: exult over my humiliation.
52 *free*: high-born.
55 *habit*: costume.
59 See Textual Notes, p. 341.
65 *unedge*: blunt.
66 *perplex*: drive her to distraction.
68 *freely*: without interruption.

More than to call me wife? Didst thou not vow
When he should die to marry me? For which
The devil in my blood, and thy protests,
Caus'd me to counsel him to undertake
A voyage to Ligorne, for that we heard
His brother there was dead, and left a daughter
Young and unfriended, who with much ado
I wished him to bring hither: he did so,
And went; and as thou know'st, died on the way.
Unhappy man, to buy his death so dear
With my advice! Yet thou for whom I did it
Forget'st thy vows, and leav'st me to my shame.

SORANZO. Who could help this?

HIPPOLITA. Who? Perjur'd man, thou couldst,
If thou hadst faith or love.

SORANZO. You are deceiv'd.
The vows I made, if you remember well,
Were wicked and unlawful; 'twere more sin
To keep them than to break them. As for me,
I cannot mask my penitence. Think thou
How much thou hast digress'd from honest shame
In bringing of a gentleman to death
Who was thy husband; such a one as he,
So noble in his quality, condition,
Learning, behaviour, entertainment, love,
As Parma could not show a braver man.

VASQUES. You do not well; this was not your promise.

SORANZO. I care not; let her know her monstrous life.
Ere I'll be servile to so black a sin
I'll be accurs'd. – Woman, come here no more,
Learn to repent and die; for by my honour

---

76 *protests*: protestations.
78 See Additional Notes, p. 351.
92 *honest shame*: honour and all sense of shame.
95 *quality, condition*: class and social position.
96 *entertainment*: hospitality.
97 *braver*: finer.
101 See Textual Notes, p. 341.

I hate thee and thy lust; you have been too foul.
[*Exit.*]

VASQUES. [*aside*] This part has been scurvily play'd.

HIPPOLITA. How foolishly this beast contemns his fate,
And shuns the use of that which I more scorn
Than I once lov'd, his love. But let him go;
My vengeance shall give comfort to his woe.
She offers to go away.

VASQUES. Mistress, mistress, Madam Hippolita, pray, a word or two!

HIPPOLITA. With me, sir?

VASQUES. With you, if you please.

HIPPOLITA. What is't?

VASQUES. I know you are infinitely mov'd now, and you think you have cause: some I confess you have, but sure not so much as you imagine.

HIPPOLITA. Indeed!

VASQUES. O, you were miserably bitter, which you follow'd even to the last syllable; faith, you were somewhat too shrewd. By my life, you could not have took my lord in a worse time since I first knew him; tomorrow you shall find him a new man.

HIPPOLITA. Well, I shall wait his leisure.

VASQUES. Fie, this is not a hearty patience, it comes sourly from you; troth, let me persuade you for once.

HIPPOLITA. [*aside*] I have it, and it shall be so; thanks, opportunity! [*To him*] Persuade me to what?

VASQUES. Visit him in some milder temper. O, if you could but master a little your female spleen, how might you win him!

HIPPOLITA. He will never love me. Vasques, thou hast been a too trusty servant to such a master,

---

106 *contemns his fate*: scorns his approaching doom.
107–8 See Textual Notes, p. 341.
109 *his woe*: the grief he has caused.
110 See Textual Notes, p. 341.
121 *shrewd*: sharp, abusive.
126 *hearty*: genuine.

and I believe thy reward in the end will fall out like mine.

VASQUES. So, perhaps, too.

HIPPOLITA. Resolve thyself it will. Had I one so true, so truly honest, so secret to my counsels, as thou hast been to him and his, I should think it a slight acquittance, not only to make him master of all I have, but even of myself.

VASQUES. O, you are a noble gentlewoman!

HIPPOLITA. Wilt thou feed always upon hopes? Well, I know thou art wise, and seest the reward of an old servant daily what it is.

VASQUES. Beggary and neglect.

HIPPOLITA. True; but Vasques, wert thou mine, and wouldst be private to me and my designs, I here protest myself, and all what I can else call mine, should be at thy dispose.

VASQUES. [*aside*] Work you that way, old mole? Then I have the wind of you. —— I were not worthy of it, by any desert that could lie within my compass. If I could –

HIPPOLITA. What then?

VASQUES. I should then hope to live in these my old years with rest and security.

HIPPOLITA. Give me thy hand. Now promise but thy silence,
And help to bring to pass a plot I have,
And here in sight of Heaven, that being done,
I make thee lord of me and mine estate.

VASQUES. Come, you are merry; this is such a happiness that I can neither think or believe.

HIPPOLITA. Promise thy secrecy, and 'tis confirm'd.

VASQUES. Then here I call our good genii for witnesses, whatsoever your designs are, or

---

143 *slight acquittance*: mean payment of a debt.
151 *be private to*: keep secret.
155 *have . . . you*: scent you, see what you intend; a hunting metaphor.
156 See Textual Notes, p. 341.
165 *merry*: just joking.
168 *good genii*: guardian spirits.
168–9 See Textual Notes, p. 341.

against whomsoever, I will not only be a special actor therein, but never disclose it till it be effected.

HIPPOLITA. I take thy word, and with that, thee for mine.
Come then, let's more confer of this anon.
On this delicious bane my thoughts shall banquet:
Revenge shall sweeten what my griefs have tasted.

Exeunt.

SCENE III

Enter RICHARDETTO *and* PHILOTIS.

RICHARDETTO. Thou seest, my lovely niece, these strange mishaps,
How all my fortunes turn to my disgrace,
Wherein I am but as a looker-on,
Whiles others act my shame and I am silent.
PHILOTIS. But uncle, wherein can this borrow'd shape
Give you content?
RICHARDETTO. I'll tell thee, gentle niece.
Thy wanton aunt in her lascivious riots
Lives now secure, thinks I am surely dead
In my late journey to Ligorne for you,
As I have caus'd it to be rumour'd out.
Now would I see with what an impudence
She gives scope to her loose adultery,
And how the common voice allows hereof;

---

170 *special*: leading.
175 *bane*: poison.
176 *tasted*: given a (salt) taste to.
4 *act*: (1) put on stage, display, (2) actively contribute to.
5 *borrow'd shape*: assumed disguise (*shape* was a theatrical term for the actor's costume).
13 *how . . . hereof*: how popular opinion judges her conduct.

Thus far I have prevail'd.
PHILOTIS. Alas, I fear
You mean some strange revenge.
RICHARDETTO. O, be not troubl'd;
Your ignorance shall plead for you in all.
But to our business: what, you learnt for certain
How Signior Florio means to give his daughter
In marriage to Soranzo?
PHILOTIS. Yes, for certain.
RICHARDETTO. But how find you young
Annabella's love
Inclin'd to him?
PHILOTIS. For aught I could perceive,
She neither fancies him or any else.
RICHARDETTO. There's mystery in that which
time must show.
She us'd you kindly?
PHILOTIS. Yes.
RICHARDETTO. And crav'd your company?
PHILOTIS. Often.
RICHARDETTO. 'Tis well; it goes as I could wish.
I am the doctor now, and as for you,
None knows you, if all fail not we shall thrive.
But who comes here?

Enter GRIMALDI.

I know him; 'tis Grimaldi,
A Roman and a soldier, near allied
Unto the Duke of Montferrato, one
Attending on the Nuncio of the Pope
That now resides in Parma, by which means
He hopes to get the love of Annabella.
GRIMALDI. Save you, sir.
RICHARDETTO. And you, sir.
GRIMALDI. I have heard
Of your approved skill, which through the city
Is freely talk'd of, and would crave your aid.

---

16 *plead . . . all*: clear you of all responsibilities.
34 *Save you*: God save you; a customary greeting, but ironic in the circumstances.

RICHARDETTO. For what, sir?
GRIMALDI. Marry, sir, for this –
But I would speak in private.
RICHARDETTO. Leave us, cousin.
Exit PHILOTIS.

GRIMALDI. I love fair Annabella, and would know
Whether in arts there may not be receipts
To move affection.
RICHARDETTO. Sir, perhaps there may,
But these will nothing profit you.
GRIMALDI. Not me?
RICHARDETTO. Unless I be mistook, you are a man
Greatly in favour with the Cardinal.
GRIMALDI. What of that?
RICHARDETTO. In duty to his grace,
I will be bold to tell you, if you seek
To marry Florio's daughter, you must first
Remove a bar 'twixt you and her.
GRIMALDI. Who's that?
RICHARDETTO. Soranzo is the man that hath her heart,
And while he lives be sure you cannot speed.
GRIMALDI. Soranzo? What, mine enemy! Is't he?
RICHARDETTO. Is he your enemy?
GRIMALDI. The man I hate
Worse than confusion;
I'll kill him straight.
RICHARDETTO. Nay, then take mine advice,
Even for his grace's sake the Cardinal.
I'll find a time when he and she do meet,
Of which I'll give you notice, and to be sure
He shall not 'scape you, I'll provide a poison
To dip your rapier's point in. If he had
As many heads as Hydra had, he dies.

---

40 *arts*: the skills of medicine.
receipts: prescriptions (for love-potions).
53 *confusion*: ruin, destruction; a frequent word in this play. See Textual Notes, p. 341.
54 See Textual Notes, p. 342.
60 *Hydra*: a many-headed beast, which grew two more heads for every one cut off. It was one of Hercules' labours to destroy this monster.

GRIMALDI. But shall I trust thee, doctor?
RICHARDETTO. As yourself;
Doubt not in aught. [*Aside*] Thus shall the fates decree:
By me Soranzo falls, that ruin'd me.

Exeunt.

SCENE IV

Enter DONADO, BERGETTO *and* POGGIO.

DONADO. Well, sir, I must be content to be both your secretary and your messenger myself. I cannot tell what this letter may work, but as sure as I am alive, if thou come once to talk with her, I fear thou wilt mar whatsoever I make.

BERGETTO. You make, uncle? Why, am not I big enough to carry mine own letter, I pray?

DONADO. Ay, ay, carry a fool's head o' thy own. Why, thou dunce, wouldst thou write a letter, and carry it thyself?

BERGETTO. Yes, that I would, and read it to her with my own mouth; for you must think, if she will not believe me myself when she hears me speak, she will not believe another's handwriting. O, you think I am a blockhead, uncle. No, sir; Poggio knows I have indited a letter myself, so I have.

POGGIO. Yes truly, sir, I have it in my pocket.

DONADO. A sweet one no doubt, pray let's see't.

BERGETTO. I cannot read my own hand very well, Poggio; read it, Poggio.

DONADO. Begin.

POGGIO. (*reads*) 'Most dainty and honey-sweet mistress, I could call you fair, and lie as fast as any that loves you, but my uncle being the elder

---

63 See Textual Notes, p. 342.
7 See Textual Notes, p. 342.
17 *indited*: written.
21 *hand*: handwriting.

man I leave it to him, as more fit for his age, and the colour of his beard. I am wise enough to tell you I can board where I see occasion, or if you like my uncle's wit better than mine, you shall marry me; if you like mine better than his, I will marry you in spite of your teeth. So, commending my best parts to you, I rest

Yours upwards and downwards, or you may choose,

Bergetto.'

BERGETTO. Ah, ha! here's stuff, uncle!

DONADO. Here's stuff indeed to shame us all. Pray, whose advice did you take in this learned letter?

POGGIO. None, upon my word, but mine own.

BERGETTO. And mine, uncle, believe it, nobody's else; 'twas mine own brain, I thank a good wit for't.

DONADO. Get you home, sir, and look you keep within doors till I return.

BERGETTO. How! That were a jest indeed; I scorn it i'faith.

DONADO. What! You do not?

BERGETTO. Judge me, but I do now.

POGGIO. Indeed, sir, 'tis very unhealthy.

DONADO. Well, sir, if I hear any of your apish running to motions and fopperies till I come back, you were as good no; look to't. *Exit.*

BERGETTO. Poggio, shall's steal to see this horse with the head in's tail?

POGGIO. Ay, but you must take heed of whipping.

BERGETTO. Dost take me for a child, Poggio? Come, honest Poggio.

Exeunt.

---

29 *board*: (1) approach a girl, (2) jest (bourd).
32 *in . . . teeth*: despite your opposition.
33 *parts*: qualities.
45 See Textual Notes, p. 342.
53 *motions*: puppet shows; regarded as childish amusements.
fopperies: follies.
54 *you . . . no*: you had better not have done so.
55–6 *horse . . . tail*: cf. I.iii.39–43 and note.

SCENE V

FRIAR. Peace! Thou hast told a tale whose every word
Threatens eternal slaughter to the soul.
I'm sorry I have heard it; would mine ears
Had been one minute deaf before the hour
That thou cam'st to me. O young man cast away
By the religious number of mine order,
I day and night have wak'd my aged eyes
Above my strength, to weep on thy behalf.
But Heaven is angry, and be thou resolv'd,
Thou art a man remark'd to taste a mischief.
Look for't; though it come late, it will come sure.

GIOVANNI. Father, in this you are uncharitable;
What I have done, I'll prove both fit and good.
It is a principle, which you have taught
When I was yet your scholar, that the frame
And composition of the mind doth follow
The frame and composition of the body.
So where the body's furniture is beauty,
The mind's must needs be virtue, which allow'd,
Virtue itself is reason but refin'd,
And love the quintessence of that. This proves
My sister's beauty, being rarely fair,
Is rarely virtuous; chiefly in her love,
And chiefly in that love, her love to me.
If hers to me, then so is mine to her;
Since in like causes are effects alike.

FRIAR. O ignorance in knowledge! Long ago,
How often have I warn'd thee, this before!
Indeed, if we were sure there were no Deity,

---

5 *cast away*: rejected and considered damned. See Textual Notes, p. 342.
6 *religious number*: religiously orthodox members.
8 See Textual Notes, p. 342.
10 *remark'd . . . mischief*: marked out to experience calamity.
15, 17 See Textual Notes, p. 342.
18 *furniture*: adornment.
21 *quintessence*: purest manifestation.

Nor Heaven nor Hell, then to be led alone
By Nature's light – as were philosophers
Of elder times – might instance some defence.
But 'tis not so. Then, madman, thou wilt find
That Nature is in Heaven's positions blind.
GIOVANNI. Your age o'errules you; had you youth like mine,
You'd make her love your Heaven, and her divine.
FRIAR. Nay, then I see th'art too far sold to Hell,
It lies not in the compass of my prayers
To call thee back; yet let me counsel thee:
Persuade thy sister to some marriage.
GIOVANNI. Marriage? Why, that's to damn her! That's to prove
Her greedy of variety of lust.
FRIAR. O fearful! If thou wilt not, give me leave
To shrive her, lest she should die unabsolv'd.
GIOVANNI. At your best leisure, father; then she'll tell you
How dearly she doth prize my matchless love;
Then you will know what pity 'twere we two
Should have been sunder'd from each other's arms.
View well her face, and in that little round
You may observe a world of variety:
For colour, lips, for sweet perfumes, her breath;
For jewels, eyes; for threads of purest gold,
Hair; for delicious choice of flowers, cheeks;
Wonder in every portion of that throne.
Hear her but speak, and you will swear the spheres
Make music to the citizens in Heaven;
But father, what is else for pleasure fram'd,

---

32 *elder*: older, pre-Christian.
instance: provide.
34 *is . . . blind*: can offer no insights into the tenets of divinity.
44 *shrive*: administer confession.
45 *At your best leisure*: whenever you like.
54 *throne*: seat of divinity, or angel (thrones were one of the nine orders of angelic beings).
55–6 See Additional Notes, p. 351.

Lest I offend your ears, shall go unnam'd.
FRIAR. The more I hear, I pity thee the more,
That one so excellent should give those parts
All to a second death. What I can do
Is but to pray; and yet I could advise thee,
Wouldst thou be rul'd.
GIOVANNI. In what?
FRIAR. Why, leave her yet,
The throne of Mercy is above your trespass;
Yet time is left you both –
GIOVANNI. To embrace each other,
Else let all time be struck quite out of number.
She is, like me, and I like her, resolv'd.
FRIAR. No more! I'll visit her. This grieves me most,
Things being thus, a pair of souls are lost.
Exeunt.

SCENE VI

Enter FLORIO, DONADO, ANNABELLA, PUTANA.

FLORIO. Where's Giovanni?
ANNABELLA. Newly walk'd abroad,
And, as I heard him say, gone to the friar,
His reverend tutor.
FLORIO. That's a blessed man,
A man made up of holiness; I hope
He'll teach him how to gain another world.
DONADO. Fair gentlewoman, here's a letter sent [*Offers a letter.*]
To you from my young cousin. I dare swear
He loves you in his soul; would you could hear
Sometimes, what I see daily, sighs and tears,
As if his breast were prison to his heart.

---

60 *parts*: abilities, excellences.
61 *a second death*: everlasting damnation, following natural death.
64 *throne of Mercy*: God as supreme ruler and merciful judge; the Friar's response to Giovanni's blasphemous praise of Annabella (54).

FLORIO. Receive it, Annabella.
ANNABELLA. Alas, good man!
[*Takes the letter.*]
DONADO. What's that she said?
PUTANA. And please you, sir, she said 'Alas, good man!'
[*aside to* DONADO] Truly, I do commend him to her every night before her first sleep, because I would have her dream of him, and she hearkens to that most religiously.
DONADO. [*aside to* PUTANA] Say'st so?
[*Gives her money.*]
Godamercy, Putana, there's something for thee, and prithee do what thou canst on his behalf; sha'not be lost labour, take my word for't.
PUTANA. [*aside to* DONADO] Thank you most heartily, sir; now I have a feeling of your mind, let me alone to work.
ANNABELLA. Guardian!
PUTANA. Did you call?
ANNABELLA. Keep this letter.
DONADO. Signior Florio, in any case bid her read it instantly.
FLORIO. Keep it for what? Pray read it me here right.
ANNABELLA. I shall, sir. *She reads.*
DONADO. How d'ye find her inclin'd, Signior?
FLORIO. Troth, sir, I know not how; not all so well
As I could wish.
ANNABELLA. Sir, I am bound to rest your cousin's debtor.
The jewel I'll return, for if he love,
I'll count that love a jewel.
DONADO. Mark you that? –
Nay, keep them both, sweet maid.
ANNABELLA. You must excuse me;
Indeed I will not keep it.
FLORIO. Where's the ring;

---

13 *And*: if it.
23 *feeling*: (1) understanding, (2) monetary reward.
30–1 *here right*: at once.

That which your mother in her will bequeath'd,
And charg'd you on her blessing not to give't
To any but your husband? Send back that.
ANNABELLA. I have it not.
FLORIO. Ha! Have it not? Where is't?
ANNABELLA. My brother in the morning took it from me;
Said he would wear't today.
FLORIO. Well, what do you say
To young Bergetto's love? Are you content
To match with him? Speak.
DONADO. There's the point indeed.
ANNABELLA. [*aside*] What shall I do? I must say something now.
FLORIO. What say? Why d'ye not speak?
ANNABELLA. Sir, with your leave,
Please you to give me freedom?
FLORIO. Yes, you have't.
ANNABELLA. Signior Donado, if your nephew mean
To raise his better fortunes in his match,
The hope of me will hinder such a hope.
Sir, if you love him, as I know you do,
Find one more worthy of his choice than me.
In short, I'm sure I sha'not be his wife.
DONADO. Why, here's plain dealing, I commend thee for't,
And all the worst I wish thee, is Heaven bless thee!
Your father yet and I will still be friends,
Shall we not, Signior Florio?
FLORIO. Yes, why not?
Look, here your cousin comes.

Enter BERGETTO *and* POGGIO.

DONADO. [*aside*] O coxcomb, what doth he make here?

---

50 *What say?*: what do you say?
51 *freedom*: free choice of husband. See Textual Notes, p. 342.
53 *raise . . . fortunes*: improve his rank or wealth.
63 *what doth he make*: what is his business.

BERGETTO. Where's my uncle, sirs?

DONADO. What's the news now?

BERGETTO. Save you, uncle, save you. You must not think I come for nothing, masters. And how, and how is't? What, you have read my letter? Ah, there I – tickl'd you i'faith!

POGGIO. [*aside to* BERGETTO] But 'twere better you had tickl'd her in another place.

BERGETTO. Sirrah sweetheart, I'll tell thee a good jest; and riddle what 'tis.

ANNABELLA. You say you'd tell me.

BERGETTO. As I was walking just now in the street, I met a swaggering fellow would needs take the wall of me; and because he did thrust me, I very valiantly call'd him rogue. He hereupon bade me draw. I told him I had more wit than so; but when he saw that I would not, he did so maul me with the hilts of his rapier that my head sung whilst my feet caper'd in the kennel.

DONADO. [*aside*] Was ever the like ass seen?

ANNABELLA. And what did you all this while?

BERGETTO. Laugh at him for a gull, till I see the blood run about mine ears, and then I could not choose but find in my heart to cry; till a fellow with a broad beard – they say he is a new-come doctor – call'd me into this house, and gave me a plaster – look you, here 'tis; and sir, there was a young wench wash'd my face and hands most excellently, i'faith I shall love her as long as I live for't – did she not, Poggio?

POGGIO. Yes, and kiss'd him too.

BERGETTO. Why la now, you think I tell a lie, uncle, I warrant.

DONADO. Would he that beat thy blood out of thy head, had beaten some wit into it; for I fear

---

70 *tickl'd*: pleased.
74 *riddle*: guess.
78 *take the wall*: take the position next the wall, the cleanest part of the street. Quarrels over this privileged place were frequent and sometimes bloody.
80–1 *more . . . so*: more intelligence than to do so.
83 *kennel*: central gutter in the street.
86 *gull*: dupe.

thou never wilt have any.

BERGETTO. O uncle, but there was a wench would have done a man's heart good to have look'd on her; by this light, she had a face methinks worth twenty of you, Mistress Annabella.

DONADO. [*aside*] Was ever such a fool born?

ANNABELLA. I am glad she lik'd you, sir.

BERGETTO. Are you so? By my troth, I thank you forsooth.

FLORIO. Sure 'twas the doctor's niece, that was last day with us here.

BERGETTO. 'Twas she, 'twas she!

DONADO. How do you know that, simplicity?

BERGETTO. Why, does not he say so? If I should have said no, I should have given him the lie, uncle, and so have deserv'd a dry beating again; I'll none of that.

FLORIO. A very modest, well-behav'd young maid
As I have seen.

DONADO. Is she indeed?

FLORIO. Indeed
She is, if I have any judgement.

DONADO. Well, sir, now you are free, you need not care for sending letters now: you are dismiss'd, your mistress here will none of you.

BERGETTO. No? Why, what care I for that; I can have wenches enough in Parma for half-a-crown apiece, cannot I, Poggio?

POGGIO. I'll warrant you, sir.

DONADO. Signior Florio,
I thank you for your free recourse you gave
For my admittance; and to you, fair maid,
That jewel I will give you 'gainst your marriage.
Come, will you go, sir?

---

107 *lik'd*: pleased.
115 *given him the lie*: accused him of lying; frequently the preliminary to a duel.
116 *dry*: severe.
118–19 See Textual Notes, p. 342.
125 *half-a-crown*: the usual price for an English prostitute.
128–32 See Textual Notes, p. 342.
131 *'gainst*: in anticipation of.

BERGETTO. Ay, marry will I. Mistress, farewell, mistress; I'll come again tomorrow. Farewell, mistress.

Exeunt DONADO, BERGETTO *and* POGGIO.

Enter GIOVANNI.

FLORIO. Son, where have you been? What, alone, alone still?
I would not have it so; you must forsake
This over-bookish humour. Well, your sister
Hath shook the fool off.

GIOVANNI. 'Twas no match for her.

FLORIO. 'Twas not indeed, I meant it nothing less;
Soranzo is the man I only like. –
Look on him, Annabella. Come, 'tis supper-time,
And it grows late. *Exit.*

GIOVANNI. Whose jewel's that?

ANNABELLA. Some sweetheart's.

GIOVANNI. So I think.

ANNABELLA. A lusty youth. –
Signior Donado gave it me to wear
Against my marriage.

GIOVANNI. But you shall not wear it;
Send it him back again.

ANNABELLA. What, you are jealous?

GIOVANNI. That you shall know anon, at better leisure.
Welcome, sweet night. The evening crowns the day.

Exeunt.

136–9 See Textual Notes, p. 342.
141 *only*: particularly.
144–7 See Textual Notes, p. 342.

ACT III

SCENE I

Enter BERGETTO *and* POGGIO.

BERGETTO. Does my uncle think to make me a baby still? No, Poggio, he shall know I have a sconce now.

POGGIO. Ay, let him not bob you off like an ape with an apple.

BERGETTO. 'Sfoot, I will have the wench, if he were ten uncles, in despite of his nose, Poggio.

POGGIO. Hold him to the grindstone, and give not a jot of ground. She hath in a manner promis'd you already.

BERGETTO. True, Poggio, and her uncle the doctor swore I should marry her.

POGGIO. He swore, I remember.

BERGETTO. And I will have her, that's more; didst see the codpiece-point she gave me, and the box of marmalade?

POGGIO. Very well; and kiss'd you, that my chops water'd at the sight on't. There's no way but to clap up a marriage in hugger mugger.

BERGETTO. I will do't, for I tell thee, Poggio, I begin to grow valiant methinks, and my courage begins to rise.

POGGIO. Should you be afraid of your uncle?

BERGETTO. Hang him, old doting rascal; no. I say I will have her.

---

3 *sconce*: head, brain.
4 *bob*: fob.
6 *'Sfoot*: by God's foot.
9–12 See Textual Notes, p. 342.
15 *codpiece-point*: tagged lace fastening the codpiece, an item of clothing well out of date by 1633.
16 *marmalade*: fruit preserve.
19 *clap . . . mugger*: hastily conclude a secret marriage.
21 *courage*: (1) bravery, (2) sexual desire.

POGGIO. Lose no time then.

BERGETTO. I will beget a race of wise men and constables, that shall cart whores at their own charges, and break the Duke's peace ere I have done myself. Come away!

Exeunt.

SCENE II

Enter FLORIO, GIOVANNI, SORANZO, ANNABELLA, PUTANA, *and* VASQUES.

FLORIO. My lord Soranzo, though I must confess
The proffers that are made me have been great
In marriage of my daughter, yet the hope
Of your still rising honours have prevail'd
Above all other jointures. Here she is,
She knows my mind, speak for yourself to her;
And hear you, daughter, see you use him nobly.
For any private speech I'll give you time.
Come, son, and you, the rest, let them alone;
Agree they as they may.

SORANZO. I thank you, sir.

GIOVANNI. [*aside to* ANNABELLA] Sister, be not all woman; think on me.

SORANZO. Vasques!

VASQUES. My lord?

SORANZO. Attend me without.

Exeunt all but SORANZO *and* ANNABELLA.

ANNABELLA. Sir, what's your will with me?

SORANZO. Do you not know
What I should tell you?

ANNABELLA. Yes, you'll say you love me.

---

28 *cart whores*: as part of their punishment, prostitutes were paraded through the streets in carts or wagons.
29 *charges*: expense.
5 *jointures*: marriage proposals.
9, 10 See Textual Notes, p. 342.
11 *be not all woman*: Giovanni fears stereotypical inconstancy.
13–14 See Textual Notes, p. 342.

SORANZO. And I'll swear it too; will you believe it?
ANNABELLA. 'Tis no point of faith.

Enter GIOVANNI *above.*

SORANZO. Have you not will to love?
ANNABELLA. Not you.
SORANZO. Whom then?
ANNABELLA. That's as the fates infer.
GIOVANNI. [*aside*] Of those I'm regent now.
SORANZO. What mean you, sweet?
ANNABELLA. To live and die a maid.
SORANZO. O, that's unfit.
GIOVANNI. [*aside*] Here's one can say that's but a woman's note.
SORANZO. Did you but see my heart, then would you swear –
ANNABELLA. That you were dead.
GIOVANNI. [*aside*] That's true, or somewhat near it.
SORANZO. See you these true love's tears?
ANNABELLA. No.
GIOVANNI. [*aside*] Now she winks.
SORANZO. They plead to you for grace.
ANNABELLA. Yet nothing speak.
SORANZO. O, grant my suit!
ANNABELLA. What is't?
SORANZO. To let me live –
ANNABELLA. Take it.
SORANZO. – still yours.
ANNABELLA. That is not mine to give.
GIOVANNI. [*aside*] One such another word would kill his hopes.
SORANZO. Mistress, to leave those fruitless strifes of wit,
Know I have lov'd you long, and lov'd you truly;

---

16 *point of faith*: article of belief essential for salvation. See Textual Notes, p. 342.
17 *infer*: contrive.
20 *woman's note*: typical female remark.
23 *winks*: turns a blind eye.
29 See Textual Notes, p. 342.

Not hope of what you have, but what you are
Have drawn me on. Then let me not in vain
Still feel the rigour of your chaste disdain.
I'm sick, and sick to th'heart.
ANNABELLA. Help! Aqua-vitae!
SORANZO. What mean you?
ANNABELLA. Why, I thought you had been sick.
SORANZO. Do you mock my love?
GIOVANNI. [*aside*] There, sir, she was too nimble.
SORANZO. [*aside*] 'Tis plain; she laughs at me! – These scornful taunts
Neither become your modesty or years.
ANNABELLA. You are no looking-glass; or if you were,
I'd dress my language by you.
GIOVANNI. [*aside*] I'm confirm'd.
ANNABELLA. To put you out of doubt, my lord, methinks
Your common sense should make you understand
That if I lov'd you, or desir'd your love,
Some way I should have given you better taste.
But since you are a nobleman, and one
I would not wish should spend his youth in hopes,
Let me advise you here to forbear your suit,
And think I wish you well, I tell you this.
SORANZO. Is't you speak this?
ANNABELLA. Yes, I myself; yet know –
Thus far I give you comfort – if mine eyes
Could have pick'd out a man, amongst all those
That sued to me, to make a husband of,
You should have been that man. Let this suffice;
Be noble in your secrecy, and wise.
GIOVANNI. [*aside*] Why now I see she loves me.
ANNABELLA. One word more.
As ever virtue liv'd within your mind,
As ever noble courses were your guide,

---

33 *Aqua-vitae*: medicinal brandy, or other spirits.
36–47 See Textual Notes, p. 342.
43 *taste*: experience of welcome.

As ever you would have me know you lov'd me,
Let not my father know hereof by you:
If I hereafter find that I must marry,
It shall be you or none.
SORANZO. I take that promise.
ANNABELLA. O, O my head!
SORANZO. What's the matter? Not well?
ANNABELLA. O, I begin to sicken!
GIOVANNI. [*aside*] Heaven forbid!
Exit from above.
SORANZO. Help, help, within there, ho! Look to your daughter,
Signior Florio.

Enter FLORIO, GIOVANNI, PUTANA.

FLORIO. Hold her up; she swoons.
GIOVANNI. Sister, how d'ye?
ANNABELLA. Sick, brother, are you there?
FLORIO. Convey her to her bed instantly, whilst I send for a physician; quickly, I say.
PUTANA. Alas, poor child!
Exeunt all but SORANZO.

Enter VASQUES.

VASQUES. My lord.
SORANZO. Oh Vasques, now I doubly am undone,
Both in my present and my future hopes.
She plainly told me that she could not love,
And thereupon soon sicken'd, and I fear
Her life's in danger.
VASQUES. [*aside*] By'r Lady, sir, and so is yours, if you knew all. [*Aloud*] 'Las, sir, I am sorry for that; may be 'tis but the maid's sickness, an overflux of youth – and then, sir, there is no such present remedy as present marriage. But hath she given you an absolute denial?

63–4 See Textual Notes, p. 342.
77 *maid's sickness*: green-sickness (chlorosis); an anaemic disease affecting young women at puberty.
78 *overflux*: overflow.
79 *present*: instant.

SORANZO. She hath and she hath not; I'm full of grief,
But what she said I'll tell thee as we go.
Exeunt.

SCENE III

Enter GIOVANNI *and* PUTANA.

PUTANA. O sir, we are all undone, quite undone, utterly undone, and sham'd forever; your sister, O your sister!

GIOVANNI. What of her? For Heaven's sake speak, how does she?

PUTANA. O that ever I was born to see this day!

GIOVANNI. She is not dead, ha, is she?

PUTANA. Dead? No, she is quick. 'Tis worse; she is with child. You know what you have done, Heaven forgive ye! 'Tis too late to repent, now Heaven help us!

GIOVANNI. With child? How dost thou know't?

PUTANA. How do I know't? Am I at these years ignorant what the meanings of qualms and water-pangs be? Of changing of colours, queasiness of stomachs, pukings, and another thing that I could name? Do not, for her and your credit's sake, spend the time in asking how and which way 'tis so. She is quick, upon my word; if you let a physician see her water you're undone.

GIOVANNI. But in what case is she?

PUTANA. Prettily amended; 'twas but a fit, which I soon espied, and she must look for often henceforward.

GIOVANNI. Commend me to her, bid her take no care;

---

8 *quick*: (1) alive, (2) pregnant.
15 *water-pangs*: frequent impulses to urinate.
16–17 *another . . . name*: an end to menstruation.
18 *credit's*: good name's.
23 *Prettily amended*: pretty well recovered.
26 *take no care*: not to worry.

Let not the doctor visit her, I charge you,
Make some excuse till I return – O me,
I have a world of business in my head! –
Do not discomfort her. – How does this news
Perplex me! – If my father come to her,
Tell him she's recover'd well; say 'twas
But some ill diet. D'ye hear, woman? Look you to't.

PUTANA. I will, sir.

Exeunt.

SCENE IV

Enter FLORIO *and* RICHARDETTO.

FLORIO. And how d'ye find her, sir?

RICHARDETTO. Indifferent well:
I see no danger, scarce perceive she's sick,
But that she told me she had lately eaten
Melons, and as she thought, those disagreed
With her young stomach.

FLORIO. Did you give her aught?

RICHARDETTO. An easy surfeit-water, nothing else.
You need not doubt her health; I rather think
Her sickness is a fullness of her blood –
You understand me?

FLORIO. I do; you counsel well,
And once within these few days will so order't
She shall be married ere she know the time.

RICHARDETTO. Yet let not haste, sir, make unworthy choice;
That were dishonour.

FLORIO. Master doctor, no,
I will not do so neither; in plain words,

30–3 See Textual Notes, p. 342.
1 *Indifferent*: tolerably, fairly.
6 *easy surfeit-water*: mild cure for indigestion.
8 *fullness . . . blood*: a case of sexual frustration; cf. I.i.32 and note.
10 *once*: at some time.

My lord Soranzo is the man I mean.
RICHARDETTO. A noble and a virtuous gentleman.
FLORIO. As any is in Parma. Not far hence
Dwells Father Bonaventure, a grave friar,
Once tutor to my son; now at his cell
I'll have 'em married.
RICHARDETTO. You have plotted wisely.
FLORIO. I'll send one straight to speak with him tonight.
RICHARDETTO. Soranzo's wise, he will delay no time.
FLORIO. It shall be so.

Enter FRIAR *and* GIOVANNI.

FRIAR. Good peace be here, and love!
FLORIO. Welcome, religious friar, you are one
That still bring blessing to the place you come to.
GIOVANNI. Sir, with what speed I could, I did my best
To draw this holy man from forth his cell
To visit my sick sister, that with words
Of ghostly comfort in this time of need
He might absolve her, whether she live or die.
FLORIO. 'Twas well done, Giovanni; thou herein
Hast show'd a Christian's care, a brother's love. –
Come, father, I'll conduct you to her chamber,
And one thing would entreat you.
FRIAR. Say on, sir.
FLORIO. I have a father's dear impression,
And wish, before I fall into my grave,
That I might see her married, as 'tis fit.
A word from you, grave man, will win her more
Than all our best persuasions.
FRIAR. Gentle sir,
All this I'll say, that Heaven may prosper her.
Exeunt.

---

21 See Textual Notes, p. 342.
29 *ghostly*: spiritual.
35 *dear impression*: loving notion.

SCENE V

Enter GRIMALDI.

GRIMALDI. Now if the doctor keep his word, Soranzo,
Twenty to one you miss your bride. I know
'Tis an unnoble act, and not becomes
A soldier's valour; but in terms of love,
Where merit cannot sway, policy must.
I am resolv'd; if this physician
Play not on both hands, then Soranzo falls.

Enter RICHARDETTO.

RICHARDETTO. You are come as I could wish; this very night
Soranzo, 'tis ordain'd, must be affied
To Annabella; and for aught I know,
Married.
GRIMALDI. How!
RICHARDETTO. Yet your patience.
The place, 'tis Friar Bonaventure's cell.
Now I would wish you to bestow this night
In watching thereabouts. 'Tis but a night;
If you miss now, tomorrow I'll know all.
GRIMALDI. Have you the poison?
RICHARDETTO. Here 'tis in this box.
Doubt nothing, this will do't; in any case,
As you respect your life, be quick and sure.
GRIMALDI. I'll speed him.
RICHARDETTO. Do; away, for 'tis not safe
You should be seen much here. – Ever my love!
GRIMALDI. And mine to you. *Exit.*
RICHARDETTO. So, if this hit, I'll laugh and hug revenge;

---

4 *terms*: circumstances.
5 *policy*: cunning.
7 *Play . . . hands*: does not double-cross me.
8–11 See Textual Notes, p. 342.
9 *affied*: betrothed.
19 *speed*: dispatch, kill.
22 *hit*: succeed.

And they that now dream of a wedding feast
May chance to mourn the lusty bridegroom's ruin.
But to my other business. Niece, Philotis!

Enter PHILOTIS.

PHILOTIS. Uncle?
RICHARDETTO. My lovely niece, you have bethought ye?
PHILOTIS. Yes, and as you counsell'd,
Fashion'd my heart to love him; but he swears
He will tonight be married, for he fears
His uncle else, if he should know the drift,
Will hinder all, and call his coz to shrift.
RICHARDETTO. Tonight? Why, best of all! But let me see,
Ay – ha – yes, – so it shall be; in disguise
We'll early to the friar's, I have thought on't.

Enter BERGETTO *and* POGGIO.

PHILOTIS. Uncle, he comes!
RICHARDETTO. Welcome, my worthy coz.
BERGETTO. Lass, pretty lass, come buss, lass; [*kisses her*] aha, Poggio!
POGGIO. There's hope of this yet.
RICHARDETTO. You shall have time enough; withdraw a little
We must confer at large.
BERGETTO. Have you not sweetmeats or dainty devices for me?
PHILOTIS. You shall have enough, sweetheart.
BERGETTO. Sweetheart! Mark that, Poggio; by my troth I cannot choose but kiss thee once more for that word 'sweetheart'. [*Kisses her*] Poggio, I have a monstrous swelling about my stomach, whatsoever the matter be.

---

30 *drift*: plan, intention.
31 *call . . . shrift*: summon his nephew (*coz*) to confession.
33 See Textual Notes, p. 342.
36 *buss*: kiss.
38, 43 See Textual Notes, p. 342.

POGGIO. You shall have physic for't, sir.
RICHARDETTO. Time runs apace.
BERGETTO. Time's a blockhead!
RICHARDETTO. Be ruled; when we have done what's fit to do,
Then you may kiss your fill, and bed her too.

SCENE VI

Enter the FRIAR *in his study, sitting in a chair,* ANNABELLA *kneeling and whispering to him, a table before them and wax lights; she weeps, and wrings her hands.*

FRIAR. I am glad to see this penance; for believe me,
You have unripp'd a soul so foul and guilty,
As I must tell you true, I marvel how
The earth hath borne you up. But weep, weep on,
These tears may do you good; weep faster yet,
Whiles I do read a lecture.
ANNABELLA. Wretched creature!
FRIAR. Ay, you are wretched, miserably wretched,
Almost condemn'd alive. There is a place –
List, daughter! – in a black and hollow vault,
Where day is never seen; there shines no sun,
But flaming horror of consuming fires;
A lightless sulphur, chok'd with smoky fogs
Of an infected darkness. In this place
Dwell many thousand thousand sundry sorts
Of never-dying deaths: there damned souls
Roar without pity; there are gluttons fed
With toads and adders; there is burning oil
Pour'd down the drunkard's throat; the usurer

---

49 *physic*: medicine.
0 s.d. See Additional Notes, p. 351.
2 *unripp'd*: torn out, exposed; a striking metaphorical anticipation of the catastrophe of the play (cf. IV.iii.53 and V.vi.59).
6 *read a lecture*: deliver a rebuke.
9 *List*: listen.

Is forc'd to sup whole draughts of molten gold;
There is the murderer forever stabb'd,
Yet can he never die; there lies the wanton
On racks of burning steel, whiles in his soul
He feels the torment of his raging lust.

ANNABELLA. Mercy, O mercy!

FRIAR. There stands these wretched things
Who have dreamt out whole years in lawless sheets
And secret incests, cursing one another.
Then you will wish each kiss your brother gave
Had been a dagger's point; then you shall hear
How he will cry, 'O, would my wicked sister
Had first been damn'd, when she did yield to lust!'
But soft, methinks I see repentance work
New motions in your heart. Say, how is't with you?

ANNABELLA. Is there no way left to redeem my miseries?

FRIAR. There is, despair not; Heaven is merciful,
And offers grace even now. 'Tis thus agreed,
First, for your honour's safety that you marry
The Lord Soranzo; next, to save your soul,
Leave off this life, and henceforth live to him.

ANNABELLA. Ay me!

FRIAR. Sigh not; I know the baits of sin
Are hard to leave. O, 'tis a death to do't.
Remember what must come! Are you content?

ANNABELLA. I am.

FRIAR. I like it well; we'll take the time.
Who's near us there?

Enter FLORIO, GIOVANNI.

FLORIO. Did you call, father?

FRIAR. Is Lord Soranzo come?

FLORIO. He stays below.

---

32 *motions*: impulses.
40 *do't*: (1) do as you are doing, (2) engage in the sexual act.
42 *take the time*: seize the opportunity.
44 *stays*: waits.

FRIAR. Have you acquainted him at full?
FLORIO. I have,
And he is overjoy'd.
FRIAR. And so are we;
Bid him come near.
GIOVANNI. [*aside*] My sister weeping, ha!
I fear this friar's falsehood. [*To them*] I will
call him. *Exit.*
FLORIO. Daughter, are you resolv'd?
ANNABELLA. Father, I am.

Enter GIOVANNI, SORANZO, *and* VASQUES.

FLORIO. My lord Soranzo, here
Give me your hand; for that I give you this.
[*Joins their hands.*]
SORANZO. Lady, say you so too?
ANNABELLA. I do, and vow
To live with you and yours.
FRIAR. Timely resolv'd.
My blessing rest on both! More to be done,
You may perform it on the morning sun.
Exeunt.

SCENE VII

Enter GRIMALDI *with his rapier drawn, and a dark lantern.*

GRIMALDI. 'Tis early night as yet, and yet too
soon
To finish such a work. Here I will lie
To listen who comes next. *He lies down.*

45–8 See Textual Notes, p. 342.
50–3 *My . . . yours*: this exchange takes the form of a legally binding betrothal, normally followed by a church service (54–5).
51 See Textual Notes, p. 342.
52–3 See Textual Notes, p. 342.
0 s.d. *dark lantern*: one in which the light could be concealed by a shutter.

Enter BERGETTO *and* PHILOTIS *disguised, and after,* RICHARDETTO *and* POGGIO.

BERGETTO. We are almost at the place, I hope, sweetheart.

GRIMALDI. [*aside*] I hear them near, and heard one say 'sweetheart'.
'Tis he; now guide my hand, some angry Justice,
Home to his bosom. [*Aloud*] Now have at you, sir!

Strikes BERGETTO *and exit.*

BERGETTO. O help, help! Here's a stitch fallen in my guts. O for a flesh-tailor quickly! – Poggio!

PHILOTIS. What ails my love?

BERGETTO. I am sure I cannot piss forward and backward, and yet I am wet before and behind. Lights, lights, ho, lights!

PHILOTIS. Alas, some villain here has slain my love!

RICHARDETTO. O, Heaven forbid it! – Raise up the next neighbours
Instantly, Poggio, and bring lights.

Exit POGGIO.

How is't, Bergetto? Slain? It cannot be!
Are you sure you're hurt?

BERGETTO. O, my belly seethes like a porridge-pot; some cold water, I shall boil over else. My whole body is in a sweat, that you may wring my shirt; feel here – Why, Poggio!

Enter POGGIO *with* OFFICERS, *and lights and halberts.*

POGGIO. Here. Alas, how do you?

RICHARDETTO. Give me a light. What's here? All blood! O sirs,

---

3 s.d. *after*: i.e. following Bergetto and Philotis.
9 *fallen*: burst.
10 *flesh-tailor*: surgeon.
19–20 See Textual Notes, p. 342.
24 s.d. *halberts*: spears with axe heads; the usual weapon carried by officers of the city watch.

Signior Donado's nephew now is slain!
Follow the murderer with all thy haste
Up to the city; he cannot be far hence.
Follow, I beseech you!

OFFICERS. Follow, follow, follow!

Exeunt OFFICERS.

RICHARDETTO. Tear off thy linen, coz, to stop his wounds. –
Be of good comfort, man.

BERGETTO. Is all this mine own blood? Nay then, good-night with me. – Poggio, commend me to my uncle, dost hear? Bid him for my sake make much of this wench. – O, I am going the wrong way sure, my belly aches so. – O, farewell, Poggio! – O! – O! – *Dies.*

PHILOTIS. O, he is dead!

POGGIO. How! Dead?

RICHARDETTO. He's dead indeed.
'Tis now too late to weep; let's have him home,
And with what speed we may find out the murderer.

POGGIO. O my master, my master, my master!

Exeunt.

SCENE VIII

Enter VASQUES *and* HIPPOLITA.

HIPPOLITA. Betroth'd?

VASQUES. I saw it.

HIPPOLITA. And when's the marriage-day?

VASQUES. Some two days hence.

HIPPOLITA. Two days? Why, man, I would but wish two hours
To send him to his last and lasting sleep.
And Vasques, thou shalt see, I'll do it bravely.

VASQUES. I do not doubt your wisdom, nor, I trust, you my secrecy. I am infinitely yours.

---

28 See Textual Notes, p. 342.
7 *bravely*: handsomely.

HIPPOLITA. I will be thine in spite of my disgrace.
So soon? O wicked man, I durst be sworn
He'd laugh to see me weep.

VASQUES. And that's a villainous fault in him.

HIPPOLITA. No, let him laugh; I'm arm'd in my resolves,
Be thou still true.

VASQUES. I should get little by treachery against so hopeful a preferment as I am like to climb to.

HIPPOLITA. Even to my bosom, Vasques. Let my youth
Revel in these new pleasures. If we thrive,
He now hath but a pair of days to live.
Exeunt.

SCENE IX

Enter FLORIO, DONADO, RICHARDETTO, POGGIO, *and* OFFICERS.

FLORIO. 'Tis bootless now to show yourself a child,
Signior Donado; what is done, is done.
Spend not the time in tears, but seek for justice.

RICHARDETTO. I must confess, somewhat I was in fault,
That had not first acquainted you what love
Pass'd 'twixt him and my niece; but as I live,
His fortune grieves me as it were mine own.

DONADO. Alas, poor creature, he meant no man harm,
That I am sure of.

FLORIO. I believe that too. –
But stay, my masters, are you sure you saw
The murderer pass here?

OFFICER. And it please you, sir, we are sure we saw a ruffian with a naked weapon in his hand, all bloody, get into my lord Cardinal's grace's gate. That we are sure of; but for fear of his

---

16–17 *against so hopeful*: in exchange for so promising.
18 *my youth*: Soranzo (cf. I.ii.103–4).
1 *bootless*: pointless.

grace, bless us! [*they cross themselves*] we durst go no further.

DONADO. Know you what manner of man he was?

OFFICER. Yes, sure I know the man, they say he is a soldier; he that lov'd your daughter, sir, an't please ye, 'twas he for certain.

FLORIO. Grimaldi, on my life!

OFFICER. Ay, ay, the same.

RICHARDETTO. The Cardinal is noble; he no doubt
Will give true justice.

DONADO. Knock someone at the gate.

POGGIO. I'll knock, sir. POGGIO *knocks.*

SERVANT. [*within*] What would ye?

FLORIO. We require speech with the lord Cardinal
About some present business; pray inform
His grace that we are here.

Enter CARDINAL *and* GRIMALDI.

CARDINAL. Why, how now, friends! What saucy mates are you
That know nor duty nor civility?
Are we a person fit to be your host?
Or is our house become your common inn,
To beat our doors at pleasure? What such haste
Is yours, as that it cannot wait fit times?
Are you the masters of this commonwealth,
And know no more discretion? O, your news
Is here before you; you have lost a nephew,
Donado, last night by Grimaldi slain.
Is that your business? Well, sir, we have knowledge on't.
Let that suffice.

GRIMALDI. In presence of your grace,
In thought I never meant Bergetto harm.
But Florio, you can tell with how much scorn
Soranzo, back'd with his confederates,
Hath often wrong'd me. I to be reveng'd
(For that I could not win him else to fight)

---

29 *present*: urgent.
31 *mates*: fellows.
37 *masters of this commonwealth*: magistrates of this community.

Had thought by way of ambush to have kill'd him,
But was unluckily therein mistook;
Else he had felt what late Bergetto did.
And though my fault to him were merely chance,
Yet humbly I submit me to your grace, [*Kneels.*]
To do with me as you please.

CARDINAL. Rise up, Grimaldi. [*He rises.*]
You citizens of Parma, if you seek
For justice, know, as Nuncio from the Pope,
For this offence I here receive Grimaldi
Into his Holiness' protection.
He is no common man, but nobly born;
Of princes' blood, though you, sir Florio,
Thought him too mean a husband for your daughter.
If more you seek for, you must go to Rome,
For he shall thither. Learn more wit, for shame.
Bury your dead. – Away, Grimaldi; leave 'em.

Exeunt CARDINAL *and* GRIMALDI.

DONADO. Is this a churchman's voice? Dwells Justice here?

FLORIO. Justice is fled to Heaven and comes no nearer.
Soranzo! Was't for him? O impudence!
Had he the face to speak it, and not blush?
Come, come, Donado, there's no help in this,
When cardinals think murder's not amiss.
Great men may do their wills, we must obey,
But Heaven will judge them for't another day.

Exeunt.

---

51 *chance*: an accidental one.
60 *mean*: undistinguished.
62 *wit*: common sense.
65 *Justice . . . nearer*: at the end of the Golden Age on earth, Astraea, goddess of justice, fled to the heavens and was placed there as the constellation Virgo.

ACT IV

SCENE I

A banquet. Hautboys. Enter the FRIAR, GIOVANNI, ANNABELLA, PHILOTIS, SORANZO, DONADO, FLORIO, RICHARDETTO, PUTANA, *and* VASQUES.

FRIAR. These holy rites perform'd, now take your times,
To spend the remnant of the day in feast;
Such fit repasts are pleasing to the saints
Who are your guests, though not with mortal eyes
To be beheld. Long prosper in this day,
You happy couple, to each other's joy!

SORANZO. Father, your prayer is heard. The hand of goodness
Hath been a shield for me against my death,
And, more to bless me, hath enrich'd my life
With this most precious jewel; such a prize
As earth hath not another like to this.
Cheer up, my love; and gentlemen, my friends,
Rejoice with me in mirth. This day we'll crown
With lusty cups to Annabella's health.

GIOVANNI. O, torture! Were the marriage yet undone, *Aside.*
Ere I'd endure this sight, to see my love
Clipp'd by another, I would dare confusion,
And stand the horror of ten thousand deaths.

VASQUES. Are you not well, sir?

GIOVANNI. Prithee, fellow, wait.
I need not thy officious diligence.

FLORIO. Signior Donado, come, you must forget
Your late mishaps, and drown your cares in wine.

---

0 s.d. *Hautboys*: oboes.
17 *Clipp'd*: embraced.
19 *wait*: attend on the guests.

SORANZO. Vasques!
VASQUES. My lord?
SORANZO. Reach me that weighty bowl.
Here, brother Giovanni, here's to you;
Your turn comes next, though now a bachelor.
Here's to your sister's happiness and mine!
[*Drinks, and offers him the bowl.*]
GIOVANNI. I cannot drink.
SORANZO. What?
GIOVANNI. 'Twill indeed offend me.
ANNABELLA. Pray, do not urge him if he be not willing.

Hautboys.

FLORIO. How now, what noise is this?

VASQUES. O sir, I had forgot to tell you. Certain young maidens of Parma, in honour to Madam Annabella's marriage, have sent their loves to her in a masque, for which they humbly crave your patience and silence.

SORANZO. We are much bound to them, so much the more
As it comes unexpected; guide them in.

Enter HIPPOLITA *and Ladies* [*masked,*] *in white robes, with garlands of willows. Music, and a dance.*

SORANZO. Thanks, lovely virgins; now might we but know
To whom we have been beholding for this love,
We shall acknowledge it.
HIPPOLITA. Yes, you shall know.
[*Unmasks.*]
What think you now?
ALL. Hippolita!
HIPPOLITA. 'Tis she.
Be not amaz'd, nor blush, young lovely bride:

---

24 *brother*: brother-in-law.
27 *offend*: (1) make me ill, (2) displease.
28 See Textual Notes, p. 342.
29 *noise*: music.
35–6 See Textual Notes, p. 342.
36 s.d. *willows*: symbolising disappointed love.
38 *love*: act of kindness. See Textual Notes, p. 342.

I come not to defraud you of your man.
[*To* SORANZO] 'Tis now no time to reckon up the talk,
What Parma long hath rumour'd of us both.
Let rash report run on; the breath that vents it
Will, like a bubble, break itself at last.
[*To* ANNABELLA] But now to you, sweet creature; lend's your hand.
Perhaps it hath been said that I would claim
Some interest in Soranzo, now your lord;
What I have right to do, his soul knows best.
But in my duty to your noble worth,
Sweet Annabella, and my cares of you,
Here take, Soranzo, take this hand from me.
I'll once more join what by the holy Church
Is finish'd and allow'd. Have I done well?

SORANZO. You have much engag'd us.

HIPPOLITA. One thing more.
That you may know my single charity,
Freely I here remit all interest
I e'er could claim, and give you back your vows;
And to confirm't – reach me a cup of wine –
My lord Soranzo, in this draught I drink
Long rest t'ye! [*Aside*] Look to it, Vasques.

VASQUES. [*aside*] Fear nothing.

He gives her a poisoned cup; she drinks.

SORANZO. Hippolita, I thank you, and will pledge
This happy union as another life. –
Wine there!

VASQUES. You shall have none, neither shall you pledge her.

HIPPOLITA. How!

VASQUES. Know now, mistress she-devil, your own mischievous treachery hath kill'd you. I must not marry you.

HIPPOLITA. Villain!

ALL. What's the matter?

---

45 *rash report*: swift gossip.
55 *allow'd*: approved.
56 *engag'd*: (1) laid under obligation, (2) betrothed.
57 *single charity*: sincere love.
64 *union*: agreement.
69–71 See Textual Notes, p. 342.

VASQUES. Foolish woman, thou art now like a firebrand, that hath kindled others and burnt thyself. *Troppo sperar, inganna*; thy vain hope hath deceiv'd thee. Thou art but dead; if thou hast any grace, pray.

HIPPOLITA. Monster!

VASQUES. Die in charity, for shame! – This thing of malice, this woman, had privately corrupted me with promise of marriage, under this politic reconciliation to poison my lord, whiles she might laugh at his confusion on his marriage-day. I promis'd her fair, but I knew what my reward should have been; and would willingly have spar'd her life, but that I was acquainted with the danger of her disposition – and now have fitted her a just payment in her own coin. There she is, she hath yet – and end thy days in peace, vile woman; as for life there's no hope, think not on't.

ALL. Wonderful justice!

RICHARDETTO. Heaven, thou art righteous.

HIPPOLITA. O, 'tis true,
I feel my minute coming. Had that slave
Kept promise – O, my torment! – thou this hour
Hadst died, Soranzo. – Heat above hell-fire! –
Yet ere I pass away – cruel, cruel flames! –
Take here my curse amongst you: may thy bed
Of marriage be a rack unto thy heart;
Burn, blood, and boil in vengeance. – O my heart,
My flame's intolerable! – Mayst thou live
To father bastards, may her womb bring forth
Monsters, and die together in your sins,
Hated, scorn'd and unpitied! – O! – O! –
Dies.

---

76 *Troppo sperar, inganna*: too much hope deceives. See Textual Notes, p. 342.

77 *but*: as good as.

80 *charity*: Christian love; an ironic reference to Hippolita's previous remark (57).

82 *under*: under the cloak of. See Textual Notes, p. 342.

90 See Textual Notes, p. 342.

95 *minute*: moment of death.

FLORIO. Was e'er so vile a creature?
RICHARDETTO. Here's the end
Of lust and pride.
ANNABELLA. It is a fearful sight.
SORANZO. Vasques, I know thee now a trusty servant,
And never will forget thee. – Come, my love,
We'll home, and thank the Heavens for this escape.
Father and friends, we must break up this mirth;
It is too sad a feast.
DONADO. Bear hence the body.
FRIAR. [*aside to* GIOVANNI] Here's an ominous change;
Mark this, my Giovanni, and take heed.
I fear the event; that marriage seldom's good,
Where the bride-banquet so begins in blood.
Exeunt.

SCENE II

Enter RICHARDETTO *and* PHILOTIS.

RICHARDETTO. My wretched wife, more wretched in her shame
Than in her wrongs to me, hath paid too soon
The forfeit of her modesty and life.
And I am sure, my niece, though vengeance hover,
Keeping aloof yet from Soranzo's fall,
Yet he will fall, and sink with his own weight.
I need not – now my heart persuades me so –
To further his confusion. There is One
Above begins to work, for, as I hear,
Debates already 'twixt his wife and him
Thicken and run to head; she, as 'tis said,
Slightens his love, and he abandons hers.

---

115 *event*: outcome.
2 See Textual Notes, p. 342.
10 *Debates*: arguments.
11 *Thicken . . . head*: multiply and come to bursting-point (as a boil might do).
12 *Slightens*: disdains.

Much talk I hear. Since things go thus, my niece,
In tender love and pity of your youth,
My counsel is that you should free your years
From hazard of these woes, by flying hence
To fair Cremona, there to vow your soul
In holiness a holy votaress.
Leave me to see the end of these extremes.
All human worldly courses are uneven;
No life is blessed but the way to Heaven.

PHILOTIS. Uncle, shall I resolve to be a nun?

RICHARDETTO. Ay, gentle niece, and in your hourly prayers
Remember me, your poor unhappy uncle.
Hie to Cremona now, as fortune leads,
Your home your cloister, your best friends your beads.
Your chaste and single life shall crown your birth;
Who dies a virgin lives a saint on earth.

PHILOTIS. Then farewell, world, and worldly thoughts adieu!
Welcome, chaste vows; myself I yield to you.

Exeunt.

SCENE III

Enter SORANZO *unbraced, and* ANNABELLA *dragged in.*

SORANZO. Come, strumpet, famous whore! Were every drop
Of blood that runs in thy adulterous veins

---

18 *votaress*: nun.
20 *uneven*: difficult, unjust.
25 *Cremona*: a town dominated by its cathedral, and within forty miles of Parma.
26 *beads*: the nun's prayer rosary.
28 See Textual Notes, p. 343.
0 s.d. *unbraced*: with his clothing (here probably his doublet) unfastened.
1 *famous*: notorious.

A life, this sword – dost see't? – should in
one blow
Confound them all. Harlot, rare, notable harlot,
That with thy brazen face maintain'st thy sin,
Was there no man in Parma to be bawd
To your loose cunning whoredom else but I?
Must your hot itch and plurisy of lust,
The heyday of your luxury, be fed
Up to a surfeit, and could none but I
Be pick'd out to be cloak to your close tricks,
Your belly-sports? Now I must be the dad
To all that gallimaufry that's stuff'd
In thy corrupted bastard-bearing womb!
Why must I?

ANNABELLA. Beastly man, why, 'tis thy fate.
I sued not to thee, for, but that I thought
Your over-loving lordship would have run
Mad on denial, had ye lent me time,
I would have told ye in what case I was.
But you would needs be doing.

SORANZO. Whore of whores!
Dar'st thou tell me this?

ANNABELLA. O yes, why not?
You were deceiv'd in me: 'twas not for love
I chose you, but for honour. Yet know this,
Would you be patient yet, and hide your shame,
I'd see whether I could love you.

SORANZO. Excellent quean!
Why, art thou not with child?

ANNABELLA. What needs all this,
When 'tis superfluous? I confess I am.

---

4 *Confound*: destroy.
5 *maintain'st*: (1) persists in, (2) defends.
8 *plurisy*: excess.
9 *heyday of your luxury*: heat of your lustfulness at its height.
11 *close*: (1) secret, (2) physically close.
13 *gallimaufry*: hodge-podge, jumble.
15 See Textual Notes, p. 343.
19 *case*: condition.
20 *doing*: active (sexually).
25 *Excellent quean*: pre-eminent harlot.

SORANZO. Tell me by whom.
ANNABELLA. Soft, sir, 'twas not in my bargain.
Yet somewhat, sir, to stay your longing stomach,
I'm content t'acquaint you with. The man,
The more than man that got this sprightly boy –
For 'tis a boy; that for your glory, sir;
Your heir shall be a son –
SORANZO. Damnable monster!
ANNABELLA. Nay, and you will not hear, I'll speak no more.
SORANZO. Yes, speak, and speak thy last.
ANNABELLA. A match, a match!
This noble creature was in every part
So angel-like, so glorious, that a woman
Who had not been but human, as was I,
Would have kneel'd to him, and have begg'd for love.
You, why you are not worthy once to name
His name without true worship, or indeed,
Unless you kneel'd, to hear another name him.
SORANZO. What was he call'd?
ANNABELLA. We are not come to that;
Let it suffice that you shall have the glory
To father what so brave a father got.
In brief, had not this chance fall'n out as't doth,
I never had been troubl'd with a thought
That you had been a creature. But for marriage,
I scarce dream yet of that.
SORANZO. Tell me his name.

---

29 *stay*: satisfy, appease.
32 See Textual Notes, p. 343.
34 *and*: if.
35 *A match*: agreed, a bargain.
38 *not been but*: was only.
45 *brave*: splendid.
48 *been a creature*: were in existence.

ANNABELLA. Alas, alas, there's all. Will you
believe?
SORANZO. What?
ANNABELLA. You shall never know.
SORANZO. How!
ANNABELLA. Never; if you do, let me be curs'd.
SORANZO. Not know it, strumpet! I'll rip up thy
heart,
And find it there.
ANNABELLA. Do, do!
SORANZO. And with my teeth
Tear the prodigious lecher joint by joint.
ANNABELLA. Ha, ha, ha, the man's merry!
SORANZO. Dost thou laugh?
Come, whore, tell me your lover, or by truth
I'll hew thy flesh to shreds! Who is't?
ANNABELLA. *Che morte più dolce che morirei
per amore?* *Sings.*
SORANZO. Thus will I pull thy hair, and thus I'll
drag
Thy lust-beleper'd body through the dust.
Yet tell his name.
ANNABELLA. *Morendo in gratia a lui, morirei
senza dolore.* *Sings.*
SORANZO. Dost thou triumph? The treasure of
the earth
Shall not redeem thee; were there kneeling kings
Did beg thy life, or angels did come down
To plead in tears, yet should not all prevail
Against my rage. Dost thou not tremble yet?
ANNABELLA. At what? To die? No, be a gallant
hangman.
I dare thee to the worst; strike, and strike home.
I leave revenge behind, and thou shalt feel't.

50, 52 See Textual Notes, p. 343.
55 *prodigious*: monstrous.
59 *Che . . . amore*: what death is sweeter than to die for love. See Textual Notes, p. 343.
63 *Morendo . . . dolore*: dying in his favour, I would die without pain. See Textual Notes, p. 343.
64 *triumph*: exult.
69 *hangman*: executioner.
71 See Textual Notes, p. 343.

SORANZO. Yet tell me ere thou diest, and tell me truly,
Knows thy old father this?
ANNABELLA. No, by my life.
SORANZO. Wilt thou confess, and I will spare thy life?
ANNABELLA. My life! I will not buy my life so dear.
SORANZO. I will not slack my vengeance.
[*Draws his sword.*]

Enter VASQUES.

VASQUES. What d'ye mean, sir?
SORANZO. Forbear, Vasques; such a damned whore
Deserves no pity.
VASQUES. Now the gods forfend!
And would you be her executioner, and kill her in your rage too? O, 'twere most unmanlike! She is your wife; what faults hath been done by her before she married you, were not against you; alas, poor lady, what hath she committed which any lady in Italy in the like case would not? Sir, you must be rul'd by your reason, and not by your fury; that were unhuman and beastly.
SORANZO. She shall not live.
VASQUES. Come, she must. You would have her confess the author of her present misfortunes, I warrant ye; 'tis an unconscionable demand, and she should lose the estimation that I, for my part, hold of her worth, if she had done it. Why sir, you ought not of all men living to know it. Good sir, be reconcil'd; alas, good gentlewoman!
ANNABELLA. Pish, do not beg for me; I prize my life
As nothing. If the man will needs be mad,

---

74 *confess*: admit your lover's name; cf. 89.
76 *slack*: delay or mitigate.
78 *forfend*: forbid.
89 See Textual Notes, p. 343.

Why let him take it.
SORANZO. Vasques, hear'st thou this?
VASQUES. Yes, and commend her for it. In this she shows the nobleness of a gallant spirit, and beshrew my heart but it becomes her rarely. [*Aside to* SORANZO] Sir, in any case smother your revenge; leave the scenting-out your wrongs to me. Be rul'd, as you respect your honour, or you mar all. [*Aloud*] Sir, if ever my service were of any credit with you, be not so violent in your distractions. You are married now; what a triumph might the report of this give to other neglected suitors! 'Tis as manlike to bear extremities, as godlike to forgive.
SORANZO. O Vasques, Vasques, in this piece of flesh,
This faithless face of hers, had I laid up
The treasure of my heart! – Hadst thou been virtuous,
Fair, wicked woman, not the matchless joys
Of life itself had made me wish to live
With any saint but thee. Deceitful creature,
How hast thou mock'd my hopes, and in the shame
Of thy lewd womb even buried me alive!
I did too dearly love thee.
VASQUES. *aside* [*to* SORANZO] This is well. Follow this temper with some passion. Be brief and moving; 'tis for the purpose.
SORANZO. Be witness to my words thy soul and thoughts,
And tell me, didst not think that in my heart
I did too superstitiously adore thee?

---

101 *beshrew*: curse.
but it becomes: if it doesn't befit.
102 *in any case*: by any means.
104 See Textual Notes, p. 343.
106 *credit*: esteem.
110 *extremities*: hardships.
121–2 See Textual Notes, p. 343.
121 *temper*: attitude, approach.
passion: display of emotion.
125 *superstitiously*: idolatrously, extravagantly.

ANNABELLA. I must confess, I know you lov'd me well.
SORANZO. And wouldst thou use me thus? O Annabella,
Be thou assur'd, whatsoe'er the villain was
That thus hath tempted thee to this disgrace,
Well he might lust, but never lov'd like me.
He doted on the picture that hung out
Upon thy cheeks, to please his humorous eye;
Not on the part I lov'd, which was thy heart,
And, as I thought, thy virtues.
ANNABELLA. O my lord!
These words wound deeper than your sword could do.
VASQUES. Let me not ever take comfort, but I begin to weep myself, so much I pity him; why, madam, I knew when his rage was overpass'd what it would come to.
SORANZO. Forgive me, Annabella. Though thy youth
Hath tempted thee above thy strength to folly,
Yet will not I forget what I should be,
And what I am, a husband; in that name
Is hid divinity. If I do find
That thou wilt yet be true, here I remit
All former faults, and take thee to my bosom.
VASQUES. By my troth, and that's a point of noble charity.
ANNABELLA. Sir, on my knees – [*Kneels.*]
SORANZO. Rise up; you shall not kneel.
Get you to your chamber, see you make no show
Of alteration; I'll be with you straight.
My reason tells me now that 'tis as common
To err in frailty as to be a woman.
Go to your chamber.
Exit ANNABELLA.

---

128 See Textual Notes, p. 343.
132 *humorous*: capricious.
145 *remit*: pardon.
151 *alteration*: (emotional) disturbance.
153 *in frailty*: through human weakness.

VASQUES. So, this was somewhat to the matter; what do you think of your heaven of happiness now, sir?

SORANZO. I carry Hell about me; all my blood
Is fir'd in swift revenge.

VASQUES. That may be, but know you how, or on whom? Alas, to marry a great woman, being made great in the stock to your hand, is a usual sport in these days; but to know what ferret it was that haunted your cony-berry, there's the cunning.

SORANZO. I'll make her tell herself, or –

VASQUES. Or what? You must not do so. Let me yet persuade your sufferance a little while. Go to her, use her mildly, win her if it be possible to a voluntary, to a weeping tune; for the rest, if all hit, I will not miss my mark. Pray, sir, go in; the next news I tell you shall be wonders.

SORANZO. Delay in vengeance gives a heavier blow. *Exit.*

VASQUES. Ah, sirrah, here's work for the nonce! I had a suspicion of a bad matter in my head a pretty whiles ago; but after my madam's scurvy looks here at home, her waspish perverseness and loud fault-finding, then I remember'd the proverb, that where hens crow and cocks hold their peace there are sorry houses. 'Sfoot, if the lower parts of a she-tailor's cunning can cover such a swelling in the stomach, I'll never blame a false stitch in a shoe whiles I live again. Up,

---

161 *great woman*: (1) woman of high rank, (2) pregnant woman.

162 *stock*: (1) body, (2) family, (3) rabbit burrow (i.e. female sexual organ).
to your hand: ready for you, already.

163 See Textual Notes, p. 343.

164 *haunted your cony-berry*: frequented the 'rabbit burrow' you own.

165 *cunning*: hunter's skill.

170 *voluntary*: (1) extempore piece of music, (2) spontaneous confession.

171 *all hit*: all goes well (the metaphor is from archery).

174 *nonce*: present occasion.

179 *proverb*: see Tilley, H778.

181 *she-tailor's*: with an indecent pun on *tail* (cf. 271).

and up so quick? And so quickly too? 'Twere a fine policy to learn by whom. This must be known; and I have thought on't.

Enter PUTANA.

Here's the way, or none. – What, crying, old mistress? Alas, alas, I cannot blame ye; we have a lord, Heaven help us, is so mad as the devil himself, the more shame for him.

PUTANA. O Vasques, that ever I was born to see this day! Doth he use thee so too, sometimes, Vasques?

VASQUES. Me! Why, he makes a dog of me; but if some were of my mind, I know what we would do. As sure as I am an honest man, he will go near to kill my lady with unkindness. Say she be with child, is that such a matter for a young woman of her years to be blam'd for?

PUTANA. Alas, good heart, it is against her will full sore.

VASQUES. I durst be sworn, all his madness is for that she will not confess whose 'tis; which he will know, and when he doth know it, I am so well acquainted with his humour, that he will forget all straight. Well, I could wish she would in plain terms tell all, for that's the way indeed.

PUTANA. Do you think so?

VASQUES. Foh, I know't; provided that he did not win her to't by force. He was once in a mind that you could tell, and meant to have wrung it out of you, but I somewhat pacified him for that, yet sure you know a great deal.

PUTANA. Heaven forgive us all, I know a little, Vasques.

VASQUES. Why should you not? Who else should? Upon my conscience, she loves you dearly, and

---

184 *so quick*: (1) so fast, (2) in such an advanced stage of pregnancy.
185 *policy*: piece of cunning. See Textual Notes, p. 343.
186 See Textual Notes, p. 343.
189 *mad*: furiously raging.
205 *humour*: obsession.
206 See Textual Notes, p. 343.

you would not betray her to any affliction for the world.

PUTANA. Not for all the world, by my faith and troth, Vasques.

VASQUES. 'Twere pity of your life if you should; but in this you should both relieve her present discomforts, pacify my lord, and gain yourself everlasting love and preferment.

PUTANA. Dost think so, Vasques?

VASQUES. Nay, I know't. Sure 'twas some near and entire friend.

PUTANA. 'Twas a dear friend indeed; but –

VASQUES. But what? Fear not to name him; my life between you and danger. Faith, I think 'twas no base fellow.

PUTANA. Thou wilt stand between me and harm?

VASQUES. Ud's pity, what else? You shall be rewarded too; trust me.

PUTANA. 'Twas even no worse than her own brother.

VASQUES. Her brother Giovanni, I warrant ye!

PUTANA. Even he, Vasques; as brave a gentleman as ever kiss'd fair lady. O, they love most perpetually.

VASQUES. A brave gentleman indeed; why, therein I commend her choice. [*Aside*] Better and better! – You are sure 'twas he?

PUTANA. Sure; and you shall see he will not be long from her too.

VASQUES. He were to blame if he would; but may I believe thee?

PUTANA. Believe me! Why, dost think I am a Turk or a Jew? No, Vasques, I have known their dealings too long to belie them now.

VASQUES. Where are you? There within, sirs!

Enter BANDITTI.

---

229 *dear*: (1) beloved, (2) costly.
232 *base*: of low birth.
234 *Ud's*: God's.
239 *brave*: splendid.
251 *belie*: lie about.

PUTANA. How now, what are these?

VASQUES. You shall know presently. Come, sirs, take me this old damnable hag, gag her instantly, and put out her eyes. Quickly, quickly!

PUTANA. Vasques, Vasques!

VASQUES. Gag her I say. 'Sfoot, d'ye suffer her to prate? What d'ye fumble about? Let me come to her. – I'll help your old gums, you toad-bellied bitch! [*He gags* PUTANA] – Sirs, carry her closely into the coal-house and put out her eyes instantly. If she roars, slit her nose; d'ye hear, be speedy and sure.

[*Exeunt* BANDITTI] *with* PUTANA.

Why, this is excellent and above expectation. Her own brother? O horrible! To what a height of liberty in damnation hath the devil train'd our age. Her brother, well! There's yet but a beginning; I must to my lord, and tutor him better in his points of vengeance. Now I see how a smooth tale goes beyond a smooth tail. But soft – What thing comes next?

Enter GIOVANNI.

Giovanni! As I would wish. My belief is strengthen'd; 'tis as firm as winter and summer.

GIOVANNI. Where's my sister?

VASQUES. Troubl'd with a new sickness, my lord; she's somewhat ill.

GIOVANNI. Took too much of the flesh, I believe.

VASQUES. Troth, sir, and you I think have e'en hit it; but my virtuous lady –

GIOVANNI. Where's she?

---

254 *presently*: instantly.
262 *closely*: secretly.
263 *slit her nose*: both a savage threat, and a not uncommon punishment for sexual offences.
264 See Textual Notes, p. 343.
267 *liberty*: licence.
train'd: lured.
271 *smooth*: deceitful.
278 *flesh*: (1) meat, (2) sexual experience.
280 *hit it*: (1) discovered the true reason, (2) enjoyed sexual intercourse.

VASQUES. In her chamber. Please you visit her; she is alone.

[GIOVANNI *gives him money.*]

Your liberality hath doubly made me your servant, and ever shall, ever –

Exit GIOVANNI.

Enter SORANZO.

Sir, I am made a man, I have plied my cue with cunning and success; I beseech you, let's be private.

SORANZO. My lady's brother's come; now he'll know all.

VASQUES. Let him know't; I have made some of them fast enough. How have you dealt with my lady?

SORANZO. Gently, as thou hast counsell'd. O, my soul
Runs circular in sorrow for revenge!
But Vasques, thou shalt know –

VASQUES. Nay, I will know no more, for now comes your turn to know. I would not talk so openly with you. Let my young master take time enough, and go at pleasure; he is sold to death, and the devil shall not ransom him. Sir, I beseech you, your privacy.

SORANZO. No conquest can gain glory of my fear.

[*Exeunt.*]

---

284 *liberality*: (1) generosity, (2) sexual licence.

286 *made a man*: a made man, assured of success.
plied my cue: played my part.

302 *No . . . fear*: possibly 'my fear will not contribute to any other man's (i.e. Giovanni's) success'. See Textual Notes, p. 343.

ACT V

SCENE I

Enter ANNABELLA *above.*

ANNABELLA. Pleasures farewell, and all ye thriftless minutes
Wherein false joys have spun a weary life;
To these my fortunes now I take my leave.
Thou precious Time, that swiftly rid'st in post
Over the world, to finish up the race
Of my last fate; here stay thy restless course,
And bear to ages that are yet unborn
A wretched woeful woman's tragedy.
My conscience now stands up against my lust
With depositions character'd in guilt,

Enter FRIAR [*below*].

And tells me I am lost. Now I confess
Beauty that clothes the outside of the face
Is cursed if it be not cloth'd with grace.
Here like a turtle, mew'd up in a cage
Unmated, I converse with air and walls,
And descant on my vile unhappiness.
O Giovanni, that hast had the spoil
Of thine own virtues and my modest fame,
Would thou hadst been less subject to those stars
That luckless reign'd at my nativity!
O, would the scourge due to my black offence

---

1 *thriftless*: profitless.
4 *in post*: at the utmost speed (with post horses).
9 *stands up against*: opposes (the metaphor is of a legal witness for the prosecution).
10 *character'd in guilt*: (1) of a guilty nature, (2) written in gilt lettering. See Textual Notes, p. 343.
14 *turtle*: turtle-dove, proverbially devoted to its mate. *mew'd up*: imprisoned.
15 *Unmated*: deprived of its mate.
16 *descant*: sing and discourse.
17 *spoil*: (1) booty, (2) despoliation.

Might pass from thee, that I alone might feel
The torment of an uncontrolled flame!
FRIAR. [*aside*] What's this I hear?
ANNABELLA. That man, that blessed friar,
Who join'd in ceremonial knot my hand
To him whose wife I now am, told me oft
I trod the path to death, and show'd me how.
But they who sleep in lethargies of lust
Hug their confusion, making Heaven unjust,
And so did I.
FRIAR. [*aside*] Here's music to the soul!
ANNABELLA. Forgive me, my good genius, and this once
Be helpful to my ends. Let some good man
Pass this way, to whose trust I may commit
This paper double-lin'd with tears and blood;
Which being granted, here I sadly vow
Repentance, and a leaving of that life
I long have died in.
FRIAR. Lady, Heaven hath heard you,
And hath by providence ordain'd that I
Should be his minister for your behoof.
ANNABELLA. Ha, what are you?
FRIAR. Your brother's friend, the friar;
Glad in my soul that I have liv'd to hear
This free confession 'twixt your peace and you.
What would you, or to whom? Fear not to speak.
ANNABELLA. Is Heaven so bountiful? Then I have found
More favour than I hop'd. Here, holy man –
Throws a letter.
Commend me to my brother, give him that,
That letter; bid him read it and repent.
Tell him that I – imprison'd in my chamber,
Barr'd of all company, even of my guardian,

---

28 *lethargies*: states of morbid drowsiness.
31 *good genius*: guardian spirit.
35 *sadly*: solemnly.
37 *died*: in a spiritual sense.
39 *behoof*: benefit.

Who gives me cause of much suspect – have time
To blush at what hath pass'd; bid him be wise,
And not believe the friendship of my lord.
I fear much more than I can speak. Good father,
The place is dangerous, and spies are busy;
I must break off – you'll do't?

FRIAR. Be sure I will,
And fly with speed. My blessing ever rest
With thee, my daughter; live to die more blest!
Exit.

ANNABELLA. Thanks to the Heavens, who have prolong'd my breath
To this good use. Now I can welcome death.
Exit.

SCENE II

Enter SORANZO *and* VASQUES.

VASQUES. Am I to be believ'd now? First marry a strumpet that cast herself away upon you but to laugh at your horns? To feast on your disgrace, riot in your vexations, cuckold you in your bride-bed, waste your estate upon panders and bawds?

SORANZO. No more, I say, no more!

VASQUES. A cuckold is a goodly tame beast, my lord.

SORANZO. I am resolv'd; urge not another word.
My thoughts are great, and all as resolute
As thunder. In mean time I'll cause our lady
To deck herself in all her bridal robes,
Kiss her, and fold her gently in my arms.
Begone – yet hear you, are the banditti ready

---

50 *Who*: which.
suspect: suspicion.
57 See Textual Notes, p. 343.
3 *horns*: the conventional attribute of the deceived husband.
4 *riot*: revel.
11 *great*: full of wrath.

To wait in ambush?
VASQUES. Good sir, trouble not yourself about other business than your own resolution; remember that time lost cannot be recall'd.
SORANZO. With all the cunning words thou canst, invite
The states of Parma to my birthday's feast;
Haste to my brother rival and his father,
Entreat them gently, bid them not to fail.
Be speedy and return.
VASQUES. Let not your pity betray you. Till my coming back, think upon incest and cuckoldry.
SORANZO. Revenge is all the ambition I aspire;
To that I'll climb or fall: my blood's on fire.
Exeunt.

SCENE III

Enter GIOVANNI.

GIOVANNI. Busy opinion is an idle fool,
That, as a school-rod keeps a child in awe,
Frights the unexperienc'd temper of the mind.
So did it me; who, ere my precious sister
Was married, thought all taste of love would die
In such a contract. But I find no change
Of pleasure in this formal law of sports.
She is still one to me, and every kiss
As sweet and as delicious as the first
I reap'd, when yet the privilege of youth
Entitl'd her a virgin. O, the glory
Of two united hearts like hers and mine!
Let poring book-men dream of other worlds,
My world, and all of happiness, is here,

---

21 *states*: dignitaries.
25 See Textual Notes, p. 343.
27 *aspire*: ardently seek.
1 *Busy opinion*: officious common belief.
idle: futile.
7 *formal . . . sports*: conventional legal sanction for sexual activities.
8 *one*: perfectly united.

And I'd not change it for the best to come:
A life of pleasure is Elysium.

Enter FRIAR.

Father, you enter on the jubilee
Of my retir'd delights. Now I can tell you,
The Hell you oft have prompted is nought else
But slavish and fond superstitious fear;
And I could prove it, too –
FRIAR. Thy blindness slays thee.
Look there, 'tis writ to thee. *Gives the letter.*
GIOVANNI. From whom?
FRIAR. Unrip the seals and see.
The blood's yet seething hot, that will anon
Be frozen harder than congealed coral.
Why d'ye change colour, son?
GIOVANNI. 'Fore Heaven, you make
Some petty devil factor 'twixt my love
And your religion-masked sorceries.
Where had you this?
FRIAR. Thy conscience, youth, is sear'd,
Else thou wouldst stoop to warning.
GIOVANNI. 'Tis her hand,
I know't; and 'tis all written in her blood.
She writes I know not what. Death? I'll not fear
An armed thunderbolt aim'd at my heart.
She writes we are discover'd – pox on dreams
Of low faint-hearted cowardice! Discover'd?
The devil we are! Which way is't possible?

---

16 *Elysium*: the classical paradise; realm of the blessed spirits.
17 *jubilee*: occasion for joyful celebration; cf. *Perkin Warbeck*, I.ii.141.
18 *retir'd*: hidden.
19 *prompted*: proposed in argument.
20 *fond*: foolish.
26 *congealed coral*: coral was thought to harden into its usual form only on being taken from the water. Red coral provides an image of frozen blood.
28 *factor*: intermediary agent.
30 *sear'd*: cauterised, incapable of feeling.
31 *stoop*: humble yourself (as a hawk 'stooped' to its trainer's lure).
34 *armed*: prepared for delivery.

Are we grown traitors to our own delights?
Confusion take such dotage; 'tis but forg'd!
This is your peevish chattering, weak old man.

Enter VASQUES.

Now, sir, what news bring you?

VASQUES. My lord, according to his yearly custom keeping this day a feast in honour of his birthday, by me invites you thither. Your worthy father, with the Pope's reverend Nuncio, and other magnificoes of Parma, have promis'd their presence; will't please you to be of the number?

GIOVANNI. Yes, tell them I dare come.

VASQUES. Dare come?

GIOVANNI. So I said; and tell him more, I will come.

VASQUES. These words are strange to me.

GIOVANNI. Say I will come.

VASQUES. You will not miss?

GIOVANNI. Yet more? I'll come! Sir, are you answer'd?

VASQUES. So I'll say. – My service to you. *Exit.*

FRIAR. You will not go, I trust.

GIOVANNI. Not go! For what?

FRIAR. O do not go! This feast, I'll gage my life,
Is but a plot to train you to your ruin;
Be rul'd, you sha'not go.

GIOVANNI. Not go? Stood Death
Threat'ning his armies of confounding plagues,
With hosts of dangers hot as blazing stars,
I would be there. Not go! Yes; and resolve
To strike as deep in slaughter as they all.
For I will go.

FRIAR. Go where thou wilt; I see

---

40 See Textual Notes, p. 343.
46 *magnificoes*: great men, nobles.
54 *miss*: fail.
59 *gage*: pledge, stake.
60 *train*: lure.
62 *confounding*: destroying.
63 *blazing stars*: comets; generally taken as omens of disaster and here associated with signs reminiscent of the apocalypse.

The wildness of thy fate draws to an end,
To a bad, fearful end. I must not stay
To know thy fall; back to Bononia I
With speed will haste, and shun this coming blow.
Parma farewell; would I had never known thee,
Or aught of thine! Well, youngman, since no prayer
Can make thee safe, I leave thee to despair.
Exit.

GIOVANNI. Despair, or tortures of a thousand Hells,
All's one to me; I have set up my rest.
Now, now, work serious thoughts on baneful plots.
Be all a man, my soul; let not the curse
Of old prescription rend from me the gall
Of courage, which enrols a glorious death.
If I must totter like a well-grown oak,
Some under-shrubs shall in my weighty fall
Be crushed to splits: with me they all shall perish. *Exit.*

SCENE IV

Enter SORANZO, VASQUES, *and* BANDITTI.

SORANZO. You will not fail, or shrink in the attempt?

VASQUES. I will undertake for their parts. – Be sure, my masters, to be bloody enough, and as unmerciful as if you were preying upon a rich

---

69 *Bononia*: cf. I.i.49 and note.
74 See Textual Notes, p. 343.
75 See Additional Notes, p. 351.
77–8 *curse . . . prescription*: Biblical curse pronounced on incest; see Deuteronomy 27.22, and Leviticus 20.17.
78 See Additional Notes, p. 351.
82 *splits*: splinters.
2 *undertake*: give an assurance.

booty on the very mountains of Liguria. For your pardons, trust to my lord; but for reward you shall trust none but your own pockets.

BANDITTI. We'll make a murder.

SORANZO. Here's gold, here's more; want nothing. What you do
Is noble, and an act of brave revenge.
I'll make ye rich, banditti, and all free.

BANDITTI. Liberty, liberty!

VASQUES. Hold, take every man a vizard. When ye are withdrawn, keep as much silence as you can possibly. You know the watchword, till which be spoken, move not, but when you hear that, rush in like a stormy flood; I need not instruct ye in your own profession.

BANDITTI. No, no, no!

VASQUES. In, then; your ends are profit and preferment – away!

[*Exeunt*] BANDITTI.

SORANZO. The guests will all come, Vasques?

VASQUES. Yes, sir, and now let me a little edge your resolution; you see nothing is unready to this great work, but a great mind in you. Call to your remembrance your disgraces, your loss of honour, Hippolita's blood, and arm your courage in your own wrongs; so shall you best right those wrongs in vengeance which you may truly call your own.

SORANZO. 'Tis well; the less I speak, the more I burn,
And blood shall quench that flame.

VASQUES. Now you begin to turn Italian! This beside; when my young incest-monger comes, he

---

5 *Liguria*: mountainous area between Parma and Genoa in north-west Italy.
8 See Textual Notes, p. 343.
9 *want*: lack.
11 *free*: free from the threat of the law.
13 *vizard*: mask.
21 See Textual Notes, p. 343.
23 *edge*: sharpen.
33 *turn Italian*: Italians had a reputation for ferocious revenge-taking.

will be sharp set on his old bit. Give him time enough, let him have your chamber and bed at liberty; let my hot hare have law ere he be hunted to his death, that if it be possible he may post to Hell in the very act of his damnation.

Enter GIOVANNI.

SORANZO. It shall be so; and see, as we would wish,
He comes himself first. – Welcome, my much-lov'd brother,
Now I perceive you honour me; you're welcome.
But where's my father?

GIOVANNI. With the other states,
Attending on the Nuncio of the Pope
To wait upon him hither. How's my sister?

SORANZO. Like a good housewife, scarcely ready yet;
You're best walk to her chamber.

GIOVANNI. If you will.

SORANZO. I must expect my honourable friends;
Good brother, get her forth.

GIOVANNI. You are busy, sir. *Exit.*

VASQUES. Even as the great devil himself would have it! Let him go and glut himself in his own destruction.

Flourish.

Hark, the Nuncio is at hand; good sir, be ready to receive him.

---

35 *sharp . . . bit*: hungry and eager for his former (sexual) food.

37 *hare*: an animal with a reputation for excessive and unnatural lustfulness.
have law: be given the start allowed before the chase began.

39 *post*: hasten.

39–40 *in . . . damnation*: Vasques intends to have Giovanni killed as he commits incest with Annabella, so ensuring the destruction of his soul as well as his body.

44 *states*: dignitaries.

49 *expect*: wait for.

53 See Textual Notes, p. 343.

Enter CARDINAL, FLORIO, DONADO, RICHARDETTO, *and Attendants.*

SORANZO. Most reverend lord, this grace hath made me proud
That you vouchsafe my house; I ever rest
Your humble servant for this noble favour.
CARDINAL. You are our friend, my lord; his Holiness
Shall understand how zealously you honour
Saint Peter's Vicar in his substitute.
Our special love to you.
SORANZO. Signiors, to you
My welcome, and my ever best of thanks
For this so memorable courtesy.
Pleaseth your grace to walk near?
CARDINAL. My lord, we come
To celebrate your feast with civil mirth,
As ancient custom teacheth; we will go.
SORANZO. Attend his grace there! Signiors, keep your way.

Exeunt.

SCENE V

Enter GIOVANNI *and* ANNABELLA *lying on a bed.*

GIOVANNI. What, chang'd so soon? Hath your new sprightly lord
Found out a trick in night-games more than we
Could know in our simplicity? Ha, is't so?
Or does the fit come on you, to prove treacherous

---

57 *vouchsafe*: deign to visit.
61 *Saint Peter's Vicar*: the Pope.
68 *keep*: continue on.
0 s.d. *Enter . . . bed*: the bed may have been pushed out on to the stage, or 'discovered' by the drawing of a curtain across the inner stage.
4 *fit*: caprice.

To your past vows and oaths?
ANNABELLA. Why should you jest
At my calamity, without all sense
Of the approaching dangers you are in?
GIOVANNI. What danger's half so great as thy revolt?
Thou art a faithless sister, else, thou know'st,
Malice, or any treachery beside,
Would stoop to my bent brows. Why, I hold fate
Clasp'd in my fist, and could command the course
Of time's eternal motion, hadst thou been
One thought more steady than an ebbing sea.
And what? You'll now be honest, that's resolv'd?
ANNABELLA. Brother, dear brother, know what I have been,
And know that now there's but a dining-time
'Twixt us and our confusion. Let's not waste
These precious hours in vain and useless speech.
Alas, these gay attires were not put on
But to some end; this sudden solemn feast
Was not ordain'd to riot in expense;
I that have now been chamber'd here alone,
Barr'd of my guardian, or of any else,
Am not for nothing at an instant freed
To fresh access. Be not deceiv'd, my brother,
This banquet is an harbinger of death
To you and me; resolve yourself it is,
And be prepar'd to welcome it.
GIOVANNI. Well then,
The schoolmen teach that all this globe of earth
Shall be consum'd to ashes in a minute.
ANNABELLA. So I have read too.
GIOVANNI. But 'twere somewhat strange
To see the waters burn; could I believe
This might be true, I could believe as well

---

11 *stoop*: yield.
17 *dining-time*: period of the midday meal. See Textual Notes, p. 343.
22 *riot*: extravagantly indulge.
28 *resolve yourself*: be assured.
30 *schoolmen*: medieval theologians.

There might be Hell or Heaven.
ANNABELLA. That's most certain.
GIOVANNI. A dream, a dream; else in this other world
We should know one another.
ANNABELLA. So we shall.
GIOVANNI. Have you heard so?
ANNABELLA. For certain.
GIOVANNI. But d'ye think
That I shall see you there, you look on me?
May we kiss one another, prate or laugh,
Or do as we do here?
ANNABELLA. I know not that,
But good, for the present, what d'ye mean
To free yourself from danger? Some way, think
How to escape; I'm sure the guests are come.
GIOVANNI. Look up, look here; what see you in my face?
ANNABELLA. Distraction and a troubl'd countenance.
GIOVANNI. Death, and a swift repining wrath. – Yet look,
What see you in mine eyes?
ANNABELLA. Methinks you weep.
GIOVANNI. I do indeed. These are the funeral tears
Shed on your grave; these furrow'd up my cheeks
When first I lov'd and knew not how to woo.
Fair Annabella, should I here repeat
The story of my life, we might lose time.
Be record, all the spirits of the air,
And all things else that are, that day and night,
Early and late, the tribute which my heart
Hath paid to Annabella's sacred love
Hath been these tears, which are her mourners now.

39–40 See Textual Notes, p. 343.
40 *prate*: casually talk.
41 *do*: (1) behave, (2) make love.
42 *good*: good brother.
47 *repining*: discontented.
51 See Textual Notes, p. 343.

Never till now did Nature do her best
To show a matchless beauty to the world,
Which, in an instant, ere it scarce was seen,
The jealous Destinies requir'd again.
Pray, Annabella, pray. Since we must part,
Go thou, white in thy soul, to fill a throne
Of innocence and sanctity in Heaven.
Pray, pray, my sister.

ANNABELLA. Then I see your drift;
Ye blessed angels, guard me!

GIOVANNI. So say I.
Kiss me. If ever after-times should hear
Of our fast-knit affections, though perhaps
The laws of conscience and of civil use
May justly blame us, yet when they but know
Our loves, that love will wipe away that rigour
Which would in other incests be abhorr'd.
Give me your hand. How sweetly life doth run
In these well-colour'd veins; how constantly
These palms do promise health! But I could chide
With Nature for this cunning flattery.
Kiss me again. – Forgive me.

ANNABELLA. With my heart.

GIOVANNI. Farewell.

ANNABELLA. Will you be gone?

GIOVANNI. Be dark, bright sun,
And make this midday night, that thy gilt rays
May not behold a deed will turn their splendour
More sooty than the poets feign their Styx!
One other kiss, my sister.

ANNABELLA. What means this?

GIOVANNI. To save thy fame, and kill thee in a kiss. *Stabs her.*
Thus die, and die by me, and by my hand.
Revenge is mine; honour doth love command.

ANNABELLA. O brother, by your hand?

---

62 See Textual Notes, p. 343.
70 *civil use*: civilised custom.
72 *rigour*: offensive violence.
82 *More . . . Styx*: the black waters of the river Styx surrounded the classical underworld.
84 *fame*: good name.

GIOVANNI. When thou art dead
I'll give my reasons for't; for to dispute
With thy – even in thy death – most lovely beauty,
Would make me stagger to perform this act
Which I most glory in.

ANNABELLA. Forgive him, Heaven – and me my sins; farewell,
Brother unkind, unkind. – Mercy, great Heaven! – O! – O! – *Dies.*

GIOVANNI. She's dead, alas, good soul; the hapless fruit
That in her womb receiv'd its life from me,
Hath had from me a cradle and a grave.
I must not dally. This sad marriage-bed,
In all her best bore her alive and dead.
Soranzo, thou hast miss'd thy aim in this;
I have prevented now thy reaching plots,
And kill'd a love for whose each drop of blood
I would have pawn'd my heart. Fair Annabella,
How over-glorious art thou in thy wounds,
Triumphing over infamy and hate!
Shrink not, courageous hand; stand up, my heart,
And boldly act my last and greater part!
Exit with the body.

SCENE VI

A Banquet. Enter CARDINAL, FLORIO, DONADO, SORANZO, RICHARDETTO, VASQUES, *and Attendants; they take their places.*

VASQUES. [*aside to* SORANZO] Remember, sir, what you have to do; be wise and resolute.

---

93 *unkind*: cruel and unnatural.
94 *hapless*: luckless.
100 *prevented*: forestalled.
reaching: clutching.
103 *over-glorious*: beautiful beyond all measure.

SORANZO. [*aside to* VASQUES] Enough, my heart is fix'd. [*To the* CARDINAL] Pleaseth your grace
To taste these coarse confections? Though the use
Of such set entertainments more consists
In custom than in cause, yet, reverend sir,
I am still made your servant by your presence.
CARDINAL. And we your friend.
SORANZO. But where's my brother Giovanni?

Enter GIOVANNI *with a heart upon his dagger.*

GIOVANNI. Here, here, Soranzo! trimm'd in reeking blood
That triumphs over death; proud in the spoil
Of love and vengeance! Fate, or all the powers
That guide the motions of immortal souls,
Could not prevent me.
CARDINAL. What means this?
FLORIO. Son Giovanni!
SORANZO. [*aside*] Shall I be forestall'd?
GIOVANNI. Be not amaz'd. If your misgiving hearts
Shrink at an idle sight, what bloodless fear
Of coward passion would have seiz'd your senses
Had you beheld the rape of life and beauty
Which I have acted? My sister, O my sister!
FLORIO. Ha! What of her?
GIOVANNI. The glory of my deed
Darken'd the midday sun, made noon as night.
You came to feast, my lords, with dainty fare.
I came to feast too, but I digg'd for food
In a much richer mine than gold or stone
Of any value balanc'd; 'tis a heart,
A heart, my lords, in which is mine entomb'd.
Look well upon't; d'ye know't?

---

4 *coarse confections*: homely dishes. See Textual Notes, p. 343.
10 *trimm'd*: adorned.
11 *spoil*: destruction and plunder.
17 *idle sight*: insignificant spectacle.
26 *balanc'd*: proven by weighing.

VASQUES. What strange riddle's this?
GIOVANNI. 'Tis Annabella's heart, 'tis; why d'ye
startle?
I vow 'tis hers; this dagger's point plough'd up
Her fruitful womb, and left to me the fame
Of a most glorious executioner.
FLORIO. Why, madman, art thyself?
GIOVANNI. Yes, father, and that times to come
may know
How as my fate I honour'd my revenge,
List, father; to your ears I will yield up
How much I have deserv'd to be your son.
FLORIO. What is't thou say'st?
GIOVANNI. Nine moons have
had their changes
Since I first throughly view'd and truly lov'd
Your daughter and my sister.
FLORIO. How! Alas,
My lords, he's a frantic madman!
GIOVANNI. Father, no.
For nine months' space, in secret I enjoy'd
Sweet Annabella's sheets; nine months I liv'd
A happy monarch of her heart and her.
Soranzo, thou know'st this; thy paler cheek
Bears the confounding print of thy disgrace,
For her too fruitful womb too soon bewray'd
The happy passage of our stol'n delights,
And made her mother to a child unborn.
CARDINAL. Incestuous villain!
FLORIO. O, his rage belies him!
GIOVANNI. It does not, 'tis the oracle of truth;
I vow it is so.
SORANZO. I shall burst with fury;
Bring the strumpet forth!
VASQUES. I shall, sir. *Exit* VASQUES.
GIOVANNI. Do, sir; have you all no faith
To credit yet my triumphs? Here I swear

---

40 *throughly*: fully.
41–2 See Textual Notes, p. 343.
48 *bewray'd*: revealed.
49 *passage*: course.
51 *rage belies him*: madness makes him a liar.

By all that you call sacred, by the love
I bore my Annabella whilst she liv'd,
These hands have from her bosom ripp'd this heart.

Enter VASQUES.

Is't true or no, sir?
VASQUES. 'Tis most strangely true.
FLORIO. Cursed man! – Have I lived to –
CARDINAL. Hold up Florio;
Monster of children, see what thou hast done,
Broke thy old father's heart! Is none of you
Dares venture on him?
GIOVANNI. Let 'em. O, my father,
How well his death becomes him in his griefs!
Why, this was done with courage; now survives
None of our house but I, gilt in the blood
Of a fair sister and a hapless father.
SORANZO. Inhuman scorn of men, hast thou a thought
T'outlive thy murders?
GIOVANNI. Yes, I tell thee, yes;
For in my fists I bear the twists of life.
Soranzo, see this heart which was thy wife's;
Thus I exchange it royally for thine, [*Stabs him.*]
And thus, and thus; now brave revenge is mine.
[SORANZO *falls.*]

VASQUES. I cannot hold any longer. You, sir, are you grown insolent in your butcheries? Have at you!

GIOVANNI. Come, I am arm'd to meet thee.

[*They*] *fight.* [GIOVANNI *is wounded.*]

VASQUES. No, will it not be yet? If this will not, another shall. Not yet? I shall fit you anon. – Vengeance!

---

67 *gilt*: (1) gilded, (2) made guilty.
71 *twists*: spun threads; Giovanni imagines himself as one of the Fates or Parcae, who spun the thread of each human life and cut it at its conclusion.
78 See Textual Notes, p. 343.
80 *fit you anon*: deal with you shortly.
81 *Vengeance*: the previously agreed watchword; cf. V.iv.15.

Enter BANDITTI.

GIOVANNI. Welcome! Come more of you, whate'er you be;
I dare your worst. –
[*They attack and wound him.*]
O, I can stand no longer; feeble arms,
Have you so soon lost strength? [*Falls.*]

VASQUES. Now you are welcome, sir! – Away, my masters, all is done. Shift for yourselves, your reward is your own; shift for yourselves.

BANDITTI. Away, away!

Exeunt BANDITTI.

VASQUES. How d'ye, my lord? See you this? How is't?

SORANZO. Dead; but in death well pleas'd that I have liv'd
To see my wrongs reveng'd on that black devil.
O Vasques, to thy bosom let me give
My last of breath; let not that lecher live – O! –
Dies.

VASQUES. The reward of peace and rest be with him, my ever dearest lord and master.

GIOVANNI. Whose hand gave me this wound?

VASQUES. Mine, sir, I was your first man; have you enough?

GIOVANNI. I thank thee; thou hast done for me but what
I would have else done on myself. Art sure
Thy lord is dead?

VASQUES. O impudent slave! As sure as I am sure to see thee die.

CARDINAL. Think on thy life and end, and call for mercy.

GIOVANNI. Mercy? Why, I have found it in this justice.

CARDINAL. Strive yet to cry to Heaven.

GIOVANNI. O, I bleed fast!

86–8 See Textual Notes, p. 343.
96–7 See Textual Notes, p. 343.
101–3 See Textual Notes, p. 343.
105 See Textual Notes, p. 343.

Death, thou art a guest long look'd-for; I embrace
Thee and thy wounds. O, my last minute comes!
Where'er I go, let me enjoy this grace,
Freely to view my Annabella's face. *Dies.*

DONADO. Strange miracle of justice!

CARDINAL. Raise up the city; we shall be murder'd all!

VASQUES. You need not fear, you shall not. This strange task being ended, I have paid the duty to the son which I have vow'd to the father.

CARDINAL. Speak, wretched villain, what incarnate fiend
Hath led thee on to this?

VASQUES. Honesty, and pity of my master's wrongs. For know, my lord, I am by birth a Spaniard, brought forth my country in my youth by Lord Soranzo's father; whom, whilst he liv'd, I serv'd faithfully; since whose death I have been to this, as I was to him. What I have done was duty, and I repent nothing but that the loss of my life had not ransom'd his.

CARDINAL. Say, fellow, know'st thou any yet unnam'd
Of counsel in this incest?

VASQUES. Yes, an old woman, sometimes guardian to this murder'd lady.

CARDINAL. And what's become of her?

VASQUES. Within this room she is; whose eyes, after her confession, I caus'd to be put out, but kept alive, to confirm what from Giovanni's own mouth you have heard. Now, my lord, what I have done you may judge of, and let your own wisdom be a judge in your own reason.

CARDINAL. Peace! First this woman, chief in these effects;

---

122 *Spaniard*: the Spanish had a contemporary reputation for cunning and ferocious enmity.

129 *Of counsel*: actively involved.

130 *sometimes*: formerly.

133 See Additional Notes, p. 351.

139 *effects*: events. See Additional Notes, p. 352.

My sentence is that forthwith she be ta'en
Out of the city, for example's sake,
There to be burnt to ashes.
DONADO. 'Tis most just.
CARDINAL. Be it your charge, Donado, see it done.
DONADO. I shall.
VASQUES. What for me? If death, 'tis welcome.
I have been honest to the son, as I was to the father.
CARDINAL. Fellow, for thee, since what thou didst was done
Not for thyself, being no Italian,
We banish thee for ever, to depart
Within three days; in this we do dispense
With grounds of reason, not of thine offence.
VASQUES. 'Tis well; this conquest is mine, and I rejoice that a Spaniard outwent an Italian in revenge. *Exit* VASQUES.
CARDINAL. Take up these slaughter'd bodies; see them buried;
And all the gold and jewels, or whatsoever,
Confiscate by the canons of the Church,
We seize upon to the Pope's proper use.
RICHARDETTO. [*discovers himself*] Your grace's pardon. Thus long I liv'd disguis'd,
To see the effect of pride and lust at once
Brought both to shameful ends.
CARDINAL. What? Richardetto. whom we thought for dead?
DONADO. Sir, was it you –
RICHARDETTO. Your friend.
CARDINAL. We shall have time
To talk at large of all; but never yet

151–2 *dispense . . . reason*: offer a dispensation on the grounds of your motives.
159 *proper*: personal.
161 *at once*: together.
165 *at large*: fully.

Incest and murder have so strangely met.
Of one so young, so rich in Nature's store,
Who could not say, *'Tis pity she's a whore*?

Exeunt.

Finis

The general commendation deserved by the actors, in their presentment of this tragedy, may easily excuse such few faults as are escaped in the printing. A common charity may allow him the ability of spelling, whom a secure confidence assures that he cannot ignorantly err in the application of sense.

---

6 *application of sense*: use of meaning.

THE

CHRONICLE

HISTORIE

OF

PERKIN VVARBECK.

A Strange Truth.

Acted (ſome-times) by the Queenes

MAIESTIES Ser ants at the

Phenix in *Drurie* lane.

Fide Honor.

By John Ford, Gent.

LONDON,

Printed by T. P. for *Hugh Beeſton*, and are to

be ſold at his Shop, neere the *Caſtle* in

Cornehill. 1634.

Title-page of the 1634 Quarto of *The Chronicle History of Perkin Warbeck*, reproduced by permission of the Provost and Fellows of King's College, Cambridge. Like the title-page of *The Broken Heart*, it carries the Latin motto which is an anagram of JOHN FORDE.

INTRODUCTORY NOTE

Sources

Ford's main sources for the historical events dramatised in *The Chronicle History of Perkin Warbeck* were Thomas Gainsford's *The True and Wonderful History of Perkin Warbeck proclaiming himself Richard the Fourth* (1618) and Francis Bacon's *The History of the Reign of King Henry the Seventh* (1622). Gainsford (d. 1624) was a journalist with an eye for striking detail; Bacon was an historian whose reading was enriched by his own experience of statecraft.

Ford conflates their accounts, often copying quite closely and incorporating the actual vocabulary of his sources, but occasionally telescoping events and rearranging their order. He does not completely confine himself to the immediate narratives by these two writers; John A-Water is modelled on the Earl of Lincoln as Gainsford describes him in an earlier part of his history, and there are indications that the dramatist occasionally consulted other authorities, Edward Hall's *The Union of the two Noble and Illustre Families of Lancaster and York* (1548) and William Warner's *Albion's England* (1586).

The play continues the story of Henry VII left at Richmond's accession by Shakespeare in *Richard III*, and there are echoes of this play and *Richard II* in Ford's writing, but *The Chronicle History of Perkin Warbeck* is far from being merely derivative. Huntly, Dalyell and Jane, the group associated with Katherine Gordon, are virtually Ford's invention, and the conception of Katherine herself, as well as those of Perkin and Henry, the opposing actor-kings, is original, transcending the characterisations found in the sources.

Stage history

The title-page of the 1634 Quarto of *The Chronicle History of Perkin Warbeck* supplies virtually all that is known about the play's original performances, given at the Phoenix, the private theatre of the Queen's company under the management of the Beestons. That the play is said to have been 'Acted (some-times)' must refer to other performances given prior to the date of publication, but their number and the date of the very first performances remain unknown.

On 19 December 1745, Ford's play was revived at the Goodman's Fields theatre, London, along with other dramas hastily put on stage to exploit popular feeling against the Jacobite rebellion led by the Young Pretender. It preceded two other plays about Perkin Warbeck, one by Macklin, intended for Drury Lane, the other by Elderton, prepared for Covent Garden. The prompt-copy is now in the Bodleian Library (Rawl. poet. 122). It was written up from a copy of the 1714 reprint of the original 1634 Quarto text of Ford's play, with cuts and alterations (including the omission of the sub-plot) intended to promote patriotic loyalty and denigrate the pretender Warbeck. Described as 'A revived historical play, not acted in the memory of man', it was performed by Shepard (Warbeck), Furnival (Henry VII), Cushing (James IV), Paget (Huntly), Mrs Hallam (Katherine) and Barnard Bourn (Skelton).

The only stage production of Ford's drama in this century was given in 1975 by the Royal Shakespeare Company at The Other Place, Stratford-upon-Avon. It was directed by Barry Kyle and John Barton, with Terence Wilton (Warbeck), Tony Church (Henry VII), Stuart Wilson (James IV), Barrie Rutter (Hialas), Oliver Ford-Davies (Huntly), Stephen Jenn (Dalyell), Celia Bannerman (Katherine), Anne Hasson (Jane), Griffith Jones (Stanley), Clement McCallin (Frion) and Sid Livingston (John A-Water). There is a detailed description of this production by J.M. Maguin in *Cahiers Élisabéthains*, 8 (1975), 65–74.

In 1969 the BBC broadcast on its Third Programme a radio version of *The Chronicle History of Perkin Warbeck*, which was repeated in 1970; and in 1977 the BBC re-broadcast the play in its *Vivat Rex* series.

Individual editions of the play

The Chronical History of Perkin Warbeck has never attracted the editorial attention given to *The Broken Heart* or to *'Tis Pity She's a Whore*. In 1714 a corrected reprint of the 1634 Quarto was issued for J. Roberts, at the Oxford Arms in Warwick Lane, London, with a prose life of Perkin Warbeck added to the play-text, and in 1896 a well-annotated school edition by J.P. Pickburn and J. Le Gay Brereton was published at Sydney by George Robertson. In 1926 Mildred Clara Struble's scholarly critical edition of the play was published at Seattle by the University of Washington Press; it contains considerable information about the historical background and sources of the drama.

Donald K. Anderson's 1965 edition in the Regents Renaissance Drama series (Nebraska: University of Nebraska Press) was based on a collation of six copies of the 1634 Quarto. Anderson outlines the historical background and discusses the characterisation and language of the play. The principal modern edition is in the Revels Plays series, edited by Peter Ure (London: Methuen, 1968). The text, based on a collation of eight copies, is fully annotated, and there are sections on the textual history, date and authorship, sources and criticism of the play. Ure provides a time chart and biographical index of the historical characters, extracts from the Gainsford source, and discussion of the relations between *Perkin Warbeck*, a lost play about Warbeck and Massinger's *Believe As You List* (1631); there is also a detailed critical discussion of the play-text.

The Chronicle History of Perkin Warbeck is contained in several play collections, the earliest of them H.M. Fitzgibbon's *Famous Elizabethan Plays* (London, 1890) and Thomas Donovan's *English Historical Plays arranged for Acting* (London and New York, 1896). It is also included in F.E. Schelling (ed.), *Typical Elizabethan Plays* (New York and London, 1926), C.R. Baskervill and others (eds.), *Elizabethan and Stuart Plays* (New York, 1934), William A. Armstrong (ed.), *Elizabethan History Plays* (London, 1965), Arthur H. Nethercot (ed.), *Stuart Plays* (New York, 1971), R.G. Lawrence (ed.), *Jacobean and Caroline Tragedies* (London, 1975), and Russell A. Marshall and Norman Rabkin (eds.), *Drama of the English Renaissance* (New York and London, 1976).

[DEDICATORY EPISTLE]

To the rightly honourable William Cavendish, Earl of Newcastle, Viscount Mansfield, Lord Bolsover and Ogle.

My Lord,

Out of the darkness of a former age (enlightened by a late both learned and an honourable pen) I have endeavoured to personate a great attempt, and in it a greater danger. In other labours you may read actions of antiquity discoursed. In this abridgement, find the actors themselves discoursing; in some kind practised as well what to speak, as speaking why to do. Your Lordship is a most competent judge in expressions of such credit, commissioned by your known ability in examining, and enabled by your knowledge in determining the monuments of time. Eminent titles may indeed inform who their owners are, not often what. To yours, the addition of that information in both cannot in any application be observed flattery, the authority being established by truth. I can only acknowledge the errors in writing mine own, the worthiness of the subject written being a perfection in the story, and of it. The custom of your Lordship's entertainments, even to strangers, is rather an example than a fashion; in which consideration,

---

Title *William . . . Ogle*: see Additional Notes, p. 352.
6 *late . . . pen*: Francis Bacon's *History of the Reign of Henry VII* (1622); Bacon died in 1626.
7 *personate*: represent dramatically.
9 *discoursed*: described, discussed.
10 *actors*: (1) participants, (2) stage performers.
12 *speaking . . . do*: explaining their reasons for their actions.
13–14 *expressions of such credit*: representations of such matters of historical truth.
14 *commissioned*: given authority.
16 *determining*: selecting.
20 *observed*: considered.
25 *entertainments*: taking into favour or service.

I dare not profess a curiosity, but am only studious that your Lordship will please, among such as best honour your goodness, to admit into your noble construction

John Ford.

---

27 *a curiosity*: any skill or cleverness.
30 *construction*: regard.

[COMMENDATORY VERSES]

I *To my own friend, Master John Ford, on his justifiable poem of Perkin Warbeck, this ode.*

They who do know me know that I,
    Unskill'd to flatter,
Dare speak this piece, in words, in matter,
A work, without the danger of the lie.
Believe me, friend, the name of this, and thee,
    Will live, your story.
Books may want faith, or merit, glory;
This neither, without judgement's lethargy.

When the arts dote, then some sick poet may
    Hope that his pen
In new-stain'd paper can find men
To roar, 'He is the wit; his noise doth sway.'
But such an age cannot be known; for all,
    Ere that time be,
Must prove such truth mortality.
So, friend, thy honour stands too fix'd to fall.

George Donne.

II *To his worthy friend, Master John Ford, upon his Perkin Warbeck.*

Let men who are writ poets lay a claim
To the Phoebean hill; I have no name,
Nor art in verse. True, I have heard some tell
Of Aganippe, but ne'er knew the well;
Therefore have no ambition with the times

Title *justifiable poem*: genuine major opus; *poem*, like *work* (4), was a title of honour.
I.4 *danger of the lie*: see *'Tis Pity She's a Whore*, II.vi.115 and note.
7 *want faith*: lack belief.
8 *lethargy*: morbid sleepiness.
12 *sway*: prevail. See Textual Notes, p. 344.
17 See Additional Notes, p. 352.

II.1 *writ poets*: acknowledged writers.
2 *Phoebean hill*: Mount Helicon, sacred to Phoebus Apollo and the Muses.
4 *Aganippe*: a spring on Mount Helicon, sacred to the Muses.

To be in print for making of ill rhymes.
But love of thee, and justice to thy pen,
Hath drawn me to this bar, with other men
To justify, though against double laws
(Waiving the subtle business of his cause),
The glorious Perkin, and thy poet's art,
Equal with his, in playing the king's part.

Ralph Eure, *Baronis primogenitus.*

III To my faithful, no less deserving, friend, the author, this indebted oblation.

Perkin is rediviv'd by thy strong hand,
And crown'd a king of new; the vengeful wand
Of greatness is forgot. His execution
May rest unmention'd, and his birth's collusion
Lie buried in the story, but his fame
Thou hast eternis'd; made a crown his game.
His lofty spirit soars yet. Had he been
Base in his enterprise, as was his sin
Conceiv'd, his title, doubtless prov'd unjust,
Had, but for thee, been silenc'd in his dust.

George Crymes, *miles.*

IV To the author, his friend, upon his Chronicle History.

These are not to express thy wit,
But to pronounce thy judgement fit
In full-fil'd phrase those times to raise
When Perkin ran his wily ways.
Still let the method of thy brain

10 See Textual Notes, p. 344.
11 *glorious*: eager for glory.
13 *Ralph . . . primogenitus*: Ralph, eldest son of William, Lord Eure.

III.1 *rediviv'd*: resurrected.
2 *wand*: sceptre.
4 *birth's collusion*: fraudulent story about his birth.
11 *George Crymes, miles*: this soldier is unidentified.

IV.1 *wit*: intellectual brilliance.
3 *full-fil'd*: carefully polished.

From Error's touch and Envy's stain
Preserve thee free, that e'er thy quill
Fair Truth may whet, and Fancy fill.
Thus Graces are with Muses met,
And practic critics on may fret;
For here thou hast produc'd a story
Which shall eclipse their future glory.

John Brograve, *Armiger.*

V *To my friend and kinsman,*
Master John Ford, the author.

Dramatic poets (as the times go) now
Can hardly write what others will allow;
The cynic snarls, the critic howls and barks,
And ravens croak, to drown the voice of larks.
Scorn those stage-harpies! This I'll boldly say:
Many may imitate, few match thy play.

John Ford, *Graiensis.*

---

8 See Textual Notes, p. 344.
10 *practic*: rough and ready, lacking theoretical knowledge.
13 See Additional Notes, p. 352.

V.2 *allow*: approve of.
5 *harpies*: fabulous and disgusting monsters, half-bird, half-woman.
7 See Additional Notes, p. 352.

PROLOGUE

Studies have, of this nature, been of late
So out of fashion, so unfollow'd, that
It is become more justice to revive
The antic follies of the times than strive
To countenance wise industry. No want
Of art doth render wit or lame or scant
Or slothful in the purchase of fresh bays,
But want of truth in them who give the praise
To their self-love, presuming to out-do
The writer, or, for need, the actors too.
But such this author's silence best befits
Who bids them be in love with their own wits.
From him to clearer judgements we can say
He shows a history, couch'd in a play.
A history of noble mention, known,
Famous, and true: most noble, 'cause our own;
Not forg'd from Italy, from France, from Spain,
But chronicl'd at home; as rich in strain
Of brave attempts as ever fertile rage
In action could beget to grace the stage.
We cannot limit scenes, for the whole land
Itself appear'd too narrow to withstand
Competitors for kingdoms. Nor is here
Unnecessary mirth forc'd, to endear
A multitude. On these two rests the fate
Of worthy expectation: Truth and State.

---

2 *unfollow'd*: less than a dozen English history plays are recorded after *Henry VIII* (1613).
3 *justice*: sensible.
4 *antic*: grotesque, ludicrous.
6 *wit*: gifted writers and performers.
7 *purchase . . . bays*: acquisition of new accolades; for *bays* see *The Broken Heart*, Prologue, 9, and note.
14 *couch'd*: set down.
17 *forg'd*: manufactured.
18 *strain*: line of offspring.
19–20 *rage In action*: passionate performance.
24 *endear*: please, attract.
26 *State*: matters of state, and stateliness, dignity.

The Scene,
THE CONTINENT OF GREAT BRITAIN

THE PERSONS PRESENTED

HENRY THE SEVENTH [King of England]
[LORD] DAUBENEY
SIR WILLIAM STANLEY
[EARL OF] OXFORD
[EARL OF] SURREY
BISHOP OF DURHAM
URSWICK Chaplain to King Henry
SIR ROBERT CLIFFORD
LAMBERT SIMNEL
HIALAS A Spanish agent
[Executioner
Post
Sheriff]
CONSTABLE
Officers, servingmen, [guards] and soldiers

JAMES THE FOURTH King of Scotland
EARL OF HUNTLY
EARL OF CRAWFORD
LORD DALYELL
MARCHMOUNT A herald
[Herald
Masquers
Servant Groom to Lady Katherine]
PERKIN WARBECK
FRION His secretary
[JOHN A-WATER] Mayor of Cork
HERON A mercer
SKELTON A tailor
ASTLEY A scrivener

WOMEN

LADY KATHERINE GORDON Wife to Perkin
COUNTESS OF CRAWFORD
JANE DOUGLAS Lady Katherine's maid
[Ladies]

Biographical notes on the characters of the play are given in a series of Additional Notes on pp. 352–4.

THE CHRONICLE HISTORY OF PERKIN WARBECK A STRANGE TRUTH

ACT I

SCENE I

[*Enter*] KING HENRY, DURHAM, OXFORD, SURREY, SIR WILLIAM STANLEY (*Lord Chamberlain*), LORD DAUBENEY. *The King supported to his throne by* STANLEY *and* DURHAM. *A Guard.*

HENRY. Still to be haunted, still to be pursu'd,
Still to be frighted with false apparitions
Of pageant majesty and new-coin'd greatness,
As if we were a mockery king in state,
Only ordain'd to lavish sweat and blood
In scorn and laughter to the ghosts of York,
Is all below our merits; yet, my lords,
My friends and counsellors, yet we sit fast
In our own royal birthright. The rent face
And bleeding wounds of England's slaughter'd people
Have been by us, as by the best physician,
At last both throughly cur'd and set in safety;
And yet for all this glorious work of peace
Ourself is scarce secure.
DURHAM. The rage of malice
Conjures fresh spirits with the spells of York;
For ninety years ten English kings and princes,

0 s.d. *supported*: with his arms upheld on those of his formal escort.
3 *pageant*: imitation.
4 *mockery*: counterfeit.
5 See Textual Notes, p. 344.
14 *malice*: hatred.

Threescore great dukes and earls, a thousand lords
And valiant knights, two hundred fifty thousand
Of English subjects have in civil wars
Been sacrific'd to an uncivil thirst
Of discord and ambition. This hot vengeance
Of the just powers above, to utter ruin
And desolation had rain'd on, but that
Mercy did gently sheathe the sword of Justice
In lending to this blood-shrunk commonwealth
A new soul, new birth, in your sacred person.

DAUBENEY. Edward the Fourth after a doubtful fortune
Yielded to nature, leaving to his sons,
Edward and Richard, the inheritance
Of a most bloody purchase; these young princes
Richard the tyrant, their unnatural uncle,
Forc'd to a violent grave. So just is Heaven,
Him hath your majesty by your own arm,
Divinely strengthen'd, pull'd from his boar's sty
And struck the black usurper to a carcass.
Nor doth the house of York decay in honours,
Though Lancaster doth repossess his right,
For Edward's daughter is King Henry's queen;
A blessed union, and a lasting blessing
For this poor panting island, if some shreds,
Some useless remnant of the house of York,
Grudge not at this content.

OXFORD. Margaret of Burgundy
Blows fresh coals of division.

SURREY. Painted fires,
Without or heat to scorch, or light to cherish.

---

23 See Textual Notes, p. 344.
27 *doubtful*: i.e. neither good nor bad.
30 *bloody purchase*: Edward's seizure of the crown by force from Henry VI.
31 *Richard . . . uncle*: Richard III.
32 See Textual Notes, p. 344.
34 *boar's sty*: Richard's armorial emblem was a boar.
38 *Edward's daughter*: Elizabeth of York.
42 *Margaret of Burgundy*: daughter of Richard, Duke of York, and sister of Edward IV (cf. 45–6).
44 See Textual Notes, p. 344.

DAUBENEY. York's headless trunk (her father), Edward's fate
(Her brother king), the smothering of her nephews
By tyrant Gloucester (brother to her nature),
Nor Gloucester's own confusion – all decrees
Sacred in Heaven – can move this woman-monster,
But that she still from the unbottom'd mine
Of devilish policies doth vent the ore
Of troubles and sedition.
OXFORD. In her age
(Great sir, observe the wonder) she grows fruitful,
Who in her strength of youth was always barren;
Nor are her births as other mothers' are,
At nine or ten months' end. She has been with child
Eight or seven years at least, whose twins being born –
A prodigy in nature; even the youngest
Is fifteen years of age at his first entrance! –
As soon as known i'th'world, tall striplings, strong,
And able to give battle unto kings;
Idols of Yorkish malice.
DAUBENEY. And but idols;
A steely hammer crushes 'em to pieces.
HENRY. Lambert, the eldest, lords, is in our service,
Preferr'd by an officious care of duty
From the scullery to a falc'ner; strange example!

---

47 *Gloucester*: before his coronation, Richard was Duke of Gloucester.
48 *confusion*: destruction.
50 *unbottom'd*: bottomless.
51 *vent*: discharge.
57 *twins*: the two impostors, Lambert Simnel and Perkin Warbeck.
58 *prodigy*: monstrosity.
62 See Textual Notes, p. 344.
65 *Preferr'd*: achieving promotion.
officious: zealous.

Which shows the difference between noble natures
And the base born. But for the upstart duke,
The new reviv'd York, Edward's second son,
Murder'd long since i'th'Tower – he lives again,
And vows to be your king.

STANLEY. The throne is fill'd, sir.

HENRY. True, Stanley, and the lawful heir sits on it;
A guard of angels and the holy prayers
Of loyal subjects are a sure defence
Against all force and counsel of intrusion.
But now, my lords, put case some of our nobles,
Our great ones, should give countenance and courage
To trim Duke Perkin, you will all confess
Our bounties have unthriftily been scatter'd
Amongst unthankful men.

DAUBENEY. Unthankful beasts,
Dogs, villains, traitors!

HENRY. Daubeney, let the guilty
Keep silence. I accuse none, though I know
Foreign attempts against a state and kingdom
Are seldom without some great friends at home.

STANLEY. Sir, if no other abler reasons else
Of duty or allegiance could divert
A headstrong resolution, yet the dangers
So lately pass'd by men of blood and fortunes
In Lambert Simnel's party must command
More than a fear, a terror to conspiracy.
The high-born Lincoln, son to De la Pole,
The Earl of Kildare, Lord Geraldine,
Francis, Lord Lovell, and the German baron,
Bold Martin Swart, with Broughton and the rest –
Most spectacles of ruin, some of mercy –
Are precedents sufficient to forewarn

---

75 *counsel of intrusion*: secret invasion plan.
76 *put case* : suppose.
78 *trim*: pretty (ironic).
79 *unthriftily*: unprofitably.
87–94 See Additional Notes, p. 354.
88 *pass'd*: undergone.
blood: high birth.

The present times, or any that live in them,
What folly, nay, what madness 'twere to lift
A finger up in all defence but yours,
Which can be but impost'rous in a title.

HENRY. Stanley, we know thou lov'st us, and thy heart
Is figur'd on thy tongue; nor think we less
Of any's here. How closely we have hunted
This cub, since he unlodg'd, from hole to hole,
Your knowledge is our chronicle. First Ireland,
The common stage of novelty, presented
This gewgaw to oppose us; there the Geraldines
And Butlers once again stood in support
Of this colossic statue. Charles of France
Thence call'd him into his protection,
Dissembl'd him the lawful heir of England;
Yet this was all but French dissimulation,
Aiming at peace with us, which being granted
On honourable terms on our part, suddenly
This smoke of straw was pack'd from France again
T'infect some grosser air. And now we learn,
Maugre the malice of the bastard Neville,
Sir Taylor, and a hundred English rebels,
They're all retir'd to Flanders, to the dam
That nurs'd this eager whelp, Margaret of Burgundy.

---

100 *Which . . . title*: i.e. the justification for defending any cause other than Henry's can only be fraudulent.
102 *figur'd*: truly imaged; ironic in view of Stanley's later behaviour.
104 *unlodg'd*: left his lair (a hunting term).
106 *novelty*: innovation, new things.
107–8 *Geraldines . . . Butlers*: great Anglo-Norman families, the Earls of Kildare and Desmond, and the Earls of Ormond.
109 *colossic statue*: giant form filled with rubbish; see Chapman's *Bussy d'Ambois*, I.i.15–17.
110 *protection*: four syllables.
111 *Dissembl'd him*: pretended that he was.
117 *Maugre*: despite.
117–18 *bastard . . . Taylor*: Sir George Neville the Bastard and Sir John Taylor were among Warbeck's supporters in Paris.

But we will hunt him there, too; we will hunt
him,
Hunt him to death even in the beldam's closet,
Though the Archduke were his buckler.
SURREY. She has styl'd him
'The fair white rose of England'.
DAUBENEY. Jolly gentleman;
More fit to be a swabber to the Flemish
After a drunken surfeit.

Enter URSWICK [*with a paper*].

URSWICK. Gracious sovereign,
Please you peruse this paper. [HENRY *reads.*]
DURHAM. The king's countenance
Gathers a sprightly blood.
DAUBENEY. Good news, believe it.
HENRY. Urswick, thine ear. – Th'ast lodg'd
him?
URSWICK. Strongly safe, sir.
HENRY. Enough. Is Barley come too?
URSWICK. No, my lord.
HENRY. No matter. Phew, he's but a running
weed,
At pleasure to be pluck'd up by the roots.
But more of this anon. I have bethought me. –
My lords, for reasons which you shall partake,
It is our pleasure to remove our court
From Westminster to th'Tower. We will lodge
This very night there; give, Lord Chamberlain,
A present order for it.
STANLEY. [*aside*] The Tower! [*Aloud*] I shall, sir.
HENRY. Come, my true, best, fast friends, these
clouds will vanish,

---

122 *beldam's closet*: witch's private chamber.
123–8 See Textual Notes, p. 344.
123 *buckler*: shield.
styl'd: titled.
125 *swabber*: ship's boy, who cleaned up the decks.
129 *him*: Sir Robert Clifford; see I.iii.
130 *Barley*: William Barley, a Hertfordshire gentleman who visited Warbeck in Flanders with Clifford, but remained loyal to Henry for some years afterwards.
131 *running*: spreading, creeping.
138 *present*: immediate.

The sun will shine at full; the heavens are
clearing.
Flourish. Exeunt.

SCENE II

Enter HUNTLY *and* DALYELL.

HUNTLY. You trifle time, sir.
DALYELL. O my noble lord,
You conster my griefs to so hard a sense
That where the text is argument of pity,
Matter of earnest love, your gloss corrupts it
With too much ill-plac'd mirth.
HUNTLY. Much mirth, Lord Dalyell?
Not so, I vow. Observe me, sprightly gallant.
I know thou art a noble lad, a handsome,
Descended from an honourable ancestry,
Forward and active, dost resolve to wrestle
And ruffle in the world by noble actions
For a brave mention to posterity.
I scorn not thy affection to my daughter,
Not I, by good St Andrew; but this bugbear,
This whoreson tale of honour – honour, Dalyell! –
So hourly chats and tattles in mine ear
The piece of royalty that is stitch'd up
In my Kate's blood, that 'tis as dangerous
For thee, young lord, to perch so near an eaglet
As foolish for my gravity to admit it.
I have spoke all at once.
DALYELL. Sir, with this truth
You mix such wormwood that you leave no hope
For my disorder'd palate e'er to relish

---

140 See Textual Notes, p. 344.
2 *conster*: construe.
hard: unfeeling.
10 *ruffle*: do battle.
13 *Andrew*: an appropriately Scottish saint.
bugbear: object of needless fear.
16 *piece*: (1) portion, (2) piece of cloth.
19 *my . . . it*: a man of my standing to allow it.

A wholesome taste again. Alas, I know, sir,
What an unequal distance lies between
Great Huntly's daughter's birth and Dalyell's fortunes.
She's the king's kinswoman, plac'd near the crown,
A princess of the blood, and I a subject.

HUNTLY. Right, but a noble subject; put in that, too.

DALYELL. I could add more; and in the rightest line
Derive my pedigree from Adam Mure,
A Scottish knight, whose daughter was the mother
To him that first begot the race of Jameses,
That sway the sceptre to this very day.
But kindreds are not ours when once the date
Of many years have swallow'd up the memory
Of their originals; so pasture fields,
Neighbouring too near the ocean, are soop'd up
And known no more. For, stood I in my first
And native greatness, if my princely mistress
Vouchsaf'd me not her servant, 'twere as good
I were reduc'd to clownery, to nothing,
As to a throne of wonder.

HUNTLY. [*aside*] Now, by St Andrew,
A spark of mettle; he has a brave fire in him.
I would he had my daughter, so I knew't not.
But't must not be so, must not. – Well, young lord,
This will not do yet; if the girl be headstrong
And will not hearken to good counsel, steal her
And run away with her, dance galliards, do,

29–33 See Additional Notes, p. 354.
32 *him*: Robert II of Scotland.
34 *kindreds*: kinships, relationships.
date: period.
37 *soop'd*: swallowed.
40 *Vouchsaf'd*: acknowledged, accepted.
41 *clownery*: the condition of a peasant.
43 *spark*: gallant.
45 See Textual Notes, p. 344.
48 *galliards*: quick, lively dances.

And frisk about the world to learn the languages.
'Twill be a thriving trade; you may set up by't.
DALYELL. With pardon, noble Gordon, this disdain
Suits not your daughter's virtue or my constancy.
HUNTLY. You are angry. – [*Aside*] Would he would beat me; I deserve it. –
Dalyell, thy hand, we're friends; follow thy courtship,
Take thine own time and speak. If thou prevail'st
With passion more than I can with my counsel,
She's thine; nay, she is thine, 'tis a fair match,
Free and allow'd. I'll only use my tongue,
Without a father's power; use thou thine.
Self do, self have; no more words, win and wear her.
DALYELL. You bless me; I am now too poor in thanks
To pay the debt I owe you.
HUNTLY. Nay, thou'rt poor
Enough. – [*Aside*] I love his spirit infinitely. –
Look ye, she comes; to her now, to her, to her!

Enter KATHERINE *and* JANE.

KATHERINE. The king commands your presence, sir.
HUNTLY. The gallant –
This, this, the lord, this servant, Kate, of yours
Desires to be your master.
KATHERINE. I acknowledge him
A worthy friend of mine.
DALYELL. Your humblest creature.
HUNTLY. [*aside*] So, so, the game's afoot. I'm in cold hunting;
The hare and hounds are parties.
DALYELL. Princely lady,
How most unworthy I am to employ

---

50 *set up*: set up a home.
62–3 See Textual Notes, p. 344.
65–8 See Textual Notes, p. 344.
69 *I'm . . . hunting*: I've lost the scent.
70 *parties*: working together.
70–1 See Textual Notes, p. 344.

My services in honour of your virtues,
How hopeless my desires are to enjoy
Your fair opinion, and much more your love,
Are only matter of despair, unless
Your goodness give large warrant to my boldness,
My feeble-wing'd ambition.

HUNTLY. [*aside*] This is scurvy.

KATHERINE. My lord, I interrupt you not.

HUNTLY. [*aside*] Indeed!
Now, on my life, she'll court him. – Nay, nay, on, sir.

DALYELL. Oft have I tun'd the lesson of my sorrows
To sweeten discord, and enrich your pity;
But all in vain. Here had my comforts sunk
And never ris'n again to tell a story
Of the despairing lover, had not now,
Even now, the earl your father –

HUNTLY. [*aside*] He means me, sure.

DALYELL. After some fit disputes of your condition,
Your highness and my lowness, giv'n a licence
Which did not more embolden than encourage
My falt'ring tongue.

HUNTLY. How, how? How's that? Embolden?
Encourage? I encourage ye? D'ye hear, sir?
A subtle trick, a quaint one! – Will you hear, man?
What did I say to you? Come, come, to th'point.

KATHERINE. It shall not need, my lord.

HUNTLY. Then hear me, Kate –
Keep you on that hand of her; I on this –
Thou stand'st between a father and a suitor,
Both striving for an interest in thy heart.
He courts thee for affection, I for duty;
He as a servant pleads, but by the privilege

---

80 *lesson*: musical exercise.
86 *disputes . . . condition*: discussions concerning your social rank.
89 See Textual Notes, p. 344.
91 *quaint*: crafty.

Of nature though I might command, my care
Shall only counsel what it shall not force.
Thou canst but make one choice; the ties of
 marriage
Are tenures not at will but during life.
Consider whose thou art, and who: a princess,
A princess of the royal blood of Scotland,
In the full spring of youth, and fresh in beauty.
The king that sits upon the throne is young
And yet unmarried, forward in attempts
On any least occasion to endanger
His person. Wherefore, Kate, as I am confident
Thou dar'st not wrong thy birth and education
By yielding to a common servile rage
Of female wantonness, so I am confident
Thou wilt proportion all thy thoughts to side
Thy equals, if not equal thy superiors.
My Lord of Dalyell, young in years, is old
In honours, but nor eminent in titles
Or in estate that may support or add to
The expectation of thy fortunes. Settle
Thy will and reason by a strength of judgement,
For, in a word, I give thee freedom; take it.
If equal fates have not ordain'd to pitch
Thy hopes above my height, let not thy passion
Lead thee to shrink mine honour in oblivion.
Thou art thine own; I have done.
DALYELL. O, you're all oracle,
The living stock and root of truth and wisdom!
KATHERINE. My worthiest lord and father, the
 indulgence
Of your sweet composition thus commands
The lowest of obedience; you have granted
A liberty so large that I want skill

---

99 *care*: loving concern.
102 *tenures . . . life*: lifelong conditions not to be changed at an individual's will.
107 *forward*: quick to act.
111 *servile rage*: slave-like passion.
113 *side*: match, keep up with.
121 *equal*: impartial.
127 *composition*: nature.
thus commands: Katherine probably kneels to her father.
129 *want*: lack.

To choose without direction of example,
From which I daily learn, by how much more
You take off from the roughness of a father,
By so much more I am engag'd to tender
The duty of a daughter. For respects
Of birth, degrees of title, and advancement,
I nor admire nor slight them; all my studies
Shall ever aim at this perfection only,
To live and die so, that you may not blush
In any course of mine to own me yours.

HUNTLY. Kate, Kate, thou grow'st upon my heart like peace,
Creating every other hour a jubilee.

KATHERINE. To you, my Lord of Dalyell, I address
Some few remaining words. The general fame
That speaks your merit, even in vulgar tongues
Proclaims it clear; but in the best, a precedent.

HUNTLY. Good wench, good girl, i'faith!

KATHERINE. For my part, trust me,
I value mine own worth at higher rate
'Cause you are pleas'd to prize it. If the stream
Of your protested service, as you term it,
Run in a constancy more than a compliment,
It shall be my delight that worthy love
Leads you to worthy actions, and these guide ye
Richly to wed an honourable name;
So every virtuous praise in after ages
Shall be your heir, and I, in your brave mention,
Be chronicl'd the mother of that issue,
That glorious issue.

HUNTLY. O that I were young again!

---

134 *respects*: considerations.
140 See Textual Notes, p. 344.
141 *jubilee*: occasion for rejoicing.
143 *general fame*: voice of public opinion.
145 *precedent*: example for others.
149 *protested*: declared, affirmed.
150 *Run . . . compliment*: continues to flow, showing constancy and not mere courtly protestation.
155 *your brave mention*: the record of your brave deeds.
156 *mother*: spiritual parent.

She'd make me court proud danger, and suck spirit
From reputation.

KATHERINE. To the present motion
Here's all that I dare answer. When a ripeness
Of more experience, and some use of time,
Resolves to treat the freedom of my youth
Upon exchange of troths, I shall desire
No surer credit of a match with virtue
Than such as lives in you. Meantime, my hopes are
Preserv'd secure, in having you a friend.

DALYELL. You are a blessed lady, and instruct
Ambition not to soar a farther flight
Than in the perfum'd air of your soft voice. –
My noble Lord of Huntly, you have lent
A full extent of bounty to this parley,
And for it shall command your humblest servant.

HUNTLY. Enough; we are still friends, and will continue
A hearty love. – O Kate, thou art mine own! –
No more; my Lord of Crawford.

Enter CRAWFORD.

CRAWFORD. From the king
I come, my Lord of Huntly, who in council
Requires your present aid.

HUNTLY. Some weighty business?

CRAWFORD. A secretary from a Duke of York,
The second son to the late English Edward,
Conceal'd I know not where these fourteen years,
Craves audience from our master, and 'tis said
The duke himself is following to the court.

158–9 *suck . . . reputation*: draw courage from a thirst for a noble fame.
159 *motion*: proposal.
162 *treat*: negotiate about.
163 *Upon*: on the occasion of.
164 *credit*: promise.
175–7 See Textual Notes, p. 344.

HUNTLY. Duke upon duke! 'Tis well, 'tis well; here's bustling
For majesty. My lord, I will along with ye.
CRAWFORD. My service, noble lady.
KATHERINE. Please ye walk, sir?
DALYELL. [*aside*] Times have their changes; sorrow makes men wise.
The sun itself must set as well as rise;
Then why not I? – Fair madam, I wait on ye.
Exeunt all.

SCENE III

Enter DURHAM, SIR ROBERT CLIFFORD, *and* URSWICK. *Lights.*

DURHAM. You find, Sir Robert Clifford, how securely
King Henry, our great master, doth commit
His person to your loyalty; you taste
His bounty and his mercy even in this,
That at a time of night so late, a place
So private as his closet, he is pleas'd
To admit you to his favour. Do not falter
In your discovery, but, as you covet
A liberal grace and pardon for your follies,
So labour to deserve it, by laying open
All plots, all persons, that contrive against it.
URSWICK. Remember not the witchcraft or the magic,
The charms and incantations, which the sorceress
Of Burgundy hath cast upon your reason!
Sir Robert, be your own friend now; discharge
Your conscience freely. All of such as love you
Stand sureties for your honesty and truth.
Take heed you do not dally with the king;

183 *bustling*: contention.
1 *securely*: confidently.
8 *discovery*: disclosure.
15 *discharge*: free from guilt.

His is wise as he is gentle.
CLIFFORD. I am miserable
If Henry be not merciful.
URSWICK. The king comes.

Enter KING HENRY.

HENRY. Clifford!
CLIFFORD. [*kneels*] Let my weak knees rot on the earth
If I appear as leprous in my treacheries,
Before your royal eyes, as to mine own
I seem a monster by my breach of truth.
HENRY. Clifford, stand up. For instance of thy safety
I offer thee my hand.
CLIFFORD. A sovereign balm
For my bruis'd soul; I kiss it with a greediness.
Sir, you are a just master, but I –
HENRY. Tell me,
Is every circumstance thou hast set down
With thine own hand within this paper true?
Is it a sure intelligence of all
The progress of our enemies' intents,
Without corruption?
CLIFFORD. True, as I wish Heaven,
Or my infected honour white again.
HENRY. We know all, Clifford, fully, since this meteor,
This airy apparition, first discradl'd
From Tournai into Portugal, and thence
Advanc'd his fiery blaze for adoration
To th'superstitious Irish; since the beard

---

25 *instance*: token.
26 *sovereign*: (1) kingly, (2) efficacious.
28–9 See Textual Notes, p. 344.
29 *circumstance*: detail.
31 *intelligence of*: piece of information about.
35 *meteor*: a common image for brilliant but short-lived achievement.
36–7 *discradl'd . . . Portugal*: Warbeck was by his own admission born in Tournai in Flanders, and later travelled to Portugal. Tournai was also the residence of his sponsor, Margaret of Burgundy, in her exile.
39 *beard*: tail.

Of this wild comet, conjur'd into France,
Sparkl'd in antic flames in Charles his court;
But shrunk again from thence, and, hid in
. darkness,
Stole into Flanders, flourishing the rags
Of painted power on the shore of Kent,
Whence he was beaten back with shame and
scorn,
Contempt, and slaughter of some naked outlaws.
But tell me, what new course now shapes Duke
Perkin?

CLIFFORD. For Ireland, mighty Henry; so
instructed
By Stephen Frion, sometimes secretary
In the French tongue unto your sacred excellence,
But Perkin's tutor now.

HENRY. A subtle villain,
That Frion! Frion, – you, my Lord of Durham,
Knew well the man.

DURHAM. French both in heart and actions!

HENRY. Some Irish heads work in this mine of
treason;
Speak 'em!

CLIFFORD. Not any of the best; your fortune
Hath dull'd their spleens. Never had counterfeit
Such a confused rabble of lost bankrupts
For counsellors: first Heron, a broken mercer,
Then John A-Water, sometimes Mayor of Cork,
Skelton, a tailor, and a scrivener
Call'd Astley; and whate'er these list to treat of
Perkin must hearken to. But Frion, cunning
Above these dull capacities, still prompts him
To fly to Scotland to young James the Fourth,

---

41 *antic*: bizarre; with an allusion to the torches used in courtly theatrical shows.
44 *painted*: counterfeit, pretended.
49 *sometimes*: former.
53 *French*: cf. I.i.112.
55 *best*: high-ranking nobility.
58 *broken mercer*: bankrupt dealer in textiles.
60 *scrivener*: secretary or money-dealer. See Additional Notes, p. 354, and Textual Notes, p. 344.
61 *list*: wish, please.

And sue for aid to him; this is the latest
Of all their resolutions.

HENRY. Still more Frion!
Pestilent adder, he will hiss out poison
As dang'rous as infectious. We must match him.
Clifford, thou hast spoke home; we give thee life.
But Clifford, there are people of our own
Remain behind untold; who are they, Clifford?
Name those and we are friends, and will to rest;
'Tis thy last task.

CLIFFORD. O sir, here I must break
A most unlawful oath to keep a just one.

HENRY. Well, well, be brief, be brief.

CLIFFORD. The first in rank
Shall be John Ratcliffe, Lord Fitzwater, then
Sir Simon Mountford and Sir Thomas Thwaites,
With William Daubeney, Cressoner, Astwood,
Worsley the Dean of Paul's, two other friars,
And Robert Ratcliffe.

HENRY. Churchmen are turn'd devils.
These are the principal?

CLIFFORD. One more remains
Unnam'd, whom I could willingly forget.

HENRY. Ha, Clifford! One more?

CLIFFORD. Great sir, do not hear him;
For when Sir William Stanley, your Lord Chamberlain,
Shall come into the list, as he is chief,
I shall lose credit with ye. Yet this lord,
Last nam'd, is first against you.

HENRY. Urswick, the light!
View well my face, sirs; is there blood left in it?

DURHAM. You alter strangely, sir.

HENRY. Alter, Lord Bishop?
Why, Clifford stabb'd me, or I dream'd he stabb'd me.

---

68 See Textual Notes, p. 344.
69 *spoke home*: made a full revelation.
78 See Textual Notes, p. 344.
83 *hear*: give audience to.
87–9 See Textual Notes, p. 344.

Sirrah, it is a custom with the guilty
To think they set their own stains off by laying
Aspersions on some nobler than themselves.
Lies wait on treasons, as I find it here.
Thy life again is forfeit; I recall
My word of mercy, for I know thou dar'st
Repeat the name no more.

CLIFFORD. I dare, and once more,
Upon my knowledge, name Sir William Stanley,
Both in his counsel and his purse, the chief
Assistant to the feigned Duke of York.

DURHAM. Most strange!

URSWICK. Most wicked!

HENRY. Yet again, once more.

CLIFFORD. Sir William Stanley is your secret enemy,
And, if time fit, will openly profess it.

HENRY. Sir William Stanley! Who? Sir William Stanley,
My chamberlain, my counsellor, the love,
The pleasure of my court, my bosom friend,
The charge and the controlment of my person,
The key and secrets of my treasury,
The all of all I am! I am unhappy.
Misery of confidence! Let me turn traitor
To mine own person, yield my sceptre up
To Edward's sister, and her bastard duke!

DURHAM. You lose your constant temper.

HENRY. Sir William Stanley!
O do not blame me; he, 'twas only he,
Who having rescu'd me in Bosworth Field
From Richard's bloody sword, snatch'd from his head
The kingly crown, and plac'd it first on mine.
He never fail'd me; what have I deserv'd
To lose this good man's heart, or he his own?

---

92 *set . . . off*: remove their own guilt.
94 *wait on*: follow, serve.
107 *The charge . . . person*: responsible for my movements and my personal security.
112 *Edward's . . . duke*: Margaret of Burgundy and Perkin Warbeck.
113 *constant temper*: steadiness of mind.

URSWICK. The night doth waste, this passion ill becomes ye;
Provide against your danger.
HENRY. Let it be so.
Urswick, command straight Stanley to his chamber.
'Tis well we are i'th'Tower; set a guard on him. –
Clifford, to bed; you must lodge here tonight,
We'll talk with you tomorrow. My sad soul
Divines strange troubles.
DAUBENEY. [*within*] Ho, the king, the king!
I must have entrance.
HENRY. Daubeney's voice; admit him.
What new combustions huddle next to keep
Our eyes from rest?

Enter DAUBENEY.

The news?
DAUBENEY. Ten thousand Cornish,
Grudging to pay your subsidies, have gather'd
A head. Led by a blacksmith and a lawyer,
They make for London, and to them is join'd
Lord Audley. As they march, their number daily
Increases; they are –
HENRY. Rascals! Talk no more;
Such are not worthy of my thoughts tonight.
To bed; and if I cannot sleep, I'll wake.
When counsels fail, and there's in man no trust,
Even then, an arm from Heaven fights for the just.

Exeunt.

---

128 *combustions huddle*: conflagrations hasten.
129–33 See Additional Notes, p. 355, and Textual Notes, p. 344.
130 *subsidies*: taxes.
131 *head*: military force.
136 See Textual Notes, p. 344.
138 See Textual Notes, p. 344.

ACT II

SCENE I

Enter above [the] COUNTESS OF CRAWFORD, KATHERINE, JANE, *with other Ladies.*

COUNTESS. Come, ladies, here's a solemn preparation
For entertainment of this English prince.
The king intends grace more than ordinary;
'Twere pity now if he should prove a counterfeit.
KATHERINE. Bless the young man, our nation would be laugh'd at
For honest souls through Christendom. My father
Hath a weak stomach to the business, madam,
But that the king must not be cross'd.
COUNTESS. He brings
A goodly troop, they say, of gallants with him;
But very modest people, for they strive not
To fame their names too much. Their godfathers
May be beholding to them, but their fathers
Scarce owe them thanks. They are disguised princes,
Brought up, it seems, to honest trades; no matter,
They will break forth in season.
JANE. Or break out,

---

2 *entertainment*: reception.
6 *honest*: ingenuous.
8 *But*: were it not.
11 *fame*: proclaim, boast about. By such behaviour they protect their family's reputation, but show no pride in their origins.
15 *break forth*: reveal their true nature.
break out: (1) erupt (as a boil might), (2) escape from prison.

For most of 'em are broken, by report. –
Flourish.
The king!
KATHERINE. Let us observe 'em and be silent.

Enter KING JAMES, HUNTLY, CRAWFORD, *and* DALYELL.

JAMES. The right of kings, my lords, extends not only
To the safe conservation of their own,
But also to the aid of such allies
As change of time and state hath oftentimes
Hurl'd down from careful crowns, to undergo
An exercise of sufferance in both fortunes.
So English Richard, surnam'd Coeur-de-Lion,
So Robert Bruce, our royal ancestor,
Forc'd by the trial of the wrongs they felt,
Both sought, and found, supplies from foreign kings
To repossess their own. Then grudge not, lords,
A much distressed prince; King Charles of France
And Maximilian of Bohemia both
Have ratified his credit by their letters.
Shall we then be distrustful? No; compassion
Is one rich jewel that shines in our crown,
And we will have it shine there.
HUNTLY. Do your will, sir.
JAMES. The young duke is at hand. Dalyell, from us
First greet him, and conduct him on; then Crawford
Shall meet him next, and Huntly last of all

16–17 See Textual Notes, p. 344.
16 *broken*: bankrupt.
22 *careful*: full of anxiety.
23 *sufferance in both fortunes*: patient endurance of good and bad fortune.
26 *trial*: experience.
27 *supplies*: reinforcements.
foreign kings: Philip II of France and Edward I of England.
31 *credit*: authenticity.

Present him to our arms. Sound sprightly music,
While majesty encounters majesty. *Hautboys.*

DALYELL *goes out, brings in* PERKIN [WARBECK] *at the door, where* CRAWFORD *entertains him, and from* CRAWFORD, HUNTLY *salutes him and presents him to the King. They embrace.* PERKIN *in state retires some few paces back. During which ceremony the Noblemen slightly salute* FRION, HERON, *a mercer,* SKELTON, *a tailor,* ASTLEY, *a scrivener, with* JOHN A-WATER, *all* PERKIN*'s followers. Salutations ended, cease music.*

WARBECK. Most high, most mighty king! That now there stands
Before your eyes, in presence of your peers,
A subject of the rarest kind of pity
That hath in any age touch'd noble hearts,
The vulgar story of a prince's ruin
Hath made it too apparent. Europe knows,
And all the western world, what persecution
Hath rag'd in malice against us, sole heir
To the great throne of old Plantagenets.
How from our nursery we have been hurried
Unto the sanctuary, from the sanctuary
Forc'd to the prison, from the prison hal'd
By cruel hands to the tormentor's fury,
Is register'd already in the volume
Of all men's tongues; whose true relation draws
Compassion, melted into weeping eyes
And bleeding souls. But our misfortunes since
Have rang'd a larger progress through strange lands,
Protected in our innocence by Heaven.

---

39 s.d. *Hautboys*: oboes.
entertains: receives.
slightly: scornfully.
A-WATER: see Textual Notes, p. 344.
44 *vulgar*: widespread, well known.
51 *hal'd*: dragged.
57 *progress*: journey; but the word was also used for a monarch's tours of his kingdom. Cf. IV.iv.36–7.

Edward the Fifth, our brother, in his tragedy
Quench'd their hot thirst of blood, whose hire to murder
Paid them their wages of despair and horror;
The softness of my childhood smil'd upon
The roughness of their task, and robb'd them farther
Of hearts to dare, or hands to execute.
Great king, they spar'd my life, the butchers spar'd it;
Return'd the tyrant, my unnatural uncle,
A truth of my dispatch. I was convey'd
With secrecy and speed to Tournai; foster'd
By obscure means, taught to unlearn myself.
But as I grew in years I grew in sense
Of fear, and of disdain; fear of the tyrant
Whose power sway'd the throne then. When disdain
Of living so unknown, in such a servile
And abject lowness, prompted me to thoughts
Of recollecting who I was, I shook off
My bondage, and made haste to let my aunt
Of Burgundy acknowledge me her kinsman,
Heir to the crown of England snatch'd by Henry
From Richard's head, a thing scarce known i'th'world.

JAMES. My lord, it stands not with your counsel now
To fly upon invectives; if you can
Make this apparent what you have discours'd,
In every circumstance, we will not study
An answer, but are ready in your cause.

WARBECK. You are a wise and just king, by the powers
Above reserv'd beyond all other aids
To plant me in mine own inheritance;

---

66 *tyrant*: Richard III.
67 *truth*: convincing account.
72 *sway'd*: controlled.
80 *stands . . . counsel*: is inconsistent with your purpose.
81 *fly upon*: resort to.
83 *study*: take time to consider.
86 *reserv'd*: set apart.

To marry these two kingdoms in a love
Never to be divorc'd while time is time.
As for the manner, first of my escape,
Of my conveyance next, of my life since,
The means and persons who were instruments,
Great sir, 'tis fit I overpass in silence;
Reserving the relation to the secrecy
Of your own princely ear, since it concerns
Some great ones living yet, and others dead,
Whose issue might be question'd. For your bounty,
Royal magnificence to him that seeks it,
We vow hereafter to demean ourself
As if we were your own and natural brother,
Omitting no occasion in our person
To express a gratitude beyond example.

JAMES. He must be more than subject who can utter
The language of a king, and such is thine.
Take this for answer: be whate'er thou art,
Thou never shalt repent that thou hast put
Thy cause, and person, into my protection.
Cousin of York, thus once more we embrace thee;
Welcome to James of Scotland! For thy safety,
Know such as love thee not shall never wrong thee.
Come, we will taste a while our court delights,
Dream hence afflictions past, and then proceed
To high attempts of honour. On, lead on!
Both thou and thine are ours, and we will guard ye.
Lead on!

Exeunt all but the LADIES *above.*

COUNTESS. I have not seen a gentleman
Of a more brave aspect or goodlier carriage;
His fortunes move not him. – Madam, you're passionate.

---

97 *Whose issue*: the legitimacy of whose children.
98 *magnificence*: generosity.
113 *attempts*: (military) enterprises.
117 *passionate*: strongly moved.

KATHERINE. Beshrew me, but his words have touch'd me home,
As if his cause concern'd me. I should pity him
If he should prove another than he seems.

Enter CRAWFORD [*above*].

CRAWFORD. Ladies, the king commands your presence instantly,
For entertainment of the duke.
KATHERINE. The duke
Must then be entertain'd, the king obey'd;
It is our duty.
COUNTESS. We will all wait on him.
Exeunt.

SCENE II

Flourish. Enter KING HENRY, OXFORD, DURHAM, SURREY.

HENRY. Have ye condemn'd my chamberlain?
DURHAM. His treasons
Condemn'd him, sir, which were as clear and manifest
As foul and dangerous. Besides, the guilt
Of his conspiracy press'd him so nearly
That it drew from him free confession
Without an importunity.
HENRY. O Lord Bishop,
This argued shame and sorrow for his folly,
And must not stand in evidence against
Our mercy, and the softness of our nature;
The rigour and extremity of law
Is sometimes too, too bitter, but we carry

---

118 *home*: deeply.
124 *wait on*: attend on.
1–6 See Textual Notes, p. 344.
4 *press'd*: oppressed; with an allusion to the contemporary torture of pressing with weights. Cf. II.iii.149–50.
nearly: closely.
5 *confession*: four syllables.

A chancery of pity in our bosom.
I hope we may reprieve him from the sentence
Of death; I hope we may.

DURHAM. You may, you may;
And so persuade your subjects that the title
Of York is better, nay, more just and lawful
Than yours of Lancaster. So Stanley holds,
Which, if it be not treason in the highest,
Then we are traitors all, perjur'd and false,
Who have took oath to Henry, and the justice
Of Henry's title; Oxford, Surrey, Daubeney,
With all your other peers of state and church,
Forsworn, and Stanley true alone to Heaven,
And England's lawful heir.

OXFORD. By Vere's old honours,
I'll cut his throat dares speak it.

SURREY. 'Tis a quarrel
T'engage a soul in.

HENRY. What a coil is here
To keep my gratitude sincere and perfect!
Stanley was once my friend, and came in time
To save my life; yet, to say truth, my lords,
The man stay'd long enough t'endanger it.
But I could see no more into his heart
Than what his outward actions did present;
And for 'em have rewarded him so fully
As that there wanted nothing in our gift
To gratify his merit, as I thought,
Unless I should divide my crown with him
And give him half; though now I well perceive
'Twould scarce have serv'd his turn without the whole.
But I am charitable, lords; let justice

---

12 *chancery*: court of appeal and equity.
18 *in the highest*: to the highest degree.
24 *Vere's*: Vere was the family name of the Earls of Oxford.
26 *coil*: tumult, row.
27 *sincere*: pure, untainted.
30 *stay'd*: delayed (to throw in his support at the battle of Bosworth Field).
33 See Textual Notes, p. 344.
35 *gratify*: reward.
38 *serv'd his turn*: satisfied him.

Proceed in execution, whiles I mourn
The loss of one whom I esteem'd a friend.
DURHAM. Sir, he is coming this way.
HENRY. If he speak to me
I could deny him nothing; to prevent it,
I must withdraw. Pray, lords, commend my favours
To his last peace, which I, with him, will pray for.
That done, it doth concern us to consult
Of other following troubles. *Exit.*
OXFORD. I am glad
He's gone; upon my life, he would have pardon'd
The traitor had he seen him.
SURREY. 'Tis a king
Compos'd of gentleness.
DURHAM. Rare and unheard of.
But every man is nearest to himself,
And that the king observes; 'tis fit he should.

Enter STANLEY, *Executioner*, URSWICK, *and* DAUBENEY.

STANLEY. May I not speak with Clifford ere I shake
This piece of frailty off?
DAUBENEY. You shall; he's sent for.
STANLEY. I must not see the king?
DURHAM. From him, Sir William,
These lords and I am sent. He bade us say
That he commends his mercy to your thoughts,
Wishing the laws of England could remit
The forfeit of your life as willingly
As he would, in the sweetness of his nature,
Forget your trespass; but, howe'er your body

---

40 *execution*: (1) operation, (2) punishment.
47, 47–50 See Textual Notes, p. 344.
52 See Textual Notes, p. 344.
51 *every . . . himself*: all men put self-interest first; a proverbial idea (Tilley, N57), ultimately derived from Terence's *Andria*, IV.i.12, *Ego proximus sum.*
54 *piece of frailty*: frail body.
57 *mercy*: compassion.

Fall into dust, he vows – the king himself
Doth vow – to keep a requiem for your soul,
As for a friend close treasur'd in his bosom.
OXFORD. Without remembrance of your errors past,
I come to take my leave, and wish you Heaven.
SURREY. And I; good angels guard ye.
STANLEY. O, the king,
Next to my soul, shall be the nearest subject
Of my last prayers. My grave Lord of Durham,
My Lords of Oxford, Surrey, Daubeney, all,
Accept from a poor dying man a farewell.
I was as you are once, great, and stood hopeful
Of many flourishing years; but fate and time
Have wheel'd about, to turn me into nothing.

Enter CLIFFORD.

DAUBENEY. Sir Robert Clifford comes: the man, Sir William,
You so desire to speak with.
DURHAM. Mark their meeting.
CLIFFORD. Sir William Stanley, I am glad your conscience,
Before your end, hath emptied every burden
Which charg'd it, as that you can clearly witness
How far I have proceeded in a duty
That both concern'd my truth, and the state's safety.
STANLEY. Mercy, how dear is life to such as hug it!
Come hither; by this token think on me.
Makes a cross on CLIFFORD*'s face with his finger.*
CLIFFORD. This token? What? I am abus'd!
STANLEY. You are not.
I wet upon your cheeks a holy sign,
The cross, the Christian's badge, the traitor's infamy.

---

74 *wheel'd about*: revolved; from the image of the wheel of fortune.
79 *charg'd*: filled, weighed down.
84 *abus'd*: wronged.

Wear, Clifford, to thy grave this painted emblem.
Water shall never wash it off, all eyes
That gaze upon thy face shall read there written
A state-informer's character, more ugly
Stamp'd on a noble name than on a base.
The Heavens forgive thee. – Pray, my lords, no change
Of words; this man and I have us'd too many.

CLIFFORD. Shall I be disgrac'd
Without reply?

DURHAM. Give losers leave to talk;
His loss is irrecoverable.

STANLEY. Once more
To all a long farewell; the best of greatness
Preserve the king. My next suit is, my lords,
To be remember'd to my noble brother,
Derby, my much griev'd brother. O, persuade him
That I shall stand no blemish to his house
In chronicles writ in another age.
My heart doth bleed for him; and for his sighs,
Tell him he must not think the style of Derby,
Nor being husband to King Henry's mother,
The league with peers, the smiles of fortune, can
Secure his peace above the state of man.
I take my leave, to travel to my dust;
Subjects deserve their deaths whose kings are just.
Come, confessor; on with thy axe, friend, on.

Exeunt [STANLEY, URSWICK, *and Executioner*].

---

90 *character*: (1) sign, (2) nature.
92 *change*: exchange.
94–6 See Textual Notes, p. 344.
97 *best of greatness*: i.e. God.
100 *Derby*: Thomas Stanley, created Earl of Derby after the battle of Bosworth; third husband of Margaret Beaufort, Henry VI's mother.
104 *style*: title.
107 *the state of man*: the human condition (of uncertainty); cf. *'Tis Pity She's a Whore*, IV.ii.20.

CLIFFORD. Was I call'd hither by a traitor's breath
To be upbraided? Lord, the king shall know it.

Enter KING HENRY *with a white staff.*

HENRY. The king doth know it, sir; the king hath heard
What he or you could say. We have given credit
To every point of Clifford's information,
The only evidence 'gainst Stanley's head.
He dies for't; are you pleas'd?
CLIFFORD. I pleas'd, my lord?
HENRY. No echoes. For your service, we dismiss
Your more attendance on the court. Take ease
And live at home; but, as you love your life,
Stir not from London without leave from us.
We'll think on your reward; away!
CLIFFORD. I go, sir. *Exit.*
HENRY. Die all our griefs with Stanley! Take this staff
Of office, Daubeney; henceforth be our chamberlain.
DAUBENEY. I am your humblest servant.
HENRY. We are follow'd
By enemies at home that will not cease
To seek their own confusion; 'tis most true
The Cornish under Audley are march'd on
As far as Winchester. But let them come,
Our forces are in readiness; we'll catch 'em
In their own toils.
DAUBENEY. Your army, being muster'd,
Consist in all, of horse and foot, at least
In number six and twenty thousand; men
Daring and able, resolute to fight,
And loyal in their truths.
HENRY. We know it, Daubeney.
For them we order thus. Oxford, in chief,
Assisted by bold Essex and the Earl
Of Suffolk, shall lead on the first battalia; –

---

112 s.d. *white staff*: the sign of office of the Lord Chancellor.
131 *toils*: snares.
138 *battalia*: squadron.

Be that your charge.
OXFORD. I humbly thank your majesty.
HENRY. The next division we assign to Daubeney.
These must be men of action, for on those
The fortune of our fortunes must rely.
The last, and main, ourself commands in person,
As ready to restore the fight at all times
As to consummate an assured victory.
DAUBENEY. The king is still oraculous.
HENRY. But, Surrey,
We have employment of more toil for thee!
For our intelligence comes swiftly to us
That James of Scotland late hath entertain'd
Perkin the counterfeit with more than common
Grace and respect; nay, courts him with rare favours.
The Scot is young and forward; we must look for
A sudden storm to England from the north,
Which to withstand, Durham shall post to Norham,
To fortify the castle and secure
The frontiers against an invasion there.
Surrey shall follow soon, with such an army
As may relieve the bishop and encounter
On all occasions the death-daring Scots.
You know your charges all; 'tis now a time
To execute, not talk. Heaven is our guard still.
War must breed peace; such is the fate of kings.
Exeunt.

SCENE III

Enter CRAWFORD *and* DALYELL.

CRAWFORD. 'Tis more than strange; my reason cannot answer

---

146 *still oraculous*: as always, divinely inspired.
148 *intelligence*: information.
149 *entertain'd*: given a welcome to.
154 *post*: hasten.
Norham: a border castle on the Tweed, near Berwick.
160 *charges*: responsibilities.

Such argument of fine imposture, couch'd
In witchcraft of persuasion, that it fashions
Impossibilities, as if appearance
Could cozen truth itself. This dukeling
mushroom
Hath doubtless charm'd the king.

DALYELL. He courts the ladies,
As if his strenth of language chain'd attention
By power of prerogative.

CRAWFORD. It madded
My very soul to hear our master's motion.
What surety both of amity and honour
Must of necessity ensue upon
A match betwixt some noble of our nation
And this brave prince, forsooth.

DALYELL. 'Twill prove too fatal;
Wise Huntly fears the threat'ning. Bless the lady
From such a ruin!

CRAWFORD. How the council privy
Of this young Phaethon do screw their faces
Into a gravity their trades, good people,
Were never guilty of! The meanest of 'em
Dreams of at least an office in the state.

DALYELL. Sure, not the hangman's; 'tis bespoke
already
For service to their rogueships. – Silence!

Enter KING JAMES *and* HUNTLY.

JAMES. Do not
Argue against our will; we have descended
Somewhat, as we may term it, too familiarly
From justice of our birthright, to examine

---

5 *cozen*: deceive.
mushroom: upstart.
6 *charm'd*: put a spell on.
8 *prerogative*: sovereign right.
9 *motion*: proposal.
10 *surety*: guarantee, bond.
amity: friendship.
14 *Bless*: may God protect.
16 *Phaethon*: see *The Broken Heart*, IV.iv.26 and note. See also Textual Notes, p. 344.

The force of your allegiance – sir, we have –
But find it short of duty.

HUNTLY. Break my heart,
Do, do king! Have my services, my loyalty –
Heaven knows, untainted ever – drawn upon me
Contempt now in mine age, when I but wanted
A minute of a peace not to be troubl'd,
My last, my long one? Let me be a dotard,
A bedlam, a poor sot, or what you please
To have me, so you will not stain your blood,
Your own blood, royal sir, though mix'd with mine,
By marriage of this girl to a straggler!
Take, take my head, sir. Whilst my tongue can wag
It cannot name him other.

JAMES. Kings are counterfeits
In your repute, grave oracle, not presently
Set on their thrones with sceptres in their fists.
But use your own detraction. 'Tis our pleasure
To give our cousin York for wife our kinswoman,
The Lady Katherine. Instinct of sovereignty
Designs the honour, though her peevish father
Usurps our resolution.

HUNTLY. O, 'tis well,
Exceeding well! I never was ambitious
Of using congées to my daughter-queen.
A queen; perhaps a quean! Forgive me, Dalyell,
Thou honourable gentleman; none here
Dare speak one word of comfort?

DALYELL. Cruel misery!

---

25 *force*: strength.
29–30 *but . . . minute*: fell short by a minute.
31 *dotard*: old fool.
32 *bedlam*: lunatic.
35 *straggler*: vagabond.
40 *use your own detraction*: be free with your calumnies.
42 *Instinct of sovereignty*: kingly instinct (that Warbeck is of royal birth).
46 *congées*: courtly obeisances.
47 *quean*: harlot; suggested by the idea of Katherine's marriage to a *straggler* (35).

CRAWFORD. The lady, gracious prince, maybe
hath settled
Affection on some former choice.
DALYELL. Enforcement
Would prove but tyranny.
HUNTLY. I thank ye heartily.
Let any yeoman of our nation challenge
An interest in the girl, then the king
May add a jointure of ascent in titles,
Worthy a free consent; now he pulls down
What old desert hath builded.
JAMES. Cease persuasions.
I violate no pawns of faiths, intrude not
On private loves; that I have play'd the orator
For kingly York to virtuous Kate, her grant
Can justify, referring her contents
To our provision. The Welsh Harry henceforth
Shall therefore know, and tremble to acknowledge,
That not the painted idol of his policy
Shall fright the lawful owner from a kingdom.
We are resolv'd.
HUNTLY. Some of thy subjects' hearts,
King James, will bleed for this!
JAMES. Then shall their bloods
Be nobly spent. No more disputes; he is not
Our friend who contradicts us.
HUNTLY. Farewell, daughter!
My care by one is lessen'd; thank the king for't,
I and my griefs will dance now.

51–2 See Textual Notes, p. 344.
53 *challenge*: lay claim to.
55 *jointure*: dowry.
58 *pawns of faiths*: pledges of betrothal.
61 *referring her contents*: handing over her (future) happiness.
62 *Welsh Harry*: Henry IV's grandfather was a Welshman, Owen Tudor.
70 See Textual Notes, p. 344.

Enter [PERKIN] WARBECK *leading* KATHERINE, *complimenting;* COUNTESS OF CRAWFORD, JANE, FRION, [JOHN A-WATER] *Mayor of Cork,* ASTLEY, HERON, *and* SKELTON.

Look, lords, look,
Here's hand in hand already!
JAMES. Peace, old frenzy!
How like a king he looks! Lords, but observe
The confidence of his aspect! Dross cannot
Cleave to so pure a metal; royal youth!
Plantagenet undoubted!
HUNTLY. [*aside*] Ho, brave youth,
But no Plantagenet, by'r Lady, yet,
By red rose or by white.
WARBECK. An union this way
Settles possession in a monarchy
Establish'd rightly, as is my inheritance.
Acknowledge me but sovereign of this kingdom,
Your heart, fair princess, and the hand of providence
Shall crown you queen of me and my best fortunes.
KATHERINE. Where my obedience is, my lord, a duty,
Love owes true service.
WARBECK. Shall I –
JAMES. Cousin, yes,
Enjoy her. From my hand accept your bride;
And may they live at enmity with comfort
Who grieve at such an equal pledge of troths.
You're the prince's wife now.
KATHERINE. By your gift, sir.
WARBECK. Thus I take seizure of mine own.
[*Embraces* KATHERINE.]
KATHERINE. I miss yet

---

71 s.d. *complimenting*: paying formal courtesies.
76 See Textual Notes, p. 344.
77 *by'r*: by our.
78 *By . . . white*: by kinship with Lancaster or York. Both families adopted a rose as their emblem.
90 *miss*: lack.

A father's blessing. Let me find it. [*Kneels*] Humbly
Upon my knees I seek it.
HUNTLY. I am Huntly,
Old Alexander Gordon, a plain subject,
Nor more nor less; and, lady, if you wish for
A blessing, you must bend your knees to Heaven,
For Heaven did give me you. Alas, alas,
What would you have me say? May all the happiness
My prayers ever su'd to fall upon you
Preserve you in your virtues! – Prithee, Dalyell,
Come with me, for I feel thy griefs as full
As mine; let's steal away and cry together.
DALYELL. My hopes are in their ruins.
Exeunt HUNTLY *and* DALYELL.
JAMES. Good kind Huntly
Is overjoy'd; a fit solemnity
Shall perfect these delights. Crawford, attend
Our order for the preparation.
Exeunt all but FRION, [JOHN A-WATER], ASTLEY, HERON, *and* SKELTON.
FRION. Now, worthy gentlemen, have I not follow'd
My undertakings with success? Here's entrance
Into a certainty above a hope.

HERON. Hopes are but hopes; I was ever confident, when I traded but in remnants, that my stars had reserv'd me to the title of a viscount at least. Honour is honour, though cut out of any stuffs.

SKELTON. My brother Heron hath right wisely deliver'd his opinion; for he that threads his needle with the sharp eyes of industry shall in time go through-stitch with the new suit of preferment.

---

93 *Alexander Gordon*: actually George Gordon; Ford took over a mistake in his sources about Huntly's name.
103 *solemnity*: ceremonial observance.
104 *attend*: wait to receive.
105 See Textual Notes, p. 344.
113 *stuffs*: materials.
117 *go through-stitch*: (1) perforate, (2) finish.

ASTLEY. Spoken to the purpose, my fine-witted brother Skelton; for as no indenture but has its counterpawn, no noverint but his condition or defeasance, so no right but may have claim, no claim but may have possession, any act of parliament to the contrary notwithstanding.

FRION. You are all read in mysteries of state,
And quick of apprehension, deep in judgement,
Active in resolution; and 'tis pity
Such counsel should lie buried in obscurity.
But why in such a time and cause of triumph
Stands the judicious Mayor of Cork so silent?
Believe it, sir, as English Richard prospers,
You must not miss employment of high nature.

A-WATER. If men may be credited in their mortality, which I dare not peremptorily aver, but they may or not be, presumptions by this marriage are then, in sooth, of fruitful expectation. Or else I must not justify other men's belief more than other should rely on mine.

FRION. Pith of experience! Those that have borne office
Weigh every word before it can drop from them.
But, noble counsellors, since now the present
Requires in point of honour (pray mistake not)
Some service to our lord, 'tis fit the Scots
Should not engross all glory to themselves
At this so grand and eminent solemnity.

SKELTON. The Scots. The motion is defied. I had rather, for my part, without trial of my country, suffer persecution under the pressing-iron of

---

120 *indenture*: deed of agreement.
121 *counterpawn*: counterpart, copy.
noverint: legal bond.
122 *defeasance*: clause defining how the contract might become void.
125 *read*: learned.
133–4 *credited in their mortality*: believed, mortal as they are.
137 *justify*: uphold.
148 *trial of my country*: i.e. trial by jury.
149 *pressing-iron*: tailor's smoothing-iron; with an allusion to execution by pressing to death with weights. Cf. II.ii.4 and note.

reproach, or let my skin be punch'd full of eyelet-holes with the bodkin of derision.

ASTLEY. I will sooner lose both my ears on the pillory of forgery.

HERON. Let me first live a bankrupt, and die in the lousy Hole of hunger, without compounding for sixpence in the pound.

A-WATER. If men fail not in their expectations, there may be spirits, also, that digest no rude affronts, master secretary Frion, or I am cozen'd; which is possible, I grant.

FRION. Resolv'd like men of knowledge. At this feast, then,
In honour of the bride, the Scots, I know,
Will in some show, some masque, or some device,
Prefer their duties. Now it were uncomely
That we be found less forward for our prince
Than they are for their lady; and by how much
We outshine them in persons of account,
By so much more will our endeavours meet with
A livelier applause. Great emperors
Have, for their recreations, undertook
Such kind of pastimes. As for the conceit,
Refer it to my study; the performance
You all shall share a thanks in. 'Twill be grateful.

HERON. The motion is allow'd. I have stole to a dancing-school when I was a prentice.

---

150 See Textual Notes, p. 345.
151 *bodkin*: needle.
155 *Hole*: the worst cell in debtors' prisons.
compounding: agreeing to settle debts by paying a fixed proportion of all claims.
158 *digest*: 'swallow', accept. See Textual Notes, p. 345.
160 *cozen'd*: deceived.
163 *device*: entertainment.
164 *Prefer*: offer, present.
167 *persons of account*: performers of distinction. Frion is proposing that they themselves take part in their masque.
169–71 *Great . . . pastimes*: Nero was the usual classical example offered in Caroline plays; cf. Massinger's *The Roman Actor*, IV.ii.224–6.
171 *conceit*: imaginative idea, theme.
173 *grateful*: pleasing.

ASTLEY. There have been Irish hubbubs, when I have made one too.

SKELTON. For fashioning of shapes, and cutting a cross-caper, turn me off to my trade again.

A-WATER. Surely there is, if I be not deceiv'd, a kind of gravity in merriment; as there is, or perhaps ought to be, respect of persons in the quality of carriage, which is, as it is construed, either so, or so.

FRION. Still you come home to me; upon occasion
I find you relish courtship with discretion,
And such are fit for statesmen of your merits.
Pray ye wait the prince, and in his ear acquaint him
With this design; I'll follow and direct ye.

Exeunt all but FRION.

O, the toil
Of humouring this abject scum of mankind!
Muddy-brain'd peasants! Princes feel a misery
Beyond impartial sufferance, whose extremes
Must yield to such abettors; yet our tide
Runs smoothly, without adverse winds. Run on!
Flow to a full sea! Time alone debates
Quarrels forewritten in the book of fates. *Exit.*

---

176 *hubbubs*: noisy entertainments.
177 *made one*: joined in.
178 *shapes*: (1) (stage) costumes, (2) dance poses.
178–9 *cutting a cross-caper*: performing a dance jump, crossing the legs; with a punning allusion to the work of a tailor, who commonly sat cross-legged.
183 *carriage*: deportment.
185 *come . . . me*: understand what I mean.
188 *wait*: attend on.
193 *extremes*: extreme necessities.
196 *debates*: abates.

ACT III

SCENE I

Enter KING HENRY, *his gorget on, his sword, plume of feathers, leading-staff, and* URSWICK.

HENRY. How runs the time of day?
URSWICK. Past ten, my lord.
HENRY. A bloody hour will it prove to some,
Whose disobedience, like the sons o'th'earth,
Throw a defiance 'gainst the face of Heaven.
Oxford, with Essex and stout De la Pole,
Have quieted the Londoners, I hope,
And set them safe from fear?
URSWICK. They are all silent.
HENRY. From their own battlements they may behold
Saint George's Fields o'erspread with armed men;
Amongst whom our own royal standard threatens
Confusion to opposers. We must learn
To practise war again in time of peace,
Or lay our crown before our subjects' feet,
Ha, Urswick, must we not?
URSWICK. The powers who seated
King Henry on his lawful throne will ever
Rise up in his defence.
HENRY. Rage shall not fright

---

0 s.d. *gorget*: armour for the throat; worn as a sign of military rank.
leading-staff: general's baton.
3 *sons o'th'earth*: the Giants, who attacked Olympus and were defeated by the gods.
5 *stout*: courageous.
De la Pole: Edmund, Earl of Suffolk, brother of John, Earl of Lincoln (see I.i.91). He later conspired against Henry.
9 *Saint George's Fields*: a large open space on the Surrey side of the Thames, between Southwark and Lambeth.
11 *Confusion*: destruction.

The bosom of our confidence. In Kent
Our Cornish rebels, cozen'd of their hopes,
Met brave resistance by that country's earl,
George Aberg'enny, Cobham, Poynings, Guildford,
And other loyal hearts; now, if Blackheath
Must be reserv'd the fatal tomb to swallow
Such stiff-neck'd abjects as with weary marches
Have travell'd from their homes, their wives and children,
To pay instead of subsidies their lives,
We may continue sovereign. Yet, Urswick,
We'll not abate one penny what in parliament
Hath freely been contributed. We must not;
Money gives soul to action. Our competitor,
The Flemish counterfeit, with James of Scotland,
Will prove what courage, need, and want can nourish
Without the food of fit supplies; but, Urswick,
I have a charm in secret that shall loose
The witchcraft wherewith young King James is bound,
And free it at my pleasure without bloodshed.

URSWICK. Your majesty's a wise king, sent from Heaven,
Protector of the just.

HENRY. Let dinner cheerfully
Be serv'd in. This day of the week is ours,
Our day of providence, for Saturday
Yet never fail'd in all my undertakings
To yield me rest at night. *A flourish.*
What means this warning?
Good fate, speak peace to Henry!

---

18 *cozen'd*: cheated.
21 *Blackheath*: a large common between Eltham and Greenwich.
23 *abjects*: outcasts.
31 *prove*: find by experience.
38–41 *This . . . night*: following Bacon, who erroneously cited Saturday as the day of the battle of Bosworth.
41 See Textual Notes, p. 345.

Enter DAUBENEY, OXFORD, *and Attendants.*

DAUBENEY. Live the king,
Triumphant in the ruin of his enemies!
OXFORD. The head of strong rebellion is cut off,
The body hew'd in pieces.
HENRY. Daubeney, Oxford,
Minions to noblest fortunes, how yet stands
The comfort of your wishes?
DAUBENEY. Briefly thus:
The Cornish, under Audley, disappointed
Of flatter'd expectation from the Kentish,
Your majesty's right-trusty liegemen, flew,
Feather'd by rage and hearten'd by presumption,
To take the field even at your palace gates,
And face you in your chamber-royal. Arrogance
Improv'd their ignorance; for they, supposing,
Misled by rumour, that the day of battle
Should fall on Monday, rather brav'd your forces
Than doubted any onset. Yet, this morning,
When in the dawning I by your direction
Strove to get Deptford Strand Bridge, there I found
Such a resistance as might show what strength
Could make; here arrows hail'd in showers upon us
A full yard long at least; but we prevail'd.
My Lord of Oxford with his fellow peers,
Environing the hill, fell fiercely on them
On the one side, I on the other, till, great sir –
Pardon the oversight – eager of doing
Some memorable act I was engag'd
Almost a prisoner, but was freed as soon

---

46 *Minions*: favourites.
49 *flatter'd*: exaggerated. See Textual Notes, p. 345.
56 *brav'd*: treated wth bravado.
57 *doubted*: feared.
59 See Textual Notes, p. 345.
64 *Environing*: circling round.
67–8 *engag'd . . . prisoner*: drawn into the fighting and almost captured.

As sensible of danger. Now the fight
Began in heat, which quenched in the blood of
Two thousand rebels, and as many more
Reserv'd to try your mercy, have return'd
A victory with safety.

HENRY. Have we lost
An equal number with them?

OXFORD. In the total
Scarcely four hundred. Audley, Flammock,
Joseph,
The ringleaders of this commotion,
Railed in ropes, fit ornaments for traitors,
Wait your determinations.

HENRY. We must pay
Our thanks where they are only due. O lords,
Here is no victory, nor shall our people
Conceive that we can triumph in their falls.
Alas, poor souls! Let such as are escap'd
Steal to the country back without pursuit.
There's not a drop of blood spilt but hath drawn
As much of mine; their swords could have
wrought wonders
On their king's part, who faintly were unsheath'd
Against their prince, but wounded their own
breasts.
Lords, we are debtors to your care; our payment
Shall be both sure and fitting your deserts.

DAUBENEY. Sir, will you please to see those rebels,
heads
Of this wild monster-multitude?

HENRY. Dear friend,
My faithful Daubeney, no. On them our justice
Must frown in terror; I will not vouchsafe
An eye of pity to them. Let false Audley
Be drawn upon an hurdle from the Newgate

---

72 *try*: experience.
have return'd: the antecedent is *fight* but the verb is attracted to the number of *rebels*.
77 *Railed*: fastened in a row.
79 *only*: alone.
86 *who faintly*: which (the swords) half-heartedly.
95 *hurdle*: sledge.
Newgate: Newgate prison.

To Tower Hill in his own coat of arms
Painted on paper, with the arms revers'd,
Defac'd and torn. There let him lose his head.
The lawyer and the blacksmith shall be hang'd,
Quarter'd, their quarters into Cornwall sent,
Examples to the rest, whom we are pleas'd
To pardon and dismiss from further quest.
My Lord of Oxford, see it done.
OXFORD. I shall, sir.
HENRY. Urswick.
URSWICK. My lord?
HENRY. To Dinham, our high treasurer,
Say we command commissions be new granted
For the collection of our subsidies
Through all the west, and that speedily.
Lords, we acknowledge our engagements due
For your most constant services.
DAUBENEY. Your soldiers
Have manfully and faithfully acquitted
Their several duties.
HENRY. For it we will throw
A largesse free amongst them, which shall hearten
And cherish up their loyalties. More yet
Remains of like employment; not a man
Can be dismiss'd till enemies abroad,
More dangerous than these at home, have felt
The puissance of our arms. O, happy kings,
Whose thrones are raised in their subjects' hearts!

Exeunt all.

SCENE II

Enter HUNTLY *and* DALYELL.

HUNTLY. Now, sir, a modest word with you, sad gentleman.

---

102 *quest*: pursuit, or judicial inquiry.
112 *largesse*: gift of money.
117 *puissance*: power.

Is not this fine, I trow, to see the gambols,
To hear the jigs, observe the frisks, b'enchanted
With the rare discord of bells, pipes and tabors,
Hotch-potch of Scotch and Irish twingle-twangles,
Like to so many quiristers of Bedlam
Trolling a catch! The feasts, the manly stomachs,
The healths in usquebaugh and bonny-clabber,
The ale in dishes never fetch'd from China,
The hundred thousand knacks not to be spoken
of,
And all this for King Oberon and Queen Mab,
Should put a soul int'ye. Look'ee, good man,
How youthful I am grown; but, by your leave,
This new queen-bride must henceforth be no
more
My daughter. No, by'r Lady, 'tis unfit!
And yet you see how I do bear this change,
Methinks courageously; then shake off care
In such a time of jollity.

DALYELL. Alas, sir,
How can you cast a mist upon your griefs,
Which, howsoe'er you shadow, but present
To any judging eye the perfect substance
Of which mine are but counterfeits?

HUNTLY. Foh, Dalyell,
Thou interrupts the part I bear in music
To this rare bridal feast; let us be merry,
Whilst flattering calms secure us against storms.

---

2 *gambols:* leaps in dancing.
3 *frisks*: lively dances.
4 *rare*: extraordinary.
tabors: small drums.
5 *twingle-twangles*: twanging the Gaelic harp.
6 *quiristers of Bedlam*: choristers from a lunatic asylum.
7 *Trolling a catch*: bellowing out a round; catches were often sung at inns.
manly stomachs: large appetites.
8 *usquebaugh and bonny-clabber*: whisky and an Irish drink of sour butter-milk and beer.
10 *knacks*: delicacies.
11 *Oberon . . . Mab*: the fairy king and queen (i.e. Warbeck and his bride).
15 See Textual Notes, p. 345.
20 *shadow*: conceal.
21 See Textual Notes, p. 345.

Tempests, when they begin to roar, put out
The light of peace, and cloud the sun's bright
eye
In darkness of despair; yet we are safe.
DALYELL. I wish you could as easily forget
The justice of your sorrows, as my hopes
Can yield to destiny.
HUNTLY. Pish, then I see
Thou dost not know the flexible condition
Of my apt nature. I can laugh, laugh heartily
When the gout cramps my joints; let but the
stone
Stop in my bladder, I am straight a-singing;
The quartan fever shrinking every limb
Sets me a-cap'ring straight; do but betray me,
And bind me a friend ever. What! I trust
The losing of a daughter, though I doted
On every hair that grew to trim her head,
Admits not any pain like one of these.
Come, thou'rt deceiv'd in me. Give me a blow,
A sound blow on the face, I'll thank thee for't.
I love my wrongs; still thou'rt deceiv'd in me.
DALYELL. Deceiv'd? O noble Huntly, my few
years
Have learnt experience of too ripe an age
To forfeit fit credulity. Forgive
My rudeness; I am bold.
HUNTLY. Forgive me first
A madness of ambition; by example
Teach me humility, for patience scorns
Lectures which schoolmen use to read to boys
Uncapable of injuries. Though old,

---

33 *apt*: adaptable. See Textual Notes, p. 345.
35 See Textual Notes, p. 345.
36 *quartan fever*: severe fever, whose fits were supposed to recur every fourth day.
37, 38 See Textual Notes, p. 345.
40 *trim*: adorn.
41 *Admits*: entails.
47 *fit credulity*: capacity for proper belief or disbelief.
50 *patience scorns*: a man who has suffered much is impatient of.
51 *schoolmen use*: academics are accustomed.

I could grow tough in fury, and disclaim
Allegiance to my king; could fall at odds
With all my fellow peers, that durst not stand
Defendants 'gainst the rape done on mine
honour.
But kings are earthly gods, there is no meddling
With their anointed bodies; for their actions,
They only are accountable to Heaven.
Yet in the puzzle of my troubl'd brain
One antidote's reserv'd against the poison
Of my distractions; 'tis in thee t'apply it.

DALYELL. Name it, O, name it quickly, sir!

HUNTLY. A pardon
For my most foolish slighting thy deserts.
I have cull'd out this time to beg it: prithee
Be gentle; had I been so, thou hadst own'd
A happy bride, but now a castaway,
And never child of mine more.

DALYELL. Say not so, sir;
It is not fault in her.

HUNTLY. The world would prate
How she was handsome. Young I know she was,
Tender, and sweet in her obedience;
But lost now; what a bankrupt am I made
Of a full stock of blessings! Must I hope
A mercy from thy heart?

DALYELL. A love, a service,
A friendship to posterity.

HUNTLY. Good angels
Reward thy charity; I have no more
But prayers left me now.

DALYELL. I'll lend you mirth, sir,
If you will be in consort.

HUNTLY. Thank ye truly.
I must; yes, yes, I must. Here's yet some ease,
A partner in affliction; look not angry.

---

53 *tough*: possibly 'hardened, violent'.
58 *for*: as regards.
65 *cull'd out*: selected.
66 *gentle*: generous.
68–9 See Textual Notes, p. 345.
78 *consort*: harmony with yourself (or with me).

DALYELL. Good noble sir. *Flourish.*
HUNTLY. O, hark! We may be quiet;
The king and all the others come, a meeting
Of gaudy sights. This day's the last of revels;
Tomorrow sounds of war. Then new exchange;
Fiddles must turn to swords. Unhappy marriage!

Enter KING JAMES, [PERKIN] WARBECK *leading* KATHERINE, CRAWFORD, COUNTESS [OF CRAWFORD], *and* JANE. HUNTLY *and* DALYELL *fall among them.*

JAMES. Cousin of York, you and your princely bride
Have liberally enjoy'd such soft delights
As a new-married couple could forethink.
Nor has our bounty shorten'd expectation;
But after all those pleasures of repose,
Or amorous safety, we must rouse the ease
Of dalliance with achievements of more glory
Than sloth and sleep can furnish. Yet, for farewell,
Gladly we entertain a truce with time,
To grace the joint endeavours of our servants.
WARBECK. My royal cousin, in your princely favour
The extent of bounty hath been so unlimited
As only an acknowledgement in words
Would breed suspicion in our state and quality.
When we shall, in the fullness of our fate –
Whose minister, Necessity, will perfect –
Sit on our own throne, then our arms, laid open
To gratitude, in sacred memory
Of these large benefits, shall twine them close
Even to our thoughts and heart without distinction.
Then James and Richard, being in effect
One person, shall unite and rule one people,
Divisible in titles only.
JAMES. Seat ye.

---

81 *may*: must. See Textual Notes, p. 345.
89 *shorten'd expectation*: fallen short of what was expected.
101 *perfect*: complete it.

Are the presenters ready?
CRAWFORD. All are ent'ring.
HUNTLY. [*aside to* DALYELL] Dainty sport toward, Dalyell. Sit; come sit,
Sit and be quiet. Here are kingly bug's-words.

Enter at one door four Scotch Antics, accordingly habited; enter at another four wild Irish in trowses, long-haired, and accordingly habited. Music. The Masquers dance.

JAMES. To all a general thanks.
WARBECK. In the next room
Take your own shapes again; you shall receive
Particular acknowledgement.
[*Exeunt the Masquers.*]
JAMES. Enough
Of merriments. Crawford, how far's our army
Upon the march?
CRAWFORD. At Heydonhall, great king;
Twelve thousand well prepar'd.
JAMES. Crawford, tonight
Post thither. We in person, with the prince,
By four o'clock tomorrow after dinner
Will be wi'ye; speed away!
CRAWFORD. I fly, my lord. [*Exit.*]
JAMES. Our business grows to head now; where's your secretary,
That he attends ye not to serve?
WARBECK. With Marchmount,
Your herald.
JAMES. Good. The proclamation's ready;

---

109 *presenters*: performers.
110 *toward*: on the way.
111 See Textual Notes, p. 355.
111 s.d. *Antics*: clowns, burlesque actors.
habited: costumed.
trowses: tight-fitting drawers.
114 *Particular*: individual.
116 *Heydonhall*: see note to IV.i.5–9.
118 *Post*: ride at full speed.
121–3 See Textual Notes, p. 345.
123 *proclamation*: a declaration of Warbeck's claim to the English throne was published in autumn 1496.

By that it will appear how the English stand
Affected to your title. – Huntly, comfort
Your daughter in her husband's absence; fight
With prayers at home for us, who for your honours
Must toil in fight abroad.

HUNTLY. Prayers are the weapons
Which men so near their graves as I do use.
I've little else to do.

JAMES. To rest, young beauties!
We must be early stirring, quickly part;
A kingdom's rescue craves both speed and art.
Cousins, good-night. *Flourish.*

WARBECK. Rest to our cousin king.

KATHERINE. Your blessing, sir.

HUNTLY. Fair blessings on your highness; sure, you need 'em.

Exeunt all but [PERKIN] WARBECK, KATHERINE, [*and* JANE].

WARBECK. Jane, set the lights down, and from us return
To those in the next room this little purse;
Say we'll deserve their loves.

JANE. It shall be done, sir. [*Exit.*]

WARBECK. Now, dearest, ere sweet sleep shall seal those eyes,
Love's precious tapers, give me leave to use
A parting ceremony; for tomorrow
It would be sacrilege to intrude upon
The temple of thy peace. Swift as the morning
Must I break from the down of thy embraces,
To put on steel, and trace the paths which lead
Through various hazards to a careful throne.

KATHERINE. My lord, I would fain go wi'ye; there's small fortune

---

125 *Affected to*: disposed towards.
136 *return*: carry in recompense.
139 See Additional Notes, p. 355.
145 *trace*: tread.
146 *careful*: full of anxiety.

In staying here behind.
WARBECK. The churlish brow
Of war, fair dearest, is a sight of horror
For ladies' entertainment. If thou hear'st
A truth of my sad ending by the hand
Of some unnatural subject, thou withal
Shalt hear how I died worthy of my right,
By falling like a king; and in the close
Which my last breath shall sound, thy name, thou fairest,
Shall sing a requiem to my soul, unwilling
Only of greater glory 'cause divided
From such a Heaven on earth as life with thee.
But these are chimes for funerals; my business
Attends on fortune of a sprightlier triumph,
For love and majesty are reconcil'd,
And vow to crown thee Empress of the West.
KATHERINE. You have a noble language, sir; your right
In me is without question, and however
Events of time may shorten my deserts
In others' pity, yet it shall not stagger
Or constancy or duty in a wife.
You must be king of me, and my poor heart
Is all I can call mine.
WARBECK. But we will live,
Live, beauteous virtue, by the lively test
Of our own blood, to let the counterfeit
Be known the world's contempt.
KATHERINE. Pray do not use
That word; it carries fate in't. The first suit
I ever made I trust your love will grant?
WARBECK. Without denial, dearest.
KATHERINE. That hereafter,
If you return with safety, no adventure

---

148 *churlish*: brutish.
152 *withal*: also.
154 *close*: final cadence.
159 *chimes*: tolling of church bells.
160 *Attends on*: serves.
166 *stagger*: daunt.
170 *lively test*: living proof.

May sever us in tasting any fortune;
I ne'er can stay behind again.
WARBECK. You're lady
Of your desires, and shall command your will.
Yet 'tis too hard a promise.
KATHERINE. What our destinies
Have rul'd out in their books we must not search,
But kneel to.
WARBECK. Then to fear when hope is fruitless
Were to be desperately miserable;
Which poverty our greatness dares not dream of,
And much more scorns to stoop to. Some few minutes
Remain yet; let's be thrifty in our hopes.
Exeunt.

SCENE III

Enter KING HENRY, HIALAS, *and* URSWICK.

HENRY. Your name is Pedro Hialas, a Spaniard?
HIALAS. Sir, a Castilian born.
HENRY. King Ferdinand,
With wise Queen Isabel, his royal consort,
Writes ye a man of worthy trust and candour.
Princes are dear to Heaven who meet with subjects
Sincere in their employments; such I find
Your commendation, sir. Let me deliver
How joyful I repute the amity

---

177 *tasting*: experiencing; a common food metaphor in Ford's writing.
178 *lady*: mistress.
179 *command your will*: have performed whatever you desire.
181 *rul'd out*: decreed.
186 *thrifty*: successful.
2 *Castilian*: Castile was one of the three divisions of medieval Spain.
7 *deliver*: express.

With your most fortunate master, who almost
Comes near a miracle in his success
Against the Moors, who had devour'd his country,
Entire now to his sceptre. We, for our part,
Will imitate his providence, in hope
Of partage in the use on't. We repute
The privacy of his advisement to us
By you, intended an ambassador
To Scotland for a peace between our kingdoms,
A policy of love, which well becomes
His wisdom and our care.

HIALAS. Your majesty
Doth understand him rightly.

HENRY. Else,
Your knowledge can instruct me; wherein, sir,
To fall on ceremony would seem useless,
Which shall not need, for I will be as studious
Of your concealment in our conference
As any counsel shall advise.

HIALAS. Then, sir,
My chief request is that, on notice given
At my dispatch in Scotland, you will send
Some learned man of power and experience
To join in treaty with me.

HENRY. I shall do it,
Being that way well provided by a servant
Which may attend ye ever.

HIALAS. If King James
By any indirection should perceive

9–12 *master . . . sceptre*: Ferdinand's capture of Granada in 1492 marked the end of Moorish power in Spain.
12 *Entire . . . sceptre*: completely under his rule.
13 *providence*: foresight.
14 *partage . . . on't*: share in profiting from it.
repute: consider.
15 *privacy of his advisement*: secret nature of his advice.
20 *Else*: if not. See Textual Notes, p. 345.
22 *fall on*: have recourse to.
27 *At my dispatch*: sent by me.
28 *power*: two syllables here and at IV.iii.102.
31 *Which*: who; the reference is to Bishop Fox.
32 *indirection*: devious means.

My coming near your court, I doubt the issue
Of my employment.
HENRY. Be not your own herald;
I learn sometimes without a teacher.
HIALAS. Good days
Guard all your princely thoughts.
HENRY. Urswick, no further
Than the next open gallery attend him. –
A hearty love go with you.
HIALAS. Your vow'd beadsman.
Exeunt URSWICK *and* HIALAS.
HENRY. King Ferdinand is not so much a fox
But that a cunning huntsman may in time
Fall on the scent; in honourable actions
Safe imitation best deserves a praise.

Enter URSWICK.

What, the Castilian's pass'd away?
URSWICK. He is,
And undiscover'd; the two hundred marks
Your majesty convey'd he gently purs'd,
With a right modest gravity.
HENRY. What was't
He mutter'd in the earnest of his wisdom?
He spoke not to be heard; 'twas about –
URSWICK. Warbeck;
How, if King Henry were but sure of subjects,
Such a wild runagate might soon be cag'd,
No great ado withstanding.
HENRY. Nay, nay; something
About my son Prince Arthur's match!
URSWICK. Right, right, sir.
He humm'd it out, how that King Ferdinand

---

33 *doubt the issue*: fear for the outcome.
35–6 See Textual Notes, p. 345.
37 *next open gallery*: nearest public gallery.
38 *beadsman*: humble servant; literally, a person paid to pray for another.
40 *cunning*: skilful, experienced.
45 *gently purs'd*: politely pocketed.
47 *earnest*: seriousness.
50 *runagate*: vagabond, fugitive.

Swore that the marriage 'twixt the Lady Catherine
His daughter, and the Prince of Wales your son,
Should never be consummated as long
As any Earl of Warwick liv'd in England,
Except by new creation.

HENRY. I remember,
'Twas so indeed. The king his master swore it?

URSWICK. Directly, as he said.

HENRY. An Earl of Warwick! –
Provide a messenger for letters instantly
To Bishop Fox. Our news from Scotland creeps,
It comes so slow. We must have airy spirits;
Our time requires dispatch. – The Earl of Warwick!
Let him be son to Clarence, younger brother
To Edward! Edward's daughter is, I think,
Mother to our Prince Arthur. Get a messenger.

Exeunt.

SCENE IV

Enter KING JAMES, [PERKIN] WARBECK, CRAWFORD, DALYELL, HERON, ASTLEY, [JOHN A-WATER], SKELTON, *and Soldiers.*

JAMES. We trifle time against these castle walls;
The English prelate will not yield. Once more
Give him a summons!

[*A trumpet is sounded for a*] *parley.*

---

58 See Additional Notes, p. 355.
60 *Directly*: precisely.
63 See Textual Notes, p. 345.
65–7 *Let . . . Arthur*: Henry is urging his son's superior dynastic claim of direct descent from Edward IV. Its weakness lay in its dependence on the female line.
0 s.d. See Textual Notes, p. 345.
1 *these castle walls*: Norham Castle, on the river Tweed (7–10), south of Berwick.

Enter above DURHAM *armed, a truncheon in his hand, and Soldiers.*

WARBECK. See, the jolly clerk
Appears, trimm'd like a ruffian.
JAMES. Bishop, yet
Set ope the ports, and to your lawful sovereign,
Richard of York, surrender up this castle,
And he will take thee to his grace; else Tweed
Shall overflow his banks with English blood,
And wash the sand that cements those hard stones
From their foundation.
DURHAM. Warlike King of Scotland,
Vouchsafe a few words from a man enforc'd
To lay his book aside, and clap on arms
Unsuitable to my age or my profession.
Courageous prince, consider on what grounds
You rend the face of peace, and break a league
With a confederate king that courts your amity.
For whom, too? For a vagabond, a straggler,
Not noted in the world by birth or name,
An obscure peasant, by the rage of Hell
Loos'd from his chains, to set great kings at strife.
What nobleman, what common man of note,
What ordinary subject hath come in,
Since first you footed on our territories,
To only feign a welcome? Children laugh at
Your proclamations, and the wiser pity
So great a potentate's abuse by one
Who juggles merely with the fawns and youth
Of an instructed compliment. Such spoils,
Such slaughters as the rapine of your soldiers
Already have committed, is enough

---

3 s.d. *truncheon*: commander's staff.
4 *trimm'd . . . ruffian*: dressed up like a city bully-boy.
5 *ports*: city gates.
22 *come in*: joined you.
24 *To . . . welcome*: even to offer a pretended welcome.
27 *juggles*: beguiles.
27–8 *fawns . . . compliment*: flatteries and formal courtesies (*compliment*) he has only recently been taught how to show.

To show your zeal in a conceited justice.
Yet, great king, wake not yet my master's vengeance;
But shake that viper off which gnaws your entrails!
I and my fellow subjects are resolv'd,
If you persist, to stand your utmost fury,
Till our last blood drop from us.

WARBECK. O sir, lend
No ear to this traducer of my honour! –
What shall I call thee, thou grey-bearded scandal,
That kick'st against the sovereignty to which
Thou owest allegiance? – Treason is bold-fac'd
And eloquent in mischief; sacred king,
Be deaf to his known malice!

DURHAM. Rather yield
Unto those holy motions which inspire
The sacred heart of an anointed body!
It is the surest policy in princes
To govern well their own, than seek encroachment
Upon another's right.

CRAWFORD. The king is serious,
Deep in his meditations.

DALYELL. Lift them up
To Heaven, his better genius!

WARBECK. Can you study,
While such a devil raves? O sir!

JAMES. Well, – Bishop,
You'll not be drawn to mercy?

DURHAM. Construe me
In like case by a subject of your own.

---

31 *conceited justice*: what you imagine to be a just cause.
37 See Textual Notes, p. 345.
41 *mischief*: evil.
43 *motions*: impulses, promptings.
48 See Textual Notes, p. 345.
49–50 See Textual Notes, p. 345.
49 *better genius*: good angel.
study: meditate.
51–2 *Construe . . . own*: interpret my behaviour by supposing what one of your own subjects would do in a similar situation.

My resolution's fix'd. King James, be counsell'd;
A greater fate waits on thee.
Exit DURHAM *with his followers.*
JAMES. Forage through
The country; spare no prey of life or goods.
WARBECK. O sir, then give me leave to yield to nature.
I am most miserable; had I been
Born what this clergyman would by defame
Baffle belief with, I had never sought
The truth of mine inheritance with rapes
Of women, or of infants murder'd, virgins
Deflower'd, old men butcher'd, dwellings fir'd,
My land depopulated, and my people
Afflicted with a kingdom's devastation.
Show more remorse, great king, or I shall never
Endure to see such havoc with dry eyes.
Spare, spare, my dear, dear England.
JAMES. You fool your piety,
Ridiculously careful of an interest
Another man possesseth. Where's your faction?
Shrewdly the bishop guess'd of your adherents,
When not a petty burgess of some town,
No, not a villager hath yet appear'd
In your assistance. That should make ye whine,
And not your country's sufferance, as you term it.
DALYELL. The king is angry.
CRAWFORD. And the passionate duke
Effeminately dolent.
WARBECK. The experience
In former trials, sir, both of mine own,
Or other princes cast out of their thrones,
Have so acquainted me how misery

---

54 *greater*: i.e. than assisting Warbeck in his ambitions.
56 *nature*: natural sorrow; Warbeck may weep at this point.
58 defame: calumny.
65 *remorse*: pity.
67 *fool your piety*: make your pity look foolish.
68 *careful of*: concerned about.
71 *petty . . . town*: minor town official.
74 *sufferance*: suffering.
76 *dolent*: sorrowful.

Is destitute of friends or of relief,
That I can easily submit to taste
Lowest reproof, without contempt or words.
JAMES. An humble-minded man!

Enter FRION.

Now, what intelligence
Speaks master secretary Frion?
FRION. Henry
Of England hath in open field o'erthrown
The armies who oppos'd him in the right
Of this young prince.
JAMES. His subsidies, you mean.
More, if you have it.
FRION. Howard, Earl of Surrey,
Backed by twelve earls and barons of the north,
An hundred knights and gentlemen of name,
And twenty thousand soldiers, is at hand
To raise your siege. Brooke, with a goodly navy,
Is admiral at sea; and Daubeney follows
With an unbroken army for a second.
WARBECK. 'Tis false! They come to side with us.
JAMES. Retreat;
We shall not find them stones and walls to cope with.
Yet, Duke of York, for such thou say'st thou art,
I'll try thy fortune to the height. To Surrey,
By Marchmount, I will send a brave defiance
For single combat; once a king will venture

---

82 *Lowest reproof*: basest ignominy.
words: an angry reply.
83 *intelligence*: news. See Textual Notes, p. 345.
87–8 See Textual Notes, p. 345.
87 *subsidies*: taxes.
92 *Brooke*: Sir Robert Willoughby, Baron de Broke, the King's Steward (V.ii.20).
94 *unbroken*: intact, undefeated (during the Cornish rebellion).
100 *once*: for once. Duelling was supposed to take place only between men of equal rank; see *'Tis Pity She's a Whore*, I.ii.3 and note.

His person to an earl, with condition
Of spilling lesser blood. Surrey is bold,
And James resolv'd.
WARBECK. O rather, gracious sir,
Create me to this glory, since my cause
Doth interest this fair quarrel; valu'd least,
I am his equal.
JAMES. I will be the man.
March softly off; where victory can reap
A harvest crown'd with triumph, toil is cheap.
Exeunt all.

ACT IV

SCENE I

Enter SURREY, DURHAM, *Soldiers, with drums and colours.*

SURREY. Are all our braving enemies shrunk back,
Hid in the fogs of their distemper'd climate,
Not daring to behold our colours wave
In spite of this infected air? Can they
Look on the strength of Cundrestine defac'd,
The glory of Heydonhall devasted, that
Of Edington cast down, the pile of Foulden
O'erthrown, and this the strongest of their forts,

101–2 *condition Of*: either 'provision to allow' or 'an agreed prohibition on'.
104 *Create me*: give me the honour of appointment to.
105 *Doth interest*: is involved in.
107 *softly*: quietly, without fanfare.
1 *braving*: vaunting, challenging.
2 *distemper'd*: intemperate.
5–9 *Cundrestine . . . demolish'd*: a list of small Scottish border castles near Berwick.
6 *devasted*: devastated.
7 *pile*: large building.

Old Ayton Castle, yielded and demolish'd,
And yet not peep abroad? The Scots are bold,
Hardy in battle; but it seems the cause
They undertake, considered, appears
Unjointed in the frame on't.

DURHAM. Noble Surrey,
Our royal master's wisdom is at all times
His fortune's harbinger; for when he draws
His sword to threaten war, his providence
Settles on peace, the crowning of an empire.

Trumpet.

SURREY. Rank all in order; 'tis a herald's sound,
Some message from King James. Keep a fix'd station.

Enter MARCHMOUNT *and another Herald in their coats.*

MARCHMOUNT. From Scotland's awful majesty we come
Unto the English general.

SURREY. To me?
Say on.

MARCHMOUNT. Thus, then: the waste and prodigal
Effusion of so much guiltless blood
As in two potent armies of necessity
Must glut the earth's dry womb, his sweet compassion
Hath studied to prevent; for which, to thee,
Great Earl of Surrey, in a single fight
He offers his own royal person, fairly
Proposing these conditions only, that
If victory conclude our master's right,
The earl shall deliver for his ransom

---

13 *Unjointed . . . frame*: badly organised; an appropriate metaphor from building.
16 *providence*: foresight.
19 s.d. *coats*: heraldic clothing.
21–2 See Textual Notes, p. 345.
23 *Effusion*: four syllables.
30 *conclude*: settle, prove.
31 *earl*: two syllables.

The town of Berwick to him, with the fishgarths.
If Surrey shall prevail, the king will pay
A thousand pounds down present for his freedom,
And silence further arms. So speaks King James.

SURREY. So speaks King James; so like a king he speaks.
Heralds, the English general returns
A sensible devotion from his heart,
His very soul, to this unfellow'd grace.
For let the king know, gentle heralds, truly,
How his descent from his great throne to honour
A stranger subject with so high a title
As his compeer in arms, hath conquer'd more
Than any sword could do. For which, my loyalty
Respected, I will serve his virtues ever
In all humility. But Berwick, say,
Is none of mine to part with. In affairs
Of princes, subjects cannot traffic rights
Inherent to the crown. My life is mine,
That I dare freely hazard; and – with pardon
To some unbrib'd vainglory – if his majesty
Shall taste a change of fate, his liberty
Shall meet no articles. If I fall, falling
So bravely, I refer me to his pleasure
Without condition; and for this dear favour,
Say, if not countermanded, I will cease
Hostility, unless provok'd.

MARCHMOUNT. This answer
We shall relate unpartially.

DURHAM. With favour,

---

32 *fishgarths*: fish farms. There was a salmon fishing industry at Berwick.
34 *present*: immediately.
38 *sensible*: deeply felt.
39 *unfellow'd*: unparalleled.
40 *gentle*: noble.
42 *stranger*: foreign.
43 *compeer*: equal.
51 *unbrib'd vainglory*: legitimate boasting.
53 *meet no articles*: not be subject to any conditions.
54 *bravely*: gloriously (because at a king's hand).
55 *dear*: precious.

Pray have a little patience. – [*Aside to* SURREY] Sir, you find
By these gay flourishes how wearied travail
Inclines to willing rest; here's but a prologue,
However confidently utter'd, meant
For some ensuing acts of peace. Consider
The time of year, unseasonableness of weather,
Charge, barrenness of profit, and occasion
Presents itself for honourable treaty,
Which we may make good use of. I will back,
As sent from you in point of noble gratitude
Unto King James, with these his heralds. You
Shall shortly hear from me, my lord, for order
Of breathing or proceeding; and King Henry,
Doubt not, will thank the service.

SURREY. To your wisdom,
Lord Bishop, I refer it.

DURHAM. Be it so then. –

SURREY. Heralds, accept this chain and these few crowns.

MARCHMOUNT. Our duty, noble general.

DURHAM. In part
Of retribution for such princely love,
My lord the general is pleas'd to show
The king your master his sincerest zeal
By further treaty, by no common man;
I will myself return with you.

SURREY. Y'oblige
My faithfullest affections t'ye, Lord Bishop.

MARCHMOUNT. All happiness attend your lordship.

[*Exeunt* DURHAM *and Heralds.*]

SURREY. Come, friends
And fellow soldiers; we, I doubt, shall meet
No enemies but woods and hills to fight with.

---

65 *Charge*: expense.
67 *back*: return.
71 *breathing*: pausing.
72–3 See Textual Notes, p. 345.
75 *Our duty*: we offer our respect.
76 *retribution*: repayment.
80 *oblige*: bind.
83 *doubt*: suspect.

Then 'twere as good to feed and sleep at home;
We may be free from danger, not secure.
Exeunt all.

SCENE II

Enter [PERKIN] WARBECK *and* FRION.

WARBECK. Frion, O Frion, all my hopes of glory
Are at a stand! The Scottish king grows dull,
Frosty and wayward, since this Spanish agent
Hath mix'd discourses with him. They are private;
I am not call'd to counsel now. Confusion
On all his crafty shrugs! I feel the fabric
Of my designs are tottering.
FRION. Henry's policies
Stir with too many engines.
WARBECK. Let his mines,
Shap'd in the bowels of the earth, blow up
Works rais'd for my defence, yet can they never
Toss into air the freedom of my birth,
Or disavow my blood, Plantagenet's!
I am my father's son still. But, O Frion,
When I bring into count with my disasters
My wife's compartnership, my Kate's, my life's,
Then, then my frailty feels an earthquake. Mischief
Damn Henry's plots, I will be England's king,
Or let my aunt of Burgundy report
My fall in the attempt deserv'd our ancestors!
FRION. You grow too wild in passion; if you will
Appear a prince indeed, confine your will
To moderation.
WARBECK. What a saucy rudeness
Prompts this distrust! If, if I will appear!

---

4 *are private*: meet privately.
6 *fabric*: building; the following verb is attracted to the intervening plural noun *designs*.
8 *engines*: plots, contrivances.
mines: underground tunnels packed with explosives.
12 *disavow*: repudiate.
19 *deserv'd*: was worthy of.

Appear a prince! Death throttle such deceits
Even in their birth of utterance; curs'd cozenage
Of trust! Ye make me mad; 'twere best, it seems,
That I should turn impostor to myself,
Be mine own counterfeit, belie the truth
Of my dear mother's womb, the sacred bed
Of a prince murder'd, and a living baffl'd!

FRION. Nay, if you have no ears to hear, I have
No breath to spend in vain.

WARBECK. Sir, sir, take heed!
Gold, and the promise of promotion, rarely
Fail in temptation.

FRION. Why to me this?

WARBECK. Nothing.
Speak what you will; we are not sunk so low
But your advice may piece again the heart
Which many cares have broken. You were wont
In all extremities to talk of comfort;
Have ye none left now? I'll not interrupt ye.
Good, bear with my distractions! If King James
Denies us dwelling here, next whither must I?
I prithee be not angry.

FRION. Sir, I told ye
Of letters, come from Ireland, how the Cornish
Stomach their last defeat, and humbly sue
That with such forces as you could partake
You would in person land in Cornwall, where
Thousands will entertain your title gladly.

WARBECK. Let me embrace thee, hug thee! Thou'st reviv'd
My comforts! If my cousin king will fail,
Our cause will never.

---

25 *cozenage*: deception.

30 *a prince . . . baffl'd*: Warbeck refers to himself as the disgraced prince; the murdered prince is Edward, his companion in the Tower of London.

33–4 *Gold . . . temptation*: a bitter hint that Warbeck now distrusts Frion's loyalty.

36 *piece*: put together.

40 *Good*: good sir.

44 *Stomach*: resent.

45 *partake*: raise.

47 *entertain*: accept.

Enter [JOHN A-WATER,] HERON, ASTLEY, [*and*] SKELTON.

Welcome, my tried friends.
You keep your brains awake in our defence. –
Frion, advise with them of these affairs,
In which be wondrous secret. I will listen
What else concerns us here; be quick and wary.
Exit WARBECK.

ASTLEY. Ah, sweet young prince! Secretary, my fellow councillors and I have consulted, and jump all in one opinion directly, that if these Scotch garboils do not fadge to our minds, we will pell-mell run amongst the Cornish choughs presently, and in a trice.

SKELTON. 'Tis but going to sea and leaping ashore, cut ten or twelve thousand unnecessary throats, fire seven or eight towns, take half a dozen cities, get into the market-place, crown him Richard the Fourth, and the business is finish'd.

A-WATER. I grant ye, quoth I, so far forth as men may do, no more than men may do; for it is good to consider, when consideration may be to the purpose. Otherwise still you shall pardon me; little said is soon amended.

FRION. Then you conclude the Cornish action
surest?

HERON. We do so, and doubt not but to thrive abundantly. Ho, my masters, had we known of the commotion when we set sail out of Ireland, the land had been ours ere this time.

SKELTON. Pish, pish, 'tis but forbearing being an earl or a duke a month or two longer; I say, and say it again, if the work go not on apace, let me never see new fashion more. I warrant ye, I

---

50 See Textual Notes, p. 345.
57 *jump*: agree.
directly: precisely.
57–8 *these . . . minds*: these Scottish commotions do not fall out as we wish. See Textual Notes, p. 345.
59 *choughs*: (1) red-billed crows (a species common in Cornwall), (2) rustics (chuffs).

warrant ye, we will have it so, and so it shall be.

ASTLEY. This is but a cold phlegmatic country, not stirring enough for men of spirit; give me the heart of England for my money.

SKELTON. A man may batten there in a week only with hot loaves and butter, and a lusty cup of muscadine and sugar at breakfast, though he make never a meal all the month after.

A-WATER. Surely, when I bore office, I found by experience that to be much troublesome was to be much wise and busy. I have observ'd how filching and bragging has been the best service in these last wars, and therefore conclude peremptorily on the design in England. If things and things may fall out as who can tell what or how, but the end will show it.

FRION. Resolv'd like men of judgement! Here to linger
More time is but to lose it. Cheer the prince
And haste him on to this; on this depends
Fame in success, or glory in our ends.

Exeunt all.

SCENE III

Enter KING JAMES; DURHAM *and* HIALAS *on either side.*

HIALAS. France, Spain, and Germany combine a league
Of amity with England; nothing wants

---

85 *batten*: grow fat.
87 *muscadine*: muscatel wine.
93 *conclude*: come to an opinion.
94–5 See Additional Notes, p. 355.
96 *but*: only.
1–4 *France . . . Henry*: Ford repeats Gainsford's confused reference to the Holy League organised by Ferdinand of Spain for the defence of Italy against the French, which Henry joined in 1496.

For settling peace through Christendom but love
Between the British monarchs, James and Henry.
DURHAM. The English merchants, sir, have been receiv'd
With general procession into Antwerp;
The Emperor confirms the combination.
HIALAS. The King of Spain resolves a marriage
For Catherine his daughter with Prince Arthur.
DURHAM. France courts this holy contract.
HIALAS. What can hinder
A quietness in England –
DURHAM. But your suffrage
To such a silly creature, mighty sir,
As is but in effect an apparition,
A shadow, a mere trifle?
HIALAS. To this union
The good of both the church and commonwealth
Invite ye.
DURHAM. To this unity, a mystery
Of providence points out a greater blessing
For both these nations than our human reason
Can search into. King Henry hath a daughter,
The Princess Margaret. I need not urge
What honour, what felicity can follow
On such affinity 'twixt two Christian kings
Inleagu'd by ties of blood; but sure I am,
If you, sir, ratify the peace propos'd,
I dare both motion and effect this marriage
For weal of both the kingdoms.
JAMES. Dar'st thou, Lord Bishop?
DURHAM. Put it to trial, royal James, by sending
Some noble personage to the English court

5–6 *The . . . Antwerp*: trade relations with Flanders had been disrupted by the Emperor Maximilian I's support for Warbeck (cf. I.i.123).
7 *combination*: treaty.
8 *resolves*: decides on.
10–11 See Textual Notes, p. 345.
11 *suffrage*: approval.
13 *apparition*: ghostly sham.
16 *To*: in addition to.
19–26 See Additional Notes, p. 355.
23 *Inleagu'd*: allied.
25 *motion*: propose.
26 *weal*: good.

By way of embassy.
HIALAS. Part of the business
Shall suit my mediation.
JAMES. Well, what Heaven
Hath pointed out to be, must be; you two
Are ministers, I hope, of blessed fate.
But herein only I will stand acquitted;
No blood of innocents shall buy my peace.
For Warbeck, as you nick him, came to me
Commended by the states of Christendom,
A prince, though in distress; his fair demeanour,
Lovely behaviour, unappalled spirit,
Spoke him not base in blood, however clouded.
The brute beasts have both rocks and caves to
fly to,
And men the altars of the church. To us
He came for refuge; kings come near in nature
Unto the gods in being touch'd with pity.
Yet, noble friends, his mixture with our blood,
Even with our own, shall no way interrupt
A general peace; only I will dismiss him
From my protection, throughout my dominions
In safety, but not ever to return.
HIALAS. You are a just king.
DURHAM. Wise, and herein happy.
JAMES. Nor will we dally in affairs of weight.
Huntly, Lord Bishop, shall with you to England,
Ambassador from us; we will throw down
Our weapons; peace on all sides now! Repair
Unto our council; we will soon be with you.
HIALAS. Delay shall question no dispatch; Heaven
crown it.
Exeunt DURHAM *and* HIALAS.

---

29 *Part of*: a share in.
35 *nick*: nickname.
36 *states*: great princes.
38 *Lovely*: affectionate.
41 *altars . . . church*: right to claim sanctuary in a church.
44 *mixture with our blood*: by Warbeck's marriage to Katherine.
55 *question no dispatch*: not put a prompt settlement into jeopardy. See Textual Notes, p. 345.

JAMES. A league with Ferdinand, a marriage
With English Margaret, a free release
From restitution for the late affronts,
Cessation from hostility! And all
For Warbeck not deliver'd, but dismiss'd!
We could not wish it better. – Dalyell!

Enter DALYELL.

DALYELL. Here, sir.
JAMES. Are Huntly and his daughter sent for?
DALYELL. Sent for
And come, my lord.
JAMES. Say to the English prince,
We want his company.
DALYELL. He is at hand, sir.

Enter [PERKIN] WARBECK, KATHERINE, JANE, FRION, HERON, SKELTON, [JOHN A-WATER,] ASTLEY.

JAMES. Cousin, our bounty, favours, gentleness,
Our benefits, the hazards of our person,
Our people's lives, our land, hath evidenc'd
How much we have engag'd on your behalf.
How trivial and how dangerous our hopes
Appear, how fruitless our attempts in war,
How windy (rather smoky) your assurance
Of party shows, we might in vain repeat.
But now obedience to the mother church,
A father's care upon his country's weal,
The dignity of state, directs our wisdom
To seal an oath of peace through Christendom,
To which we are sworn already. 'Tis you
Must only seek new fortunes in the world,
And find an harbour elsewhere. As I promis'd
On your arrival, you have met no usage
Deserves repentance in your being here;

---

58 *affronts*: hostilities.
62–3 See Textual Notes, p. 345.
64 See Textual Notes, p. 345.
72 *party shows*: demonstrations of political support.
73 *obedience . . . church*: the Borgia Pope, Alexander VI, was canvassing support for the Holy League.
78 *only*: alone.

But yet I must live master of mine own.
However, what is necessary for you
At your departure I am well content
You be accommodated with, provided
Delay prove not my enemy.

WARBECK. It shall not,
Most glorious prince. The fame of my designs
Soars higher than report of ease and sloth
Can aim at. I acknowledge all your favours,
Boundless and singular; am only wretched
In words as well as means to thank the grace
That flow'd so liberally. Two empires firmly
You're lord of: Scotland and Duke Richard's
heart.
My claim to mine inheritance shall sooner
Fail than my life to serve you, best of kings.
And witness Edward's blood to me, I am
More loth to part with such a great example
Of virtue than all other mere respects.
But, sir, my last suit is, you will not force
From me what you have given, this chaste lady,
Resolv'd on all extremes.

KATHERINE. I am your wife;
No human power can or shall divorce
My faith from duty.

WARBECK. Such another treasure
The earth is bankrupt of.

JAMES. I gave her, cousin,
And must avow the gift; will add withal
A furniture becoming her high birth
And unsuspected constancy; provide
For your attendance. We will part good friends.

Exeunt KING [JAMES] *and* DALYELL.

---

88 *report of*: (my) reputation for.
96 *Edward's*: Edward IV's.
98 *mere*: insignificant.
101 *Resolv'd on all extremes*: determined to face all extremities.
106 *furniture*: provision.
107 *unsuspected*: free from all suspicion.
108 *your attendance*: servants to attend you. See Textual Notes, p. 345.

WARBECK. The Tudor hath been cunning in his plots;
His Fox of Durham would not fail at last.
But what? Our cause and courage are our own.
Be men, my friends, and let our cousin king
See how we follow fate as willingly
As malice follows us. You're all resolv'd
For the west parts of England?
ALL. Cornwall, Cornwall!
FRION. The inhabitants expect you daily.
WARBECK. Cheerfully
Draw all our ships out of the harbour, friends;
Our time of stay doth seem too long, we must
Prevent intelligence; about it suddenly.
ALL. A prince, a prince, a prince!
Exeunt [HERON, SKELTON, ASTLEY, *and* JOHN A-WATER].
WARBECK. Dearest, admit not into thy pure thoughts
The least of scruples, which may charge their softness
With burden of distrust. Should I prove wanting
To noblest courage now, here were the trial.
But I am perfect, sweet; I fear no change,
More than thy being partner in my sufferance.
KATHERINE. My fortunes, sir, have arm'd me to encounter
What chance soe'er they meet with. – Jane, 'tis fit
Thou stay behind, for whither wilt thou wander?
JANE. Never till death will I forsake my mistress,
Nor then, in wishing to die with ye gladly.
KATHERINE. Alas, good soul!
FRION. Sir, to your aunt of Burgundy
I will relate your present undertakings;
From her expect on all occasions welcome.
You cannot find me idle in your services.

---

119 *Prevent intelligence*: forestall the news of our coming.
suddenly: at once.
120 See Textual Notes, p. 345.
125 *perfect*: not lacking in courage.
126 *More*: other.
sufferance: suffering.

WARBECK. Go, Frion, go! Wise men know how to soothe
Adversity, not serve it. Thou hast waited
Too long on expectation; never yet
Was any nation read of so besotted
In reason as to adore the setting sun.
Fly to the Archduke's court; say to the duchess,
Her nephew, with fair Katherine his wife,
Are on their expectation to begin
The raising of an empire. If they fail,
Yet the report will never. Farewell, Frion.
Exit FRION.
This man, Kate, has been true, though now of late
I fear too much familiar with the Fox.

Enter HUNTLY *and* DALYELL.

HUNTLY. I come to take my leave. You need not doubt
My interest in this sometime child of mine;
She's all yours now, good sir. – O poor lost creature,
Heaven guard thee with much patience! If thou canst
Forget thy title to old Huntly's family,
As much of peace will settle in thy mind
As thou canst wish to taste, but in thy grave.
[*Weeps.*]
Accept my tears yet, prithee; they are tokens
Of charity, as true as of affection.
KATHERINE. This is the cruell'st farewell!
HUNTLY. Love, young gentleman,
This model of my griefs. She calls you husband;
Then be not jealous of a parting kiss,
It is a father's not a lover's off'ring. –
Take it, my last. [*Kisses her*] I am too much a child.

---

137 *waited (on)*: served, attended.
145 *report*: fame (of the attempt).
151 *with*: by giving you.
155–6 *tokens . . . affection*: as true tokens of pitiful love as they are of paternal affection.
158 *model*: imitation, epitome.

Exchange of passion is to little use.
So I should grow too foolish. Goodness guide
thee! *Exit* HUNTLY.
KATHERINE. Most miserable daughter! Have you
aught
To add, sir, to our sorrows?
DALYELL. I resolve,
Fair lady, with your leave, to wait on all
Your fortunes in my person, if your lord
Vouchsafe me entertainment.
WARBECK. We will be bosom friends, most noble
Dalyell,
For I accept this tender of your love
Beyond ability of thanks to speak it. –
Clear thy drown'd eyes, my fairest; time and
industry
Will show us better days, or end the worst.
Exeunt all.

SCENE IV

Enter OXFORD *and* DAUBENEY.

OXFORD. No news from Scotland yet, my lord?
DAUBENEY. Not any
But what King Henry knows himself. I thought
Our armies should have march'd that way; his
mind,
It seems, is alter'd.
OXFORD. Victory attends
His standard everywhere.
DAUBENEY. Wise princes, Oxford,
Fight not alone with forces. Providence
Directs and tutors strength; else elephants
And barbed horses might as well prevail
As the most subtle stratagems of war.

---

162 *passion*: grief.
163 *So*: thus.
168 *entertainment*: acceptance.
6 *Providence*: foresight.
8 *barbed*: armoured.

OXFORD. The Scottish king show'd more than common bravery
In proffer of a combat hand to hand
With Surrey.
DAUBENEY. And but show'd it. Northern bloods
Are gallant being fir'd, but the cold climate,
Without good store of fuel, quickly freezeth
The glowing flames.
OXFORD. Surrey, upon my life,
Would not have shrunk an hair's-breadth.
DAUBENEY. May he forfeit
The honour of an English name and nature
Who would not have embrac'd it with a greediness
As violent as hunger runs to food.
'Twas an addition any worthy spirit
Would covet next to immortality,
Above all joys of life. We all miss'd shares
In that great opportunity.

Enter KING HENRY *and* URSWICK, *whispering*.

OXFORD. The king!
See, he comes smiling.
DAUBENEY. O, the game runs smooth
On his side, then, believe it; cards well shuffled
And dealt with cunning bring some gamester thrift,
But others must rise losers.
HENRY. The train takes?
URSWICK. Most prosperously.
HENRY. I knew it should not miss.
He fondly angles who will hurl his bait
Into the water 'cause the fish at first
Plays round about the line and dares not bite. –
Lords, we may reign your king yet. Daubeney, Oxford,

---

20 *addition*: mark of honour added to a coat of arms.
23–4 See Textual Notes, p. 345.
26 *thrift*: success.
27 *train takes*: lure works; a metaphor from drag-hunting.
29 *fondly*: foolishly.

Urswick, must Perkin wear the crown?
DAUBENEY. A slave!
OXFORD. A vagabond!
URSWICK. A glow-worm!
HENRY. Now, if Frion,
His practis'd politician, wear a brain
Of proof, King Perkin will in progress ride
Through all his large dominions. Let us meet him
And tender homage, ha, sirs? Liegemen ought
To pay their fealty.
DAUBENEY. Would the rascal were,
With all his rabble, within twenty miles
Of London.
HENRY. Further off is near enough
To lodge him in his home. I'll wager odds
Surrey and all his men are either idle
Or hasting back; they have not work, I doubt,
To keep them busy.
DAUBENEY. 'Tis a strange conceit, sir.
HENRY. Such voluntary favours as our people
In duty aid us with, we never scatter'd
On cobweb parasites, or lavish'd out
In riot or a needless hospitality.
No undeserving favourite doth boast
His issues from our treasury; our charge
Flows through all Europe, proving us but steward
Of every contribution, which provides
Against the creeping canker of disturbance.
Is it not rare, then, in this toil of state
Wherein we are embark'd, with breach of sleep,

---

36 *proof*: tested and proven ability.
progress: royal procession.
39 *fealty*: homage.
rascal: (1) low-bred fellow, (2) young or inferior stag (leading to the hunting metaphor in 42).
42 *lodge*: discover (the lair of a buck).
44 *doubt*: suspect.
45 *conceit*: idea.
46 *favours*: i.e. sums of money.
49 *riot*: extravagant living.
51 *charge*: expenditure.
55 *rare*: extraordinary.

Cares, and the noise of trouble, that our mercy
Returns nor thanks nor comfort? Still the west
Murmur and threaten innovation,
Whisper our government tyrannical,
Deny us what is ours, nay, spurn their lives,
Of which they are but owners by our gift.
It must not be.
OXFORD. It must not, should not.

Enter a POST.

HENRY. So then.
To whom?
POST. This packet to your sacred majesty.
HENRY. Sirrah, attend without.
[*Exit the* POST.]
OXFORD. News from the north, upon my life.
DAUBENEY. Wise Henry
Divines aforehand of events; with him
Attempts and execution are one act.
HENRY. Urswick, thine ear. Frion is caught, the man
Of cunning is outreach'd; we must be safe.
Should reverend Morton our archbishop move
To a translation higher yet, I tell thee
My Durham owns a brain deserves that see.
He's nimble in his industry, and mounting.
Thou hear'st me?
URSWICK. And conceive your Highness fitly.
HENRY. Daubeney and Oxford, since our army stands
Entire, it were a weakness to admit
The rust of laziness to eat amongst them.
Set forward toward Salisbury; the plains

---

59 *innovation*: revolution. The word has five syllables.
63 s.d. POST: courier. See Textual Notes, p. 345.
63–4 See Textual Notes, p. 345.
71 *Morton*: John Morton, Henry's Chancellor of the Exchequer and Archbishop of Canterbury from 1486 to 1500.
72 *translation . . . yet*: promotion to the Papacy, or to Heaven (by death).
73 *see*: office of a bishop, or, as here, archbishop.
74 *mounting*: ambitious.
75 *conceive*: understand.

Are most commodious for their exercise.
Ourself will take a muster of them there,
And or disband them with reward or else
Dispose as best concerns us.

DAUBENEY. Salisbury?
Sir, all is peace at Salisbury.

HENRY. Dear friend,
The charge must be our own; we would a little
Partake the pleasure with our subjects' ease. –
Shall I entreat your loves?

OXFORD. Command our lives.

HENRY. You're men know how to do, not to forethink.
My bishop is a jewel tried and perfect;
A jewel, lords. The post who brought these letters
Must speed another to the Mayor of Exeter. –
Urswick, dismiss him not.

URSWICK. He waits your pleasure.

HENRY. Perkin a king? A king!

URSWICK. My gracious lord?

HENRY. Thoughts busied in the sphere of royalty
Fix not on creeping worms without their stings,
Mere excrements of earth. The use of time
Is thriving safety, and a wise prevention
Of ills expected. We're resolv'd for Salisbury.
Exeunt all.

SCENE V

A general shout within. Enter [PERKIN] WARBECK, DALYELL, KATHERINE, *and* JANE.

WARBECK. After so many storms as wind and seas
Have threaten'd to our weather-beaten ships,
At last, sweet fairest, we are safe arriv'd

---

81 *take a muster*: conduct a review.
85 *charge*: responsibility.
96 *excrements*: superfluous outgrowths.
96–7 *use . . . Is*: proper management of time results in.

On our dear mother earth, ingrateful only
To Heaven and us in yielding sustenance
To sly usurpers of our throne and right.
These general acclamations are an omen
Of happy process to their welcome lord.
They flock in troops, and from all parts with wings
Of duty fly, to lay their hearts before us.
Unequall'd pattern of a matchless wife,
How fares my dearest yet?

KATHERINE. Confirm'd in health,
By which I may the better undergo
The roughest face of change. But I shall learn
Patience to hope, since silence courts affliction,
For comforts to this truly noble gentleman –
Rare unexampl'd pattern of a friend! –
And my beloved Jane, the willing follower
Of all misfortunes.

DALYELL. Lady, I return
But barren crops of early protestations,
Frost-bitten in the spring of fruitless hopes.

JANE. I wait but as the shadow to the body;
For, madam, without you let me be nothing.

WARBECK. None talk of sadness; we are on the way
Which leads to victory. Keep cowards thoughts
With desperate sullenness! The lion faints not,
Lock'd in a grate, but, loose, disdains all force
Which bars his prey; and we are lion-hearted,
Or else no king of beasts. (*Another shout*) Hark, how they shout

---

8 *process*: progress.
14–16 *I . . . comforts*: since they silently (uncomplainingly) attend me in my affliction, I will teach (*learn*) myself to hope patiently, so that I can administer comfort.
20 *early protestations*: premature avowals.
22 *wait*: attend.
25 *Keep*: dwell.
26 *desperate sullenness*: despairing melancholy.
27 *grate*: cage.
28 *bars*: bars him from.
29 See Textual Notes, p. 345.

Triumphant in our cause! Bold confidence
Marches on bravely, cannot quake at danger.

Enter SKELTON.

SKELTON. Save King Richard the Fourth; save thee, king of hearts! The Cornish blades are men of mettle; have proclaim'd through Bodmin and the whole county my sweet prince monarch of England. Four thousand tall yeomen, with bow and sword, already vow to live and die at the foot of King Richard.

Enter ASTLEY.

ASTLEY. The mayor, our fellow counsellor, is servant for an emperor. Exeter is appointed for the rendezvous, and nothing wants to victory but courage and resolution. *Sigillatum et datum Septembris, anno regni regis primo, et cetera; confirmatum est.* All's cock-sure.

WARBECK. To Exeter, to Exeter, march on!
Commend us to our people; we in person
Will lend them double spirits. Tell them so.

SKELTON *and* ASTLEY. King Richard, King Richard!

[*Exeunt* SKELTON *and* ASTLEY.]

WARBECK. A thousand blessings guard our lawful arms!
A thousand horrors pierce our enemies' souls!
Pale fear unedge their weapons' sharpest points,
And when they draw their arrows to the head,
Numbness shall strike their sinews. Such advantage
Hath majesty in its pursuit of justice,

---

32 *Save*: God preserve.
33 *blades*: (1) fine fellows, (2) swords.
34 *mettle*: (1) courage, (2) metal.
Bodmin: Cornish town north-west of Plymouth. See Textual Notes, p. 345.
41 *wants*: is lacking.
42–4 *Sigillatum . . . est*: sealed and dated on September the tenth, in the first year of the king's reign, etc.; confirmed.
44 *cock-sure*: absolutely certain.

That on the proppers-up of Truth's old throne
It both enlightens counsel and gives heart
To execution; whiles the throats of traitors
Lie bare before our mercy. O divinity
Of royal birth! How it strikes dumb the tongues
Whose prodigality of breath is brib'd
By trains to greatness! Princes are but men,
Distinguish'd by the fineness of their frailty.
Yet not so gross in beauty of the mind;
For there's a fire more sacred purifies
The dross of mixture. Herein stands the odds:
Subjects are men on earth; kings, men and gods.
Exeunt all.

ACT V

SCENE I

Enter KATHERINE *and* JANE *in riding-suits, with one* SERVANT.

KATHERINE. It is decreed; and we must yield to fate,
Whose angry justice, though it threaten ruin,
Contempt, and poverty, is all but trial
Of a weak woman's constancy in suffering.
Here in a stranger's and an enemy's land,
Forsaken and unfurnish'd of all hopes
But such as wait on misery, I range

---

57 *execution*: action.
61 *trains to greatness*: great men's crowds of servants.
62 *frailty*: mortal condition.
63 *gross*: common.
64–5 *purifies . . . mixture*: purges the worthless matter (ordinary humanity) of its contaminating elements.
65 *odds*: difference.
7 *range*: wander about.

To meet affliction whereso'er I tread.
My train and pomp of servants is reduc'd
To one kind gentlewoman and this groom. –
Sweet Jane, now whither must we?
JANE. To your ships,
Dear lady, and turn home.
KATHERINE. Home! I have none.
Fly thou to Scotland; thou hast friends will weep
For joy to bid thee welcome. But, O Jane,
My Jane, my friends are desperate of comfort,
As I must be of them; the common charity,
Good people's alms and prayers of the gentle,
Is the revenue must support my state.
As for my native country, since it once
Saw me a princess in the height of greatness
My birth allow'd me, here I make a vow
Scotland shall never see me, being fallen
Or lessen'd in my fortunes. Never, Jane,
Never to Scotland more will I return.
I could be England's queen – a glory, Jane,
I never fawn'd on – yet the king who gave me
Hath sent me with my husband from his presence;
Deliver'd us suspected to his nation;
Render'd us spectacles to time and pity.
And is it fit I should return to such
As only listen after our descent
From happiness enjoyed to misery
Expected, though uncertain? Never, never!
Alas, why dost thou weep, and that poor creature
Wipe his wet cheeks too? Let me feel alone
Extremities, who know to give them harbour.
Nor thou nor he has cause. You may live safely.

---

15 *desperate*: without hope.
17 *gentle*: possibly 'kind-hearted'.
18 *state*: (1) condition, (2) 'greatness'.
25 See Textual Notes, p. 345.
26 *gave me*: i.e. in marriage.
28 *his nation*: Warbeck's England.
31 *listen after*: are eager to hear of.

JANE. There is no safety whiles your dangers, madam,
Are every way apparent.
SERVANT. Pardon, lady;
I cannot choose but show my honest heart;
You were ever my good lady.
KATHERINE. O dear souls,
Your shares in grief are too, too much!

Enter DALYELL.

DALYELL. I bring,
Fair princess, news of further sadness yet
Than your sweet youth hath been acquainted with.
KATHERINE. Not more, my lord, than I can welcome. Speak it;
The worst, the worst I look for.
DALYELL. All the Cornish
At Exeter were by the citizens
Repuls'd, encounter'd by the Earl of Devonshire
And other worthy gentlemen of the country.
Your husband march'd to Taunton, and was there
Affronted by King Henry's chamberlain,
The king himself in person, with his army,
Advancing nearer to renew the fight
On all occasions. But the night before
The battles were to join, your husband, privately,
Accompanied with some few horse, departed
From out the camp, and posted none knows whither.
KATHERINE. Fled without battle given?
DALYELL. Fled, but follow'd
By Daubeney, all his parties left to taste
King Henry's mercy – for to that they yielded –

46–50 *All . . . Taunton*: see Additional Notes, p. 355.
51 *Affronted*: confronted.
chamberlain: Lord Daubeney.
55 *battles*: armies.
59 *parties*: supporters.

Victorious without bloodshed.
KATHERINE. O, my sorrows!
If both our lives had prov'd the sacrifice
To Henry's tyranny, we had fall'n like princes,
And robb'd him of the glory of his pride.
DALYELL. Impute it not to faintness or to weakness
Of noble courage, lady, but foresight;
For by some secret friend he had intelligence
Of being bought and sold by his base followers.
Worse yet remains untold.
KATHERINE. No, no, it cannot.
DALYELL. I fear you are betray'd. The Earl of Oxford
Runs hot in your pursuit.
KATHERINE. He shall not need;
We'll run as hot in resolution, gladly
To make the earl our jailor.
JANE. Madam, madam,
They come, they come!

Enter OXFORD, *with followers.*

DALYELL. Keep back, or he who dares
Rudely to violate the law of honour
Runs on my sword.
KATHERINE. Most noble sir, forbear. –
What reason draws you hither, gentlemen?
Whom seek ye?
OXFORD. All stand off. With favour, lady,
From Henry, England's king, I would present
Unto the beauteous princess, Katherine Gordon,
The tender of a gracious entertainment.
KATHERINE. We are that princess, whom your master-king
Pursues with reaching arms to draw into
His power. Let him use his tyranny,

73–4 See Textual Notes, p. 345.
75 *Rudely*: discourteously.
81 *tender*: offer.
entertainment: welcome.

We shall not be his subjects.
OXFORD. My commission
Extends no further, excellentest lady,
Than to a service; 'tis King Henry's pleasure
That you, and all that have relation t'ye,
Be guarded as becomes your birth and greatness.
For rest assur'd, sweet princess, that not aught
Of what you do call yours shall find disturbance,
Or any welcome other than what suits
Your high condition.
KATHERINE. By what title, sir,
May I acknowledge you?
OXFORD. Your servant, lady,
Descended from the line of Oxford's earls,
Inherits what his ancestors before him
Were owners of.
KATHERINE. Your king is herein royal,
That by a peer so ancient in desert
As well as blood commands us to his presence.
OXFORD. Invites ye, princess, not commands.
KATHERINE. Pray use
Your own phrase as you list; to your protection
Both I and mine submit.
OXFORD. There's in your number
A nobleman whom fame hath bravely spoken.
To him the king my master bade me say
How willingly he courts his friendship; far
From an enforcement more than what in terms
Of courtesy so great a prince may hope for.
DALYELL. My name is Dalyell.
OXFORD. 'Tis a name hath won
Both thanks and wonder from report. My lord,
The court of England emulates your merit,
And covets to embrace ye.
DALYELL. I must wait on

85–6 See Textual Notes, p. 345.
93 *condition*: birth, rank.
103 *fame hath bravely spoken*: public report has spoken of highly.
106 See Textual Notes, p. 345.
110 *emulates*: is jealous of.

The princess in her fortunes.
OXFORD. Will you please,
Great lady, to set forward?
KATHERINE. Being driven
By fate, it were in vain to strive with Heaven.
Exeunt all.

SCENE II

Enter KING HENRY, SURREY, URSWICK, *and a guard of Soldiers.*

HENRY. The counterfeit, King Perkin, is escap'd;
Escape so let him. He is hedg'd too fast
Within the circuit of our English pale
To steal out of our ports, or leap the walls
Which guard our land; the seas are rough, and wider
Than his weak arms can tug with. Surrey, henceforth
Your king may reign in quiet. Turmoils past,
Like some unquiet dream, have rather busied
Our fancy than affrighted rest of state.
But, Surrey, why, in articling a peace
With James of Scotland, was not restitution
Of losses, which our subjects did sustain
By the Scotch inroads, question'd?
SURREY. Both demanded
And urg'd, my lord; to which the king replied,
In modest merriment but smiling earnest,
How that our master Henry was much abler
To bear the detriments than he repay them.
HENRY. The young man, I believe, spake honest truth;

3 *pale*: territory.
9 *fancy*: imagination.
rest of state: national peace.
10 *articling a peace*: arranging a peace treaty.
17 *detriments*: losses.
18 *young*: James was twenty-five.

He studies to be wise betimes. Has, Urswick,
Sir Rhys ap Thomas and Lord Brooke our Steward
Return'd the western gentlemen full thanks
From us for their tried loyalties?

URSWICK. They have;
Which, as if health and life had reign'd amongst 'em,
With open hearts they joyfully receiv'd.

HENRY. Young Buckingham is a fair-natur'd prince,
Lovely in hopes, and worthy of his father.
Attended by an hundred knights and squires
Of special name, he tender'd humble service,
Which we must ne'er forget. And Devonshire's wounds,
Though slight, shall find sound cure in our respect.

Enter DAUBENEY, *with* [PERKIN] WARBECK, HERON, JOHN A-WATER, ASTLEY, SKELTON.

DAUBENEY. Life to the king, and safety fix his throne!
I here present you, royal sir, a shadow
Of majesty, but in effect a substance
Of pity; a young man, in nothing grown
To ripeness but th'ambition of your mercy:
Perkin, the Christian world's strange wonder.

HENRY. Daubeney,
We observe no wonder. I behold, 'tis true,
An ornament of nature, fine and polish'd,

---

19 *betimes*: early in his life.
20 *Sir . . . Steward*: Thomas was a great Welsh magnate; for Brooke see the note to III.iv.92.
22 See Textual Notes, p. 345.
25 *Young Buckingham*: Edward Stafford, third Earl of Buckingham (1478–1521); his *father* (26) was executed by Richard III.
26 *Lovely in hopes*: of great promise.
28 *special*: distinguished.
30 *respect*: esteem.
34 *young man*: Warbeck was about thirty-four.
36–7 See Textual Notes, p. 345.

A handsome youth indeed, but not admire him.
How came he to thy hands?
DAUBENEY. From sanctuary
At Beaulieu, near Southhampton, register'd,
With these few followers, for persons privileg'd.
HENRY. I must not thank you, sir! You were to blame
To infringe the liberty of houses sacred.
Dare we be irreligious?
DAUBENEY. Gracious lord,
They voluntarily resign'd themselves
Without compulsion.
HENRY. So? 'Twas very well;
'Twas very, very well. – Turn now thine eyes,
Young man, upon thyself, and thy past actions!
What revels, in combustion through our kingdom,
A frenzy of aspiring youth hath danc'd,
Till, wanting breath, thy feet of pride have slipp'd
To break thy neck.
WARBECK. But not my heart; my heart
Will mount till every drop of blood be frozen
By death's perpetual winter. If the sun
Of majesty be darken'd, let the sun
Of life be hid from me, in an eclipse
Lasting and universal. Sir, remember
There was a shooting in of light when Richmond,
Not aiming at a crown, retir'd, and gladly,
For comfort to the Duke of Bretaine's court.
Richard, who sway'd the sceptre, was reputed
A tyrant then; yet then a dawning glimmer'd
To some few wand'ring remnants, promising day

---

39 *admire*: wonder at.
41 *Beaulieu*: a great Cistercian monastery in Hampshire. See Textual Notes, p. 345.
42 *for*: as being.
50 *combustion*: violent commotion.
59 *Richmond*: Henry IV's title before his defeat of Richard III.
60–1 *retir'd . . . court*: see Additional Notes, pp. 355–6. See Textual Notes, p. 345.

When first they ventur'd on a frightful shore
At Milford Haven –
DAUBENEY. Whither speeds his boldness?
Check his rude tongue, great sir!
HENRY. O, let him range.
The player's on the stage still, 'tis his part;
He does but act. What follow'd?
WARBECK. Bosworth Field;
Where, at an instant, to the world's amazement,
A morn to Richmond and a night to Richard
Appear'd at once. The tale is soon applied.
Fate, which crown'd these attempts when least assur'd,
Might have befriended others, like resolv'd.
HENRY. A pretty gallant! Thus your aunt of Burgundy,
Your duchess-aunt, inform'd her nephew; so,
The lesson, prompted and well conn'd, was moulded
Into familiar dialogue, oft rehears'd,
Till, learnt by heart, 'tis now receiv'd for truth.
WARBECK. Truth in her pure simplicity wants art
To put a feigned blush on. Scorn wears only
Such fashion as commends to gazers' eyes
Sad ulcerated novelty, far beneath
The sphere of majesty. In such a court,
Wisdom and gravity are proper robes

65–6 See Additional Notes, p. 356.
65 *frightful*: terrifying.
69 *Bosworth Field*: the battlefield near Leicester where Richmond defeated and killed Richard III.
72 *at once*: simultaneously.
77 *prompted*: by Margaret of Burgundy as teacher and stage prompter; a dual metaphor continued in *dialogue* and *rehears'd* (78).
conn'd: memorised.
78 *familiar*: (1) easily understood (by a pupil), (2) well-known (by an actor).
rehears'd: (1) repeated, (2) practised for stage performance.
80–1 *Truth . . . on*: Truth was often imaged as an unashamedly naked woman.
wants: lacks.
83 *Sad ulcerated novelty*: Warbeck means himself.

By which the sovereign is best distinguish'd
From zanies to his greatness.
HENRY. Sirrah, shift
Your antic pageantry, and now appear
In your own nature, or you'll taste the danger
Of fooling out of season.
WARBECK. I expect
No less than what severity calls justice,
And politicians safety; let such beg
As feed on alms. But if there can be mercy
In a protested enemy, then may it
Descend to these poor creatures, whose engagements
To th'bettering of their fortunes have incurr'd
A loss of all; to them, if any charity
Flow from some noble orator, in death
I owe the fee of thankfulness.
HENRY. So brave! –
What a bold knave is this! Which of these rebels
Has been the Mayor of Cork?
DAUBENEY. This wise formality. –
Kneel to the king, ye rascals! [*They kneel.*]
HENRY. Canst thou hope
A pardon, where thy guilt is so apparent?
A-WATER. Under your good favours, as men are men they may err. For I confess, respectively, in taking great parts, the one side prevailing, the other side must go down. Herein the point is clear, if the proverb hold that hanging goes by destiny, that it is to little purpose to say this thing or that shall be thus or thus; for as the fates will have it, so it must be, and who can help it?

---

87 *zanies to*: imitators of; from the name of the comic servant in the *commedia dell'arte*.
87–8 *shift . . . pageantry*: change the costume of your clownish play-acting.
94 *protested*: declared.
95 *engagements*: involvement (with me).
98 *orator*: advocate.
101 *wise formality*: pompous idiot.
105 *respectively*: respectfully.
108–9 *hanging . . . destiny*: see Tilley, W232.

DAUBENEY. O blockhead! Thou a privy councillor?
Beg life, and cry aloud, 'Heaven save King Henry!'

A-WATER. Every man knows what is best, as it happens. For my own part, I believe it is true, if I be not deceiv'd, that kings must be kings, and subjects subjects. But which is which, you shall pardon me for that. Whether we speak or hold our peace, all are mortal; no man knows his end.

HENRY. We trifle time with follies.

[HERON, A-WATER, ASTLEY, SKELTON.] Mercy, mercy!

HENRY. Urswick, command the dukeling and these fellows
To Digby, the Lieutenant of the Tower.
With safety let them be convey'd to London.
It is our pleasure no uncivil outrage,
Taunts or abuse be suffer'd to their persons;
They shall meet fairer law than they deserve.
Time may restore their wits, whom vain ambition
Hath many years distracted.

WARBECK. Noble thoughts
Meet freedom in captivity. – The Tower!
Our childhood's dreadful nursery!

HENRY. No more.

URSWICK. Come, come, you shall have leisure to bethink ye.

Exit URSWICK *with* PERKIN [WARBECK] *and his followers.*

HENRY. Was ever so much impudence in forgery?
The custom, sure, of being styl'd a king
Hath fasten'd in his thought that he is such.
But we shall teach the lad another language;
'Tis good we have him fast.

DAUBENEY. The hangman's physic

---

121 *trifle*: waste. See Textual Notes, p. 345.
123 *Digby*: Sir John Digby.
131 *Our*: either the royal plural, or Warbeck's recollection of his brother Edward's and his own imprisonment.
133 *forgery*: fraudulent deceit.
134 *styl'd*: called.
137 *physic*: medicine.

Will purge this saucy humour.
HENRY. Very likely;
Yet we could temper mercy with extremity,
Being not too far provok'd.

Enter OXFORD, KATHERINE *in her richest attire,* [DALYELL,] JANE, *and Attendants.*

OXFORD. Great sir, be pleas'd
With your accustom'd grace to entertain
The Princess Katherine Gordon.
HENRY. Oxford, herein
We must beshrew thy knowledge of our nature.
A lady of her birth and virtues could not
Have found us so unfurnish'd of good manners
As not, on notice given, to have met her
Half-way in point of love. – Excuse, fair cousin,
The oversight! [KATHERINE *goes to kneel.*]
O fie, you may not kneel;
'Tis most unfitting. First, vouchsafe this welcome,
A welcome to your own, for you shall find us
But guardian to your fortune and your honours.
KATHERINE. My fortunes and mine honours are weak champions,
As both are now befriended, sir; however,
Both bow before your clemency.
HENRY. Our arms
Shall circle them from malice. [*Embraces* KATHERINE] A sweet lady!
Beauty incomparable! Here lives majesty
At league with love.
KATHERINE. O sir, I have a husband!
HENRY. We'll prove your father, husband, friend, and servant;
Prove what you wish to grant us. – Lords, be careful

---

139 *temper*: admix.
extremity: extreme severity.
140 See Textual Notes, p. 345.
143 *beshrew*: blame.
149 *vouchsafe*: accept.

A patent presently be drawn for issuing
A thousand pounds from our exchequer yearly
During our cousin's life. – Our queen shall be
Your chief companion, our own court your home,
Our subjects all your servants.
KATHERINE. But my husband?
HENRY. By all descriptions, you are noble Dalyell,
Whose generous truth hath fam'd a rare observance!
We thank ye; 'tis a goodness gives addition
To every title boasted from your ancestry,
In all most worthy.
DALYELL. Worthier than your praises,
Right princely sir, I need not glory in.
HENRY. Embrace him, lords. –
[*The Lords embrace* DALYELL.]
[*To* KATHERINE]. Whoever calls you mistress
Is lifted in our charge; a goodlier beauty
Mine eyes yet ne'er encounter'd.
KATHERINE. Cruel misery
Of fate, what rests to hope for?
HENRY. Forward, lords,
To London. – Fair, ere long I shall present ye
With a glad object: peace, and Huntly's blessing.
Exeunt all.

---

160 *patent . . . drawn*: official document be prepared immediately.
166 *generous . . . observance*: noble fidelity has brought fame to your splendid and devoted service.
172 *lifted . . . charge*: raised up as an object of our special care.
176 *object*: sight.

SCENE III

Enter CONSTABLE *and Officers,* [PERKIN] WARBECK, URSWICK, *and* LAMBERT SIMNEL *like a falconer. A pair of stocks.*

CONSTABLE. Make room there! Keep off, I require ye, and none come within twelve foot of his majesty's new stocks, upon pain of displeasure. Bring forward the malefactors. Friend, you must to this gear, no remedy. Open the hole, and in with his legs; just in the middle hole, there, that hole.

[WARBECK *is put in the stocks.*]

Keep off, or I'll commit you all. Shall not a man in authority be obeyed? So, so there, 'tis as it should be. Put on the padlock, and give me the key; off, I say, keep off!

URSWICK. Yet, Warbeck, clear thy conscience. Thou hast tasted
King Henry's mercy liberally. The law
Has forfeited thy life; an equal jury
Have doom'd thee to the gallows. Twice, most wickedly,
Most desperately, hast thou escap'd the Tower,
Inveigling to thy party with thy witchcraft
Young Edward, Earl of Warwick, son to Clarence,
Whose head must pay the price of that attempt.
Poor gentleman; unhappy in his fate,
And ruin'd by thy cunning! So a mongrel
May pluck the true stag down. Yet, yet, confess
Thy parentage; for yet the king has mercy.

LAMBERT. You would be Dick the Fourth; very likely!
Your pedigree is publish'd; you are known

---

0 s.d. *falconer*: cf. I.i.64–6.
8 *commit*: imprison.
12 *Yet*: even now.
14 *equal*: impartial.
15–19 *Twice . . . attempt*: see Additional Notes, p. 356.

For Osbeck's son of Tournai, a loose runagate,
A landloper. Your father was a Jew,
Turn'd Christian merely to repair his miseries.
Where's now your kingship?

WARBECK. Baited to my death?
Intolerable cruelty! I laugh at
The Duke of Richmond's practice on my fortunes.
Possession of a crown ne'er wanted heralds.

LAMBERT. You will not know who I am?

URSWICK. Lambert Simnel,
Your predecessor in a dangerous uproar;
But, on submission, not alone receiv'd
To grace, but by the king vouchsaf'd his service.

LAMBERT. I would be Earl of Warwick; toil'd and ruffl'd
Against my master, leapt to catch the moon,
Vaunted my name Plantagenet, as you do.
An earl, forsooth! Whenas in truth I was,
As you are, a mere rascal. Yet his majesty,
A prince compos'd of sweetness – Heaven protect him! –
Forgave me all my villainies, repriev'd
The sentence of a shameful end, admitted
My surety of obedience to his service;
And I am now his falconer, live plenteously,
Eat from the king's purse, and enjoy the sweetness
Of liberty and favour, sleep securely.
And is not this now better than to buffet
The hangman's clutches, or to brave the cordage
Of a tough halter, which will break your neck?
So, then, the gallant totters. Prithee, Perkin,
Let my example lead thee. Be no longer
A counterfeit; confess, and hope for pardon!

---

26 *runagate*: vagabond.
27 *landloper*: wanderer.
29 *Baited*: tormented (like an animal).
31 *practice on* : intrigue against.
37 *ruffl'd*: fought.
44–5 *admitted My surety*: accepted my pledge.
49 *buffet*: beat against.
52 *totters*: swings, is hanged.

WARBECK. For pardon! Hold, my heart-strings,
whiles contempt
Of injuries, in scorn, may bid defiance
To this base man's foul language. Thou poor
vermin!
How dar'st thou creep so near me? Thou an
earl?
Why, thou enjoy'st as much of happiness
As all the swinge of slight ambition flew at.
A dunghill was thy cradle. So a puddle,
By virtue of the sunbeams, breathes a vapour
T'infect the purer air, which drops again
Into the muddy womb that first exhal'd it.
Bread and a slavish ease, with some assurance
From the base beadle's whip, crown'd all thy
hopes.
But, sirrah, ran there in thy veins one drop
Of such a royal blood as flows in mine,
Thou wouldst not change condition to be second
In England's state, without the crown itself!
Coarse creatures are incapable of excellence.
But let the world, as all to whom I am
This day a spectacle, to time deliver,
And by tradition fix posterity,
Without another chronicle than truth,
How constantly my resolution suffer'd
A martyrdom of majesty.

LAMBERT. He's past
Recovery; a Bedlam cannot cure him.

URSWICK. Away, inform the king of his behaviour.

---

56 *injuries*: calumnies.
60 *swinge*: impetus.
flew at: the image is of a hawk (a less than royal bird) hunting.
62 *breathes*: exhales.
66 *base beadle's whip*: the beadle was a minor official, one of whose duties was to punish petty offenders by flogging.
74 *by . . . posterity*: by handing down my story establish for posterity.
76 *constantly*: steadfastly.
78 *Bedlam*: hospital for the insane; cf. III.ii.6 and note.

LAMBERT. Perkin, beware the rope; the hangman's coming.

Exit [LAMBERT] SIMNEL.

URSWICK. If yet thou hast no pity of thy body,
Pity thy soul!

Enter KATHERINE, JANE, DALYELL, *and* OXFORD.

JANE. Dear lady!
OXFORD. Whither will ye,
Without respect of shame?
KATHERINE. Forbear me, sir,
And trouble not the current of my duty! –
O my lov'd lord! Can any scorn be yours
In which I have no interest? – Some kind hand
Lend me assistance, that I may partake
Th'infliction of this penance. – My life's dearest,
Forgive me; I have stay'd too long from tend'ring
Attendance on reproach, yet bid me welcome.
WARBECK. Great miracle of constancy! My miseries
Were never bankrupt of their confidence
In worst afflictions, till this; now I feel them.
Report and thy deserts, thou best of creatures,
Might to eternity have stood a pattern
For every virtuous wife, without this conquest.
Thou hast outdone belief; yet may their ruin
In after-marriages be never pitied
To whom thy story shall appear a fable.
Why wouldst thou prove so much unkind to greatness
To glorify thy vows by such a servitude?
I cannot weep, but trust me, dear, my heart
Is liberal of passion. – Harry Richmond!

---

80 See Textual Notes, p. 345.
83 *Without respect*: careless.
Forbear me: leave me alone.
84 *trouble*: disturb.
90 *reproach*: (your) disgrace.
93 See Textual Notes, p. 345.
94 *Report*: (your) fame.

A woman's faith hath robb'd thy fame of triumph.
OXFORD. Sirrah, leave off your juggling, and tie
up
The devil that ranges in your tongue.
URSWICK. Thus witches,
Possess'd, even to their deaths deluded, say
They have been wolves, and dogs, and sail'd
in egg-shells
Over the sea, and rid on fiery dragons;
Pass'd in the air more than a thousand miles
All in a night. The enemy of mankind
Is powerful but false, and falsehood confident.
OXFORD. Remember, lady, who you are; come
from
That impudent impostor.
KATHERINE. You abuse us!
For when the holy churchman join'd our hands,
Our vows were real then; the ceremony
Was not in apparition, but in act. –
Be what these people term thee, I am certain
Thou art my husband. No divorce in Heaven
Has been su'd out between us; 'tis injustice
For any earthly power to divide us.
Or we will live, or let us die, together.
There is a cruel mercy.
WARBECK. Spite of tyranny,
We reign in our affections, blessed woman!
Read in my destiny the wrack of honour;
Point out, in my contempt of death, to memory
Some miserable happiness; since herein,
Even when I fell, I stood enthron'd a monarch
Of one chaste wife's troth, pure and uncorrupted.
Fair angel of perfection, immortality
Shall raise thy name up to an adoration;

---

105 *juggling*: deception, pretence.
107 See Textual Notes, p. 346.
109 *rid*: rode.
110 *Pass'd*: travelled.
111 *The enemy of mankind*: the Devil.
117 *apparition*: appearance only.
118 *Be what*: whatever.
120 *su'd out*: applied for.
125 *wrack*: destruction, ruin.

Court every rich opinion of true merit;
And saint it in the calendar of virtue,
When I am turn'd into the self-same dust
Of which I was first form'd.

OXFORD. The lord ambassador,
Huntly, your father, madam, should he look on
Your strange subjection, in a gaze so public,
Would blush on your behalf, and wish his country
Unleft for entertainment to such sorrow.

KATHERINE. Why art thou angry, Oxford? I must be
More peremptory in my duty. – Sir,
Impute it not unto immodesty
That I presume to press you to a legacy,
Before we part for ever.

WARBECK. Let it be, then,
My heart, the rich remains of all my fortunes.

KATHERINE. Confirm it with a kiss, pray.

WARBECK. O, with that
I wish to breathe my last! Upon thy lips,
Those equal twins of comeliness, I seal
The testament of honourable vows. [*Kisses her.*]
Whoever be that man that shall unkiss
This sacred print next, may he prove more thrifty
In this world's just applause, not more desertful.

KATHERINE. By this sweet pledge of both our souls, I swear
To die a faithful widow to thy bed,
Not to be forc'd or won. O, never, never!

Enter SURREY, DAUBENEY, HUNTLY, *and* CRAWFORD.

DAUBENEY. Free the condemned person, quickly free him. –

---

132 *rich*: high.
133 *saint . . . virtue*: be enrolled as a saint, commemorated on a saint's day in the Church's calendar.
139 *entertainment to*: experience, reception of.
147 See Textual Notes, p. 346.
151 *thrifty*: fortunate in receiving.
156–86 See Additional Notes, p. 356.

What has he yet confess'd?
URSWICK. Nothing to purpose;
But still he will be king.
SURREY. Prepare your journey
To a new kingdom, then. – Unhappy madam,
Wilfully foolish! – See, my lord ambassador,
Your lady daughter will not leave the counterfeit
In this disgrace of fate.
HUNTLY. I never pointed
Thy marriage, girl, but yet, being married,
Enjoy thy duty to a husband freely.
Thy griefs are mine. I glory in thy constancy;
And must not say I wish that I had miss'd
Some partage in these trials of a patience.
KATHERINE. You will forgive me, noble sir?
HUNTLY. Yes, yes;
In every duty of a wife, and daughter,
I dare not disavow thee. – To your husband,
For such you are, sir, I impart a farewell
Of manly pity; what your life has pass'd through,
The dangers of your end will make apparent.
And I can add, for comfort to your sufferance,
No cordial but the wonder of your frailty
Which keeps so firm a station. – We are parted.
WARBECK. We are. A crown of peace renew thy age,
Most honourable Huntly. – Worthy Crawford,
We may embrace; I never thought thee injury.
CRAWFORD. Nor was I ever guilty of neglect
Which might procure such thought. I take my leave, sir.
[*They embrace.*]
WARBECK. To you, Lord Dalyell – what? Accept a sigh;

---

159 See Textual Notes, p. 346.
162 *disgrace*: disfavour.
pointed: arranged.
165 See Textual Notes, p. 346.
167 *partage*: share.
174 *sufferance*: suffering.
175 *cordial*: restorative medicine.
177 See Textual Notes, p. 346.
179 *thought*: intended even in a thought.

'Tis hearty and in earnest.
DALYELL. I want utterance;
My silence is my farewell.
KATHERINE. Oh! – Oh! –
JANE. Sweet madam,
What do you mean? My lord, your hand.
DALYELL. Dear lady,
Be pleas'd that I may wait ye to your lodging.
Exit KATHERINE, [*supported by*] DALYELL [*and*] JANE.

Enter Sheriff and Officers [*with*] SKELTON, ASTLEY, HERON, *and* [JOHN A-WATER,] *with halters about their necks.*

OXFORD. Look ye; behold your followers, appointed
To wait on ye in death.
WARBECK. Why, peers of England,
We'll lead 'em on courageously. I read
A triumph over tyranny upon
Their several foreheads. Faint not in the moment
Of victory! Our ends, and Warwick's head,
Innocent Warwick's head – for we are prologue
But to his tragedy – conclude the wonder
Of Henry's fears; and then the glorious race
Of fourteen kings, Plantagenets, determines
In this last issue male. Heaven be obey'd.
Impoverish time of its amazement, friends,
And we will prove as trusty in our payments
As prodigal to nature in our debts.
Death? Pish, 'tis but a sound, a name of air,
A minute's storm, or not so much. To tumble
From bed to bed, be massacred alive
By some physicians for a month or two
In hope of freedom from a fever's torments,

---

183 *want utterance*: lack the ability to speak.
186 *wait*: attend on. See Textual Notes, p. 346.
186 s.d. SKELTON . . . A-WATER: in historical fact, only John A-Water and his son were executed.
194 *wonder*: extraordinary spectacle.
196 *determines*: ends.
199 *payments*: i.e. of the debt of life, owed to nature.
203 *massacred*: mutilated.

Might stagger manhood; here, the pain is pass'd
Ere sensibly 'tis felt. Be men of spirit!
Spurn coward passion! So illustrious mention
Shall blaze our names, and style us Kings o'er
Death.

DAUBENEY. Away – impostor beyond precedent!
No chronicle records his fellow.

Exeunt [Sheriff], all Officers and Prisoners.

HUNTLY. I have
Not thoughts left; 'tis sufficient in such cases
Just laws ought to proceed.

Enter KING HENRY, DURHAM, *and* HIALAS.

HENRY. We are resolv'd.
Your business, noble lords, shall find success
Such as your king importunes.

HUNTLY. You are gracious.

HENRY. Perkin, we are inform'd, is arm'd to die;
In that we'll honour him. Our lords shall follow
To see the execution; and from hence
We gather this fit use: that public states,
As our particular bodies, taste most good
In health, when purged of corrupted blood.

Exeunt all.

Finis

---

206 *stagger manhood*: make manly courage fail.
207 *sensibly*: acutely.
208 *passion*: emotion.
209 *blaze*: proclaim.
style: title.
214 *success*: outcome.
219 *use*: moral lesson.
220 *As*: like.
taste: experience.

Epilogue

Here has appear'd, though in a several fashion,
The threats of majesty, the strength of passion,
Hopes of an empire, change of fortunes; all
What can to theatres of greatness fall,
Proving their weak foundations. Who will please,
Among such several sights, to censure these
No births abortive, nor a bastard brood –
Shame to a parentage, or fosterhood –
May warrant by their loves all just excuses,
And often find a welcome to the Muses.

Finis

---

1 *several fashion*: mode suitable to each.
6 *several*: varied.
censure: judge.
9 *warrant*: give assurance of.
10 *to*: to the company of. In the final couplet, Ford invites the applause of the audience, and assures them of a future welcome in the theatre.

NOTES

TEXTUAL NOTES

The Broken Heart

Prologue 6 *courts*: Gifford; *Courts'*

Cast List 14 LEMOPHIL: Q (though the name is consistently given as Hemophil(l) in the play until V.ii.124); Lenophil conj. Brooke and Paradise. None of these forms can easily be reconciled with Ford's translation 'glutton', but the clear evidence of correction in the Cast List in the case of Grausis gives the form Lemophil used there superior textual authority.

23 GRAUSIS: Q (corrected): GRANSIS Q (uncorrected, and throughout the play-text). In this case, the etymology confirms the corrected form.

I.i.15 *Not that,*: Weber; Not, that

I.i.18 *broach'd*: Weber; brauch't

I.i.31 *of union*: Q (corrected); of holy vnion Q (uncorrected)

I.i.55 *humanity*: after Weber; humanity.

I.i.83 *Athens.*: Weber; *Athens*

I.i.93–4 *however* / Worthy,: Gifford; how euer worthy, /

I.ii.20 *Pephnon*: Spencer; Pephon

I.ii.37 *thankfulness*: Weber; thankefulnesse,

I.ii.82 *sacrifices, . . . reason*: Weber; *sacrifices* . . . *Reason*;

I.ii.89 *slights*: Weber; sleights

I.ii.108 *creatures . . . valour*: Q; creatures of spirit. / Valour conj. this edition

I.ii.111 *you*: Weber; yon

I.ii.113 *You*: Weber; Yon

I.ii.116 s.h. LEMOPHIL: conj. Spencer; *Phil.*

I.ii.120 *all together*: Gifford; altogether

I.ii.133 *feathers*: Weber; Fathers

I.ii.143 s.d. *Exeunt* . . . PHILEMA: Gifford; follows 145 in Q

I.ii.146 *slight*: Weber; sleight

I.iii.37 *secure.*: Spencer; secure,

I.iii.50 s.d. *Walks*: Gifford; *Walke*

I.iii.182 *acts*: Sturgess; Arts

II.i.29 *their*: Weber; the

II.i.62–3 *Why,. . . soul!*: Sturgess; Why . . . soule?

II.i.127 s.d. *Enter* PHULAS: Dyce; follows *Now*? in Q

II.ii.64 *We*: Q (corrected); She Q (uncorrected)

II.iii.5 *nature once*: Gifford; nature Q. The emendation, which is no more than intelligent guesswork, restores the metre but does not address the awkward bridge from line 4 to line 5. It is possible that an intervening line has been omitted by the printer.

II.iii.9 *little skill*: Weber; skill

II.iii.16 s.d. *Exit* PROPHILUS: Weber; follows *hour* (15) in Q

II.iii.31 *On Vesta's altars*: Oliphant; The holiest Artars

II.iii.32 *The holiest*: Oliphant; On *Vesta's*

II.iii.124 *I'll*: *Modern British Drama*; I'e
frenzy: Brooke and Paradise; French

III.i.11 *heart*: Gifford; hearts

III.i.35 *nature*;: Weber; nature

III.i.39 *basis*: Weber; Bases

III.i.41 *or*: Gifford; of

III.i.54 s.d. *Exit* ORGILUS: Dyce; follows *thrifty*. (53) in Q
III.i.72 *Your*: Weber; You
III.ii. Q does not mark this scene division.
III.ii.55 *Of . . . untroubl'd*: Mitford; The vntroubled of Country toyle, drinkes
III.ii.61 *Whiles*: Baskervill; Which
III.ii.71 *act*: Weber; art
III.ii.93 *or nearness*: Lamb; or Q. Other guesses at the word omitted or lost from the type-line include 'closeness', 'bond' and 'tie'.
III.ii.95 *'Tis . . . sister,*: Gifford; as . . . Sister:
III.ii.128 *noble.*: Morris; noble,
III.ii.159 *silent*: Weber; sinlent
III.ii.184 *your judgement*: Gifford; iudgement
III.ii.206 *a'*: Harrier; a
III.iii. Q does not mark this scene division.
III.iii.5 *grave*: Dyce: graues
III.iv Q does not mark this scene division.
III.iv.11 *wish*: Weber; with
III.v. Q does not mark this scene division.
III.v.35 *enjoin*: conj. Dyce; enjoy
III.v.36 s.h. PENTHEA: Weber; not in Q
III.v.96 *revel in*: Lamb; reuell
IV.i.25 *be denied*: Weber; beny'd
IV.i.88 *less rash*: Gifford; rash
IV.ii. Q does not mark this scene division.
IV.ii.35 *deities*: Gifford; deities:
IV.ii.44 *madness*: conj. Maxwell; words
IV.ii.54 *dearth*: this edition; death
IV.ii.57 *been*: Weber; bee
IV.ii.65 *roof*: Weber; root
IV.ii.67 *impost'rous*: Spencer (impostorous); Impostors
IV.ii.81 *sun*: Weber; Swan
IV.ii.85–6 *ye, begins / To*: after Gifford; 'ee) / Begins to
IV.ii.107 *bandy*: Dyce; bawdy
IV.ii.111 *too*: Weber; to Q. Although this emendation completes the sense of the half-line, it is likely that Orgilus's remark was completed in a following line omitted by the printer.
IV.ii.112 s.h. PENTHEA: Weber; not in Q
IV.ii.161 *think.*: Weber; thinke
IV.ii.177 *angry*: Weber; augury
IV.iii. Q does not mark this scene division.
IV.iii.27 *too,*: Merivale; to
IV.iii.30 *sir –* : after Gifford; Sir;
IV.iii.63 *trifle*: Dyce; trifle;
IV.iii.75 *for*: Weber; foe
IV.iii.76 *never!*: Weber; neuer
IV.iii.87 *'cause*: Weber; cause
IV.iii.89 *fortunes,*: Harrier; fortuness
IV.iii.96 *Wear*: Weber; Were
IV.iii.139 s.d. *Soft . . . music*: Weber; follows 140 in Q
IV.iv. Q does not mark this scene division.
IV.iv.59 s.d. *Stabs*: Weber; *kils*
IV.iv.64 *success.*: after Weber; successe
V.i.7 *too*: Weber; to

V.i.12 *doubles*: Gifford; doublers
V.ii.9 *you*: Q (corrected); you with Q (uncorrected)
V.ii.54 *rend*: Gifford; rent
V.ii.74 *slight*: Weber; sleight
V.ii.109 *these*: this edition; this
V.ii.111 *expectation*: Weber; expection
V.ii.123 s.h. NEARCHUS: Gifford; *Org.*
V.iii. Q does not mark this scene division.
V.iii.0 s.d. *Music . . . which*: Spencer; *during which musicke of Recorders*
crown'd;: Weber; *crown'd*
V.iii.23 *infinite*: Weber; infinites
V.iii.51–2 *Philema . . . Chrystalla*: this edition; *Christalla . . . Philema*
V.iii.64 *mother's*: Lamb; mother
V.iii.83 *The outward*: Gifford; *outward*

'Tis Pity She's a Whore

The Quarto text is divided into Acts only; all scene divisions are editorial.
I.ii.26 *mean*: Q (corrected); meaned Q (uncorrected)
I.ii.47 *thy*: Sturgess; this
I.ii.49 *had not*: Dodsley; had
I.ii.62 *villainy*: Dodsley; villaine
I.ii.162 s.d. *Exeunt*: Weber; *Exit*
I.ii.165 *ruin*: Gifford; ruin,
I.ii.185–7 *Yes . . . well*: this edition; Yes . . . Sister? / Howsoeuer . . . well.
I.ii.213 *The*: Dodsley; they
I.ii.229 *strike*: Dodsley; strick
I.ii.252 *brother*,: Dodsley; brother
I.ii.253 *sister*,: Dodsley; sister
I.ii.282 *swear't*;: this edition; swear't
I.iii.15 *you*: Dodsley; yon
I.iii.29 *How*: Weber; *Pog.* How
I.iii.45 *thither*: Gifford; hither
II.i.15 *then?*: Roper; then,
II.i.24 *jesting*.: Dodsley; iesting
II.i.55–60 *So . . . time*: Weber; as prose Q
II.i.71–2 *Sir . . . command*: Weber; one line in Q
II.ii.1 s.h. SORANZO: Ellis; not in Q
II.ii.7 *thee*: Dodsley; the
II.ii.59 *thy*: Q (corrected); the Q (uncorrected)
II.ii.102 *accurs'd*: Bawcutt; a Coarse Q (corrected); a Curse Q (uncorrected)
II.ii.107–8 *that . . . lov'd*,: Weber; that, . . . lou'd
II.ii.110 *mistress*,: Q (corrected); Mistress Q (uncorrected)
II.ii.156 *lie within*: Dyce; lye – – – – within
II.ii.168–9 *for witnesses*: Dodsley; foe-witnesses
II.iii.53 *Worse than confusion*: this line is a short one whether 'confusion' is spoken with three or four syllables. There is no satisfactory way of adjusting it and no sign of a lacuna in the text so I retain the Quarto reading in preference to any of the many editorial rearrangements of the passage.

II.iii.54 *kill*: Q (corrected); tell Q (uncorrected)
II.iii.63 *ruin'd*: Q (corrected); min'd Q (uncorrected)
II.iv.7 *Why,*: Dyce; Why
II.iv.45 *look you*: Dodsley; looke yon
II.v.5 *cast away*: this edition; cast-away,
II.v.8 *my*: Dodsley; thy
II.v.15 *frame*: Dodsley; Fame
II.v.17 *the body*: Gifford; body
II.vi.51 *freedom?*: Gifford; freedome.
have't: Roper; haue
II.vi.118–19 *A . . . seen*: Weber; one line in Q
II.vi.128–32 *Signior . . . sir*: Dyce; as prose Q
II.vi.136–9 *Son . . . off*: Weber; as prose Q
II.vi.136 *still*: Gifford; still, still
II.vi.144–7 *A . . . again*: Gifford; A . . . me / To . . . Marriage. / But . . . againe
III.i.9–12 *She . . . her*: Weber; Shee . . . already. / True . . . Doctor / Swore . . . her
III.i.11 s.h. BERGETTO: Dodsley; *Pog.*
III.ii.9 *son, . . . rest,*: this edition; sonne . . . rest
III.ii.10 *Agree they*: Gifford; Agree
III.ii.13–14 *Do . . . tell you*: Weber; one line in Q
III.ii.16 *no*: Gifford; not
III.ii.29 *Know*: Dodsley; I know
III.ii.36–47 *'Tis . . . this*: Reed; as prose in Q
III.ii.63–4 *Help . . . Florio*: this edition; Helpe . . . ho. / *Gio*. Looke . . . *Florio*
III.iii.30–3 *Do . . . to't*: this edition; Doe . . . mee! / If . . . well, / Say . . . *Woeman*, / Looke . . . to't
III.iii.30 *does* : Dodsley; doe
III.iv.21 *I'll . . . tonight*: Weber; I'le . . . straight / To . . . to night
III.v.8–11 *You . . . Married*: Reed; as prose Q
III.v.33 *Ay*: Dodsley; I
III.v.38 s.h. POGGIO: Bawcutt; *Phi.*
III.v.43 *shall have*: Gifford; shall
III.vi.45–8 I . . . *him*: Weber; I . . . ouer-ioy'd. / And . . . neere. / My . . . him
III.vi.51 *hand*;: Reed; hand,
III.vi.52–3 *I . . . yours*: Weber; one line in Q
III.vii.19–20 *How . . . hurt*: Gifford; How . . . slaine? / It . . . hurt
III.vii.28 *thy*: this edition; the
IV.i.28 s.d. *Hautboys*: Gifford; follows 36 in Q
IV.i.35–6 *We . . . in*: Gifford; as prose Q
IV.i.36 s.d. *a dance*: Weber; *a Daunce. Dance.*
IV.i.38 *this*: Q (corrected): thy Q (uncorrected)
IV.i.69–71 *Know . . . you*: Weber; Know . . . treachery / Hath . . . you
IV.i.76 *inganna*: Weber; *niganna*
IV.i.82 *marriage*: Dodsley; malice
IV.i.90 *yet — and*: Q. Two long dashes in Q here probably show a loss of text. Bawcutt suggests that *yet* may be a misprint for *that* or *it* (the 'just payment'), but the sense would still require some such phrase as 'Now repent'.
IV.ii.2 *hath*: Q (corrected); hath hath Q (uncorrected)

IV.ii.28 *lives*: Dodsley; liue
IV.iii.15 *why*: Roper, Q (corrected catchword); Shey Q; Say Dodsley, Q (uncorrected catchword)
IV.iii.32 *boy*;: Bawcutt; Boy
your glory: McIlwraith; glory
IV.iii.50 *Alas . . . believe*: this edition; Alas . . . all / Will . . . beleeue
IV.iii.52 *Never*; *if*: Bawcutt; Neuer, / If
IV.iii.59 *più*: Weber; *pluis*
morirei: Bawcutt; *morirere* Q (corrected); *morire* Q (uncorrected)
IV.iii.63 *a lui*: Roper; *Lei* Q; *Dei* Weber
IV.iii.71 *I leave*: Q (corrected); leaue Q (uncorrected)
IV.iii.89 *author*: Dyce; authors
IV.iii.104 *your*: Dodsley; hour
IV.iii.121–2 *Follow . . . purpose*: as prose Weber; Follow . . . passion, / Bee . . . purpose
IV.iii.128 *thou*: Gifford; thus
IV.iii.163 *ferret*: Dodsley; *Secret*
IV.iii.185 *whom.*: Weber; whom
IV.iii.186 s.d. *Enter* PUTANA: Weber; follows 190 in Q
IV.iii.206 *Well,*: Dodsley; Well
IV.iii.264 s.d. *Exeunt* BANDITTI: Dodsley; *Exit* Q (where the direction follows 'expectation' (265)
IV.iii.302 s.d. *Exeunt*: Reed; *Exit*
V.i.10 *depositions*: Dodsley; dispositions
V.i.10 s.d. *Enter* FRIAR: Q (corrected); not in Q (uncorrected)
V.i.57 *blest*: Dodsley; blessed
V.ii.25 *you.*: this edition; you
V.iii.40 s.d. *Enter* VASQUES: Dyce; follows 41 in Q
V.iii.74 s.h. GIOVANNI: Dodsley; not in Q
V.iv.8 s.h. BANDITTI: this edition; *Ban. omnes* (shortened to *Omnes* at 12 and 19)
V.iv.21 s.d. *Exeunt*: Reed; *Exit*
V.iv.53 s.d. *Flourish*: Q (uncorrected); precedes 55 s.d. Q (corrected)
V.v.17 *dining*: Q (corrected); dying Q (uncorrected)
V.v.39–40 *That . . . laugh*: Reed; That . . . there, / You . . . mee, / May . . . another, / Prate . . . laugh
V.v.51 *woo*: Q (corrected); woe Q (uncorrected)
V.v.62 *requir'd*: Q (corrected); require Q (uncorrected)
V.vi.4 *confections?*: Walley; Confections.
V.vi.41–2 *How . . . madman*: McIlwraith; one line in Q
V.vi.78 s.d. *They . . . wounded*: Sturgess; *Fight* Q (following 77)
V.vi.86–8 *Now . . . yourselves*: as prose Weber; Now . . . Sir, / Away . . . done, / Shift . . . owne, / Shift . . . selues
V.vi.96–7 *The . . . master*: as prose Weber; The . . . him, / My . . . Maister
V.vi. 101–3 *I . . . dead*: Bawcutt; as prose Q
V.vi.105 *thee*: Dodsley; the

The Chronicle History of Perkin Warbeck

The Quarto text is divided into Acts only; all scene divisions are editorial.

Commendatory Verses I.12 *wit*: Weber; WIT'S
II.10 *Waiving*: Anderson; Waving
IV.8 *whet*: Ure; wett
I.i.5 *blood*: 1714; blond
I.i.23 *rain'd*: 1714; raign'd
I.i.32 *grave. So . . . Heaven,*: Dyce; graue, so . . . Heauen.
I.i.44 *or heat to*: 1714; to heate or
I.i.62 s.h. DAUBENEY: Gifford; *Ox*:
I.i.123–8 *Though . . . blood*: Weber; Tho . . . Buckler. / Shee . . . *England*. / Iollie . . . Swabber / To . . . surfet. / Gracious . . . paper. / The . . . bloud
I.i.140 s.d. *Flourish*: Ure; centred after end of scene in Q
I.ii.45 *But't*: Weber; But
I.ii.62–3 *Nay . . . infinitely*: Weber; one line in Q
I.ii.65–8 *The gallant . . . mine*: Weber; The . . . this / Servant . . . Maister / I . . . mine
I.ii.70–1 *Princely . . . employ*: Weber; one line in Q
I.ii.89 *falt'ring*: this edition; faulting
How . . . Embolden: Weber; How . . . that? / Embolden
I.ii.140 *heart like peace*: Q (corrected); heart, Q (uncorrected)
I.ii.175–7 *From . . . aid*: Weber; From . . . *Huntley*, / Who . . . ayde
I.iii.28–9 *Tell . . . down*: Weber; one line in Q
I.iii.60 *Skelton*: Dyce; *Sketon* throughout Q
I.iii.68 *infectious*: Dyce; infections
him: Dyce; 'em
I.iii.78 *Cressoner*: Pickburn; *Chessoner*
I.iii.87–9 *Urswick . . . Bishop*: Weber; *Vrswick* . . . Sirs, / Is . . . alter / Strangely . . . Bishop
I.iii.129 s.d. *Enter* DAUBENEY: Gifford; follows *newes* in Q
I.iii.129–34 *Ten . . . more*: Weber; Ten . . . your / Subsidies . . . a / Blacksmith . . . *London*, / And . . . march, / Their . . . are – / Rascalls . . . more
I.iii.136 *To bed; and . . . wake*: Gifford; And . . . wake: – to bed
I.iii.138 s.d. *Exeunt*: Q reads *Exeunt. / Finis Actus primi.*
II.i.16–17 *For . . . king*: Weber; one line in Q
II.i.16 s.d. *Flourish*: Weber; follows *silent* (17) in Q
II.i.39 s.d. A-WATER: Weber; a Watring
II.ii.1–6 *His . . . importunity*: Weber; His . . . as / Cleere . . . dangerous: / Besides . . . him / So . . . free / Confession . . . importunitie
II.ii.33 *him*: 1714; 'em
II.ii.47 s.d. *Exit*: Gifford; *Exeunt*
II.ii.47–50 *I . . . of*: Weber; I . . . would / Haue . . . him. / 'Tis . . . gentlenesse. / Rare . . . of
II.ii.52 s.d. *Enter . . .* DAUBENEY: Q; some editors add a Confessor, but Urswick might shrive Stanley, and takes no further part in the scene following Stanley's dismissal to execution.
II.ii.94–6 *Shall . . . more*: Weber; Shall . . . loosers / Leaue . . . more
II.iii.16 Phaethon: 1714 (Phaeton); Phueton
II.iii.51–2 *Enforcement . . . tyranny*: Weber; one line in Q
II.iii.70 *for't*,: Q reads for't, *Enter*.
II.iii.76 *youth*: Weber; Lady
II.iii.105 s.d. JOHN A-WATER: Ure; *Major*

II.iii.150 *punch'd*: Gifford; pincht
II.iii.158 *digest*: Weber; disgest
III.i.41 s.d. *A flourish*: Weber; follows 42 in Q
III.i.49 *expectation*: Ure; expectation,
III.i.59 *Deptford*: Weber; *Dertford*
III.ii.15 *My*: Q (corrected); Any Q (uncorrected)
III.ii.21 *To any*: Q (corrected); To Q (uncorrected)
III.ii.33 *apt nature*: Q (corrected: ap't nature); nature Q (uncorrected)
III.ii.35 *Stop*: Q (corrected); Stoppes Q (uncorrected)
III.ii.37 *do but*: Q (corrected); do Q (uncorrected)
III.ii.38 *ever.*: Q (corrected); ever, Q (uncorrected)
III.ii.68–9 *Say . . . her*: Weber; one line in Q
III.ii.81 s.d. *Flourish*: Baskervill; follows 85 in Q
III.ii.121–3 *Our . . . herald*: Weber; Our . . . your / Secretarie . . . serue? / With . . . Herald
III.iii.20–1 *Else . . . sir*: Weber; one line in Q
III.iii.35–6 *Good . . . thoughts*: Weber; one line in Q
III.iii.63 *so*: Q (corrected); too Q (uncorrected)
III.iv.0. s.d. JOHN A-WATER: Weber; Major
III.iv.37 *No*: Weber; Me
traducer: Gifford; *seducer*
III.iv.48 *meditations*: Gifford; meditation
III.iv.49–50 *Can . . . sir*: Weber; one line in Q
III.iv.83 s.d. *Enter* FRION: Dyce; follows 82 in Q
III.iv.87–8 *His . . . it*: Weber; one line in Q
IV.i.21–2 *To . . . on*: Weber; one line in Q
IV.i.72–3 *To . . . it*: Weber; one line in Q
IV.ii.50 s.d. *Enter . . .* SKELTON: Weber; follows *friends* in Q
JOHN A-WATER: Ure; *Major*
IV.ii.57 *these*: Gifford; this
IV.iii.10–11 *What . . . England*: Weber; one line in Q
IV.iii.55 *Delay . . . it*: Weber; Delay . . . dispatch, / Heaven . . . it
IV.iii.62–3 *Sent . . . lord*: Weber; one line in Q
IV.iii.64 s.d. JOHN A-WATER: Ure; *Major*
IV.iii.108 s.d. *Exeunt*: Weber; *Exit*
IV.iii.120 s.d. HERON . . . A-WATER: Ure; *Counsellors*
IV.iv.23–4 *The . . . smiling*: Weber; one line in Q
IV.iv.63 s.d. *Enter a* POST: Weber; follows *whom* (64) in Q
IV.iv.63–4 *So . . . whom*: Weber; one line in Q
IV.v.29 s.d. *Another shout*: Weber; follows *shout* in Q
IV.v.34 *Bodmin*: Dyce; *Bodnam*
V.i.25 *I could*: this edition; Could I
V.i.73–4 *Madam . . . come*: Weber; one line in Q
V.i.85–6 *My . . . lady*: Weber; one line in Q
V.i.106 *enforcement*: Ure; enforcement,
V.ii.22 s.h. URSWICK: Weber; *Sur*:
V.ii.36–7 *Daubeney . . . true*: Weber; one line in Q
V.ii.41 *Beaulieu*: Weber; *Beweley*
V.ii.61 *Bretaine's*: Weber; *Britaines*
V.ii.121 s.h. HERON . . . SKELTON: Dyce; *Omnes*.
V.ii.140 s.d. DALYELL: Gifford; not in Q, but Dalyell has a speaking part in this scene (165–72)
V.iii.80 s.d. *Exit . . .* SIMNEL: Gifford; follows *soule* (82) in Q
V.iii.93 *this; now*: Dyce; *this now*,

V.iii.107 *to their*: Gifford; to
V.iii.147 *last!*: after Weber; last
V.iii.159 *then . . . madam*: Weber; then, (vnhappie Madam)
V.iii.165 *Thy*: Weber; The
V.iii.177 *We are.*: Gifford; Wee are
V.iii.186 s.d. *Exit . . .* JANE: after Gifford; *Exeunt Daliell, Katherine, Iane*
JOHN A-WATER: Ure; Mayor

ADDITIONAL NOTES

The Broken Heart

Dedicatory Epistle

Title *William . . . Marshall*: Ford dedicated his Spartan play to a distinguished soldier. Craven (1608–97) was the eldest son of a Lord Mayor of London. He left Oxford University for military service with the Prince of Orange against the Spanish. Charles I knighted him in 1627, then created him Baron Craven of Hamstead Marshall, a Berkshire town near Newbury. In 1631 he commanded English troops fighting in Germany in support of the Elector Frederick. He returned to England after Frederick's death in 1632, where he became the dedicatee of a number of classical, military and religious works. A royalist during the Civil War and Commonwealth, he also supported Elizabeth of Bohemia, Frederick's widow and a daughter of James I. In 1664, Charles II created him Viscount Craven of Uffington and Earl of Craven, and he became one of the early Fellows of the Royal Society.

Cast List

THE SPEAKERS' NAMES: two of the names in this list have a legendary or historical basis. Amyclas was a legendary king of Sparta, though Ford may have taken the name from a Spartan king in Sir Philip Sidney's *Arcadia* (1593). Nearchus was a friend and admiral of Alexander the Great. Ford seems to have invented the remaining names from Greek elements, though his own glosses on Ithocles, Lemophil and Groneas remain unexplained, and Amelus actually means 'neglectful' rather than 'trusty'. Most of the following derivations are taken from Ure:

Ithocles: 'straight' and 'honour'
Orgilus: 'inclined to anger'
Bassanes: 'torment'
Armostes: 'one who governs', from the title (*harmostes*) of a Spartan viceroy sent to rule a subject city (see V.iii.43–4)
Crotolon: 'a rattling noise'
Prophilus: 'very dear'
Nearchus: 'young leader'
Tecnicus: 'artistic, skilful'
Lemophil: the form of this name is uncertain (see the Textual Notes, p. 339); suggested derivations are 'gluttonous', 'lover of the wine vat' (*Lenophil*) and 'blood-lover' (*Hemophil*)
Groneas: 'hollow vessel'
Phulas: 'keeping watch'
Calantha: 'beautiful' and 'flower'
Penthea: 'lamentation'
Euphrania: 'one who gladdens'
Chrystalla: 'ice, crystal'
Philema: 'kiss'
Grausis: 'old woman'
Thrasus: 'courage' and 'bold'
Aplotes: 'simplicity'

I.ii.13 *Laconia*: the south-eastern district of the Peloponnese, ruled over by the city of Sparta; also called Lacedemonia (16). It was bordered on the north-west by Messenia, whose chief city was Messene (15). Historically, these two city-states fought two long wars in the eighth and seventh centuries B.C., a conflict which ended in a Spartan victory in 668 B.C.

I.iii.100 *talking to himself*: Orgilus is perhaps to be thought of as arguing aloud with the book he is reading, rather than debating with an imaginary intellectual opponent. At 104 he pretends to address his master, Tecnicus.

II.i.21–2 *I . . . eye*: Phulas will guard Penthea like Argus, the hundred-eyed guardian of Hera. In art, Argus was frequently represented dressed in robes covered in eyes.

II.i.50–2 *since . . . out*: captive lions and dancing bears might be seen in Ford's London, rather than in classical Sparta, but this is only one example of the way in which the dramatist mingles elements of Greek, Roman and English culture throughout the play.

II.i.62–3 *Why . . . soul!*: some editors accept the strained interrogative construction of Q, or take the sentence as incomplete, so making Bassanes pensive at this point. But he is responding to Phulas's reported *she-news* (59), arguing that female beauty itself should be taken as *apparent proof* (58) of inevitable infidelity.

II.ii.3–5 *Ambition . . . ruin*: the image is based on the fact that for sport or for training purposes birds were blinded by having their eyelids sewn together (*seeled*). This caused the loss of all sense of direction, and on release they would fly upwards until they collapsed from exhaustion and fell to the ground.

II.iii.149–51 *Then . . . account*: Gifford assigned these lines to Penthea as 'evidently the continuation of [her] ideas in the former speech'. But the warning about present conduct is typical of Bassanes' suspicious nature, and Prophilus's response is a veiled rebuke (151–2).

III.i.40–50 *He . . . honour*: Tecnicus's speech is intended as an oblique warning to Orgilus not to elevate self-satisfaction (including the satisfactions of revenge) into a moral virtue, as well as providing a thematic statement about the nature of true and false honour. The philosopher contrasts the value judgements derived from personal opinion, itself founded on emotion and concerned with the random flow of events, with those issuing from knowledge, based on reason and concerned with universal certainties.

III.ii.20–1 *Soldiers . . . effeminate*: according to Plutarch, the Spartans banned certain types of music as likely to weaken the moral fibre of their citizens (an argument not unknown in our own society). Bassanes is thinking of the soldier Ithocles.

III.iv.65 *greater ceremony*: a formal marriage service, confirming the plighting of troth which is the ceremony conducted here, and which Penthea and Orgilus had celebrated before Ithocles imposed the match with Bassanes.

III.v.56 *married maids*: although editors have suspected textual corruption here, there is a clear antithesis with *virgin wives* (52). The wives are *virgin* in their faithful love; the *married maids* are those who have taken vows of physical chastity. Compare the term 'Bride of Christ' applied to Christian nuns.

IV.i.102–4 *painted . . . lion*: the image is grotesque (horses do not harass lions), but conveys Ithocles' passionate anger well enough. He is the provoked lion, muzzled by Nearchus's privileged position as royal guest. Nearchus is the young horse (animal symbol of youthful folly and rudeness) wearing the highly decorated trappings of royalty. Ford may have had in mind contemporary paintings and pictures of royal riders on richly caparisoned horses.

IV.ii.110 *Spare your hand*: Penthea takes Orgilus's hand, though he at first pulls back. In her madness she goes on to express openly her frustrated feelings for him, kissing and embracing him (112–13). Yet she remains partly aware of the reaction of those around her (114).

IV.ii.129–31 *All . . . ears*: Penthea seems to transfer her own exhausted physical condition to Orgilus, the *married bachelor* (131); the pale purple of the amethyst here symbolises enervation of health and passion. Fashionable young Elizabethan men wore such gems in their ears, and the actor playing Orgilus may do so too. Penthea's distracted mind is presented by means of a dense verbal texture; so, *lost his colour* (128) gives rise to the striking image of the *straying heart* (129), and the lover's cold lips, his mouth (127), becomes in turn a pale cranny and a faintly coloured gem.

IV.ii.164–6 *to . . . fumes*: Bassanes is not being excessively fanciful. Sherman found a contemporary ballad in the Shirburn collection celebrating a girl who was said to have lived for sixteen years on the scent of perfumes, and Burton, in *The Anatomy of Melancholy*, II.5.i.5, reports that ''tis a question commonly controverted in our schools, *an odores nutriant* [whether fumes can provide nourishment]'.

IV.iii.65 *loose for strait*: a pregnant woman would replace her usual tight-waisted gown with an ample, unwaisted garment. But Orgilus is also punning on *loose* (unchaste) and *strait* = straight (strictly virtuous).

IV.iii.88 *Have . . . Divinely*: this implies a previous off-stage encounter (cf. IV.ii.186–9), where the couple mutually declared their love, and Calantha promised to ask the king's consent to her marriage.

IV.iv.0 s.d. *engine*: mechanism. This contrivance is capable of trapping its occupant by the arms. The real and fictional use of such trick chairs for murderous or erotic purposes is usefully reviewed in an appendix in the Revels edition of *The Broken Heart* by T.J.B. Spencer, pp. 224–8.

V.iii.51–3 *I . . . temple*: one would expect Philema ('Kiss') to marry, and Chrystalla ('Ice' or 'Crystal') to become a Vestal Virgin, and the names are metrically interchangeable. Given the dramatist's care in inventing appropriate names for his characters, it is difficult to believe that Ford here forgot their significance or that Calantha intends an ironic reversal of their roles. The text of Q contains an unusual proportion of errors, and there is no sign of authorial correction or supervision of the printer's work, so I have taken the names of the two attendants as having been interchanged by a careless compositor and corrected them accordingly.

V.iii.75 *They . . . heartstrings*: one of many versions of a line from Seneca's *Hippolytus* (607), *curae leves locuntur, ingentes stupent* (small troubles can be spoken, great ones find no voice).

'Tis Pity She's a Whore

Dedicatory Epistle

Title *John . . . Turvey*: although he speaks of 'a particular engagement' to John Mordaunt (19), nothing is known of Ford's relationship with this patron, the son of an old Catholic family, and a courtier who became for a time the favourite of James I. Mordaunt married Elizabeth Howard, a Protestant heiress, and was converted to Anglicanism by Archbishop Ussher in 1625. On his father's death in 1608 he had become the fifth Viscount Mordaunt, and he was created first Earl of Peterborough by Charles I in 1628. He raised a regiment for Parliament in 1642, and was made General of the Ordnance, but he died of consumption in the same year.

Commendatory Verse

11 *Thomas Ellice*: Thomas Ellice (b. 1607) was a brother of Robert Ellice of Gray's Inn, one of the dedicatees of *The Lover's Melancholy* (1629). Thomas entered Gray's Inn in 1626, and wrote a commendatory poem for Davenant's tragedy *Albovine* (1629). His career has not been traced further. See 'Robert and Thomas Ellice, friends of Ford and Davenant', Mary Hobbs, *Notes and Queries*, new series 21 (1974), 292–3.

Cast List

THE ACTORS' NAMES: the names of Ford's characters come from a variety of sources, most of them of a literary nature. Bonaventura and Poggio were famous Italian writers frequently mentioned, as Roper notes, in Burton's *The Anatomy of Melancholy*. Soranzo and Bergetto are names found in Whetstone's *Heptameron of Civil Discourses* (1582), and Richardetto (Richardet) occurs in the story by de Rosset in his *Histoires Tragiques de Nostre Temps* (1615) which was probably Ford's principal source for his play. Florio and Putana are derived from John Florio's Italian dictionary, *A World of Words* (1598), where there is an entry for *putana*, a whore. Grimaldi is a turbulent Italian commander in Massinger's play *The Renegado* (1624). Hippolita combines the name (and nature) of Hippolyta, Queen of the Amazons, with that of Hippolyte, lustful wife of Acastus. Philotis is derived from Greek φιλστηζ, meaning 'love, affection'; cf. the Greek-derived names in *The Broken Heart*.

I.ii.22–3 *Brave my lord*: my brave lord. Vasques is being sarcastic, provoking Grimaldi verbally and threatening him physically. Finally Grimaldi goes to draw his sword at 24 and is immediately attacked by Vasques. Some editors take Q's – *braue my Lord, – you'le fight* to mean, 'Are you getting brave enough, my lord, to fight me?' Others take it to mean, 'Do you dare challenge my master? Will you fight me after all?', and punctuate accordingly. I understand Vasques as saying, 'My supposedly brave lord, you *are* going to fight me.' The dashes in Q may be intended to indicate intervals of provocative swordplay by Vasques.

II.i.63 *perfection*: perfect beauty or accomplishments. Spencer points out that much of the language in this passage is given an ironic or sexual colouring because of the previous scene of love-making between Annabella and Giovanni. Such charged words include *virtue, perfection* (by sexual experience) (63); *music, content* (66); *know, parts* (accomplishments *and* sexual organs) (67); *touch an instrument* and *done't* (78).

II.ii.5 *Sannazar*: Jacopo Sannazaro (1455–1530) was a Neopolitan pastoral and love poet. His prose and verse romance *Arcadia* (1501–4) was well known in England. He wrote a famous short poem in Latin praising Venice, for which he received a lavish reward from the city. This was reported in Thomas Coryat's *Crudities* (1611), and in a letter written in 1621 by James Howell to a member of the Middle Temple, where Ford himself was in residence.

II.ii.78 *A voyage to Ligorne*: a journey (by land) to the sea-port of Leghorn (Italian, *Livorno*), about one hundred miles from Parma. The route was mountainous and infested with brigands; cf. V.iv.2–4.

II.v.55–6 *the spheres . . . Heaven*: the concentric spheres which constituted the created universe in pre-Copernican astronomy were thought to make through their motion a perfectly harmonious music, inaudible to human beings; see *The Merchant of Venice*, V.i, and cf. *The Broken Heart*, II.iii.19.

III.vi.0 s.d. *in his study*: there is some textual uncertainty about the location of this scene, and several editors since Weber have omitted this phrase and placed the action in Annabella's bedroom, mainly on the grounds that the room is upstairs (44) and the Friar has previously been directed to Annabella's *chamber* (III.iv.33). But the phrase occurs in an elaborate stage direction which is undoubtedly authorial, and in the immediately preceding scene Richardetto and Grimaldi speak of a betrothal in Friar Bonaventura's *cell* (III.v.8–12). Such a place might be thought of as approached from below if it was a room in a larger building, rather than an isolated single-chambered dwelling. It is possible that the original sequence and location of scenes have become obscured by textual cuts or changes made by the author or the stage company which first produced the play. It is odd, for instance, that in III.iv.17–25 Florio greets Bonaventura with no surprise after he has spoken of him as if he was some distance away, and still to be approached to conduct the marriage *at his cell*.

V.iii.75 *set up my rest*: chosen my final play; from the card game Primero, in which the player finally 'stands' or 'sets up his rest' when he decides to venture the result of the game on the cards in his hand.

V.iii.78 *gall*: bitterness of spirit. The use of oak-galls in the manufacture of ink leads to the idea of writing down in the roll of honour Giovanni's intended deed of 'courage', and probably generates the following image of a falling oak tree (80).

V.vi.133 *Within this room*: Vasques might point off-stage to the coal-house where Putana had been taken (IV.iii.262), but it is also possible for her to be brought forward at this point for the audience to see and the Cardinal to condemn.

V.vi.139 *this . . . effects*: this woman, who played the leading part in these events. The Cardinal must mean Putana, since there would be little point to Giovanni's question addressed to Vasques (60) if the Spaniard had carried the body of Annabella on-stage. Since the Cardinal has had no opportunity to discover the truth about Putana's part in the affair, Ford must intend his savage judgement of her to afford another instance of human injustice and irrationality in a leader of the society which Giovanni has challenged and defied.

The Chronicle History of Perkin Warbeck

Dedicatory Epistle

Title *William . . . Ogle*: Cavendish (1592–1672) was made a Knight of the Bath in 1610 and Viscount Mansfield in 1620. Charles I created him Baron Cavendish of Bolsover and first Earl of Newcastle in 1628. In 1629 he inherited the title Baron Ogle and was made a Marquess in 1643. A poet, dramatist and patron of writers, he supported Jonson, Shirley and Davenant, and collaborated in writing plays with Shirley, Dryden and Shadwell. During the Civil War, he led the royalist forces in the north, and went into exile in 1644. On his return to England, he was created Duke of Newcastle and retired with his wife, the authoress Margaret Lucas, to a life of literary and philosophical study. That he was both a nephew of the first Earl of Devonshire (to whose widow Ford addressed the elegy *Fame's Memorial*) and a patron of Ford's associates may explain the dramatist's approach to him.

Commendatory Verses

I.17 *George Donne*: the second son of the poet and divine John Donne, born in 1605. He wrote commendatory verses for plays by Ford, Massinger and Heywood, and contributed to *Jonsonus Virbius* (1638), a collection of elegies commemorating Ben Jonson.

IV.13 *John Brograve*: a son of the attorney Sir John Brograve (died 1613), and, like Ford, a member of one of the Inns of Court – in this case, Gray's Inn, where the dramatist had several friends. Brograve describes himself as *Armiger*, that is, entitled to bear heraldic arms by reason of his father's knighthood, bestowed by James I.

V.7 *John Ford, Graiensis*: Ford's older cousin, and, like Brograve, a Gray's Inn man. Ford included him among the dedicatees of *The Lover's Melancholy* (1629), and dedicated *Love's Sacrifice* (1633) to him. In that dedication he speaks of his cousin with special affection.

Cast List

4 *Henry*: Henry Tudor (1457–1509), Lancastrian ruler of England after the defeat of the Yorkist King Richard III at the battle of Bosworth Field in 1485.

5 *Daubeney*: Giles, first Baron Daubeney (D'Aubigny), a Lancastrian supporter made a privy councillor and later Lord

Chamberlain (1495). In 1497 he commanded the royal forces against the Scots and against a Cornish rebellion.

6 *Stanley*: Sir William Stanley (1435–95), a wealthy nobleman who threw in his decisive support for Henry at Bosworth, and was appointed Lord Chamberlain in 1485. He was executed in 1495 on suspicion of supporting Perkin Warbeck.

7 *Oxford*: John de Vere (1443–1513), thirteenth Earl of Oxford, High Constable of England and one of Henry's chief military and political leaders.

8 *Surrey*: Thomas Howard (1443–1524), Earl of Surrey and High Treasurer of England; he was responsible for keeping the border with Scotland secure.

9 *Durham*: Richard Fox (1448–1528), successively Bishop of Exeter, Durham and Winchester; Henry's Secretary of State, and a skilful diplomat.

10 *Urswick*: Christopher Urswick (1448–1522), a cleric and diplomat who became Dean of York, and later of Windsor.

11 *Clifford*: Sir Robert Clifford, youngest son of Sir Thomas Clifford (1414–55) and brother of the so-called 'Butcher of Wakefield', John Lord Clifford, Sheriff of Westmorland (1435–61), whose estates were confiscated and shared between Sir William Stanley and Richard of Gloucester on his death at Towton.

12 *Simnel*: Lambert Simnel was the figurehead in a Yorkist plot against Henry. He claimed to be the Earl of Warwick, Edward IV's nephew, and was actually crowned Edward VI in Dublin in 1486. The next year he landed in England with an army, but was defeated and captured; he became a servant in Henry's household.

13 *Hialas*: Don Pedro de Ayala, an experienced ambassador sent by Ferdinand and Isabella of Spain to negotiate a marriage between their daughter Catherine and Prince Arthur. In 1496 Ferdinand sent him to Scotland on a successful mission to reunite James and Henry in a common front against France.

19 *James*: the Scottish king who died at Flodden. During his reign (1488–1513) Scotland's military strength was increased. Though he renewed alliance with France and for a time supported Perkin Warbeck, he made peace with England in 1502 and married Margaret, Henry VII's daughter.

20 *Huntly*: George (Alexander, in Ford's source, Gainsford) Gordon, second Earl of Huntly. He was one of James's privy councillors, and Lord High Chancellor from 1498.

21 *Crawford*: it is uncertain whether Ford had in mind David or John Lindsay, fifth or sixth Earl of Crawford. The fifth Earl, who died in 1495, was created Duke of Montrose by James III in 1488.

22 *Dalyell*: a fictitious character, but there was such a Scottish family (Dalyell or Dalzell), and it has been suggested that Ford may have known some of its members.

23 *Marchmount*: a Scottish herald named in Gainsford.

25 *Masquers*: the text calls for eight masquers, but four of them may have been played by A-Water, Heron, Skelton and Astley; see II.iii.167 and note.

27 *Warbeck*: Perkin Warbeck (?1474–99) was a Fleming who,

probably at the instigation of Margaret of York, Duchess of Burgundy, claimed that he was Richard Duke of York, and had survived imprisonment in the Tower of London by Richard III. He was received by the French King Charles VIII, and recognised as King of England by the Emperor Maximilian I, Archduke of Austria, who in 1495 backed an abortive landing at Deal, in Kent. Warbeck next took his fleet to Ireland and briefly laid siege to Waterford, then sailed to Scotland where he was welcomed by James IV and married to the king's relative, Lady Katherine Gordon. He accompanied James on an unsuccessful foray into England, but was later turned away by the king. In 1497 he headed a rebellion in Cornwall, but was defeated and taken at Beaulieu. After escaping from custody in 1499 he was recaptured and compelled to make a public confession. When he continued to plot with the Earl of Warwick in the Tower of London, he and the Earl were executed.

28 *Frion*: Stephen Frion, Henry's French Secretary, who shifted allegiance to Charles VIII of France and was appointed Perkin Warbeck's chief aide by the king.

29 *A-Water*: John A-Water (or Walters) was twice Mayor of Cork; he was hung in 1499 for his part in Warbeck's rebellion.

30 *Heron*: John Heron (Herne), a London merchant who fled to Ireland to avoid his creditors and backed Warbeck's bid for the crown.

31 *Skelton*: Edward (or Richard) Skelton, a tailor, and one of Warbeck's councillors. Ford's spelling of the name, Sketon, comes from a misprint in Gainsford; all other historical sources call him Skelton, which is the form adopted in this text.

32 *Astley*: Nicholas Astley, a copy-clerk or money-dealer; another of Warbeck's advisers. Like Heron and Skelton he took sanctuary with Warbeck in 1497, and seems to have escaped further punishment.

34 *Katherine Gordon*; although some modern historians believe that Katherine Gordon was the daughter of the Earl of Huntly by his third wife, Elizabeth Lady Gray, Ford's sources took it that she was Huntly's eldest daughter by his second wife, Princess Annabella Stewart, youngest daughter of James I, and was therefore a kinswoman of James IV. She was married to Warbeck in 1496; after his death she subsequently married three more husbands, and died in 1537.

35 *Countess of Crawford*: either Elizabeth Hamilton or Mariota Home; see note to 21 above.

36 *Jane Douglas*: daughter of the fifth Earl of Angus, and younger sister of the poet Gavin Douglas.

I.i.87–94 *dangers . . . rest*: alluding to the defeat at Stoke, near Newark, of the Yorkist leaders supporting Lambert Simnel's 1487 invasion. They included the Earl of Lincoln, Richard III's cousin; the Earl of Kildare, Henry's own Lord Deputy in Ireland, and his brother Thomas Lord Geraldine; Viscount Lovell, Sir Thomas Broughton and the German mercenary leader Swart.

I.ii.29–33 *I . . . day*: although Dalyell is an unhistorical character, his account of the line of descent of the Stuart kings is accurate as far as it goes. The first Stuart king of Scotland, Robert II, married Elizabeth Mure, daughter of Sir Adam Mure, and it was from this union that 'the race of Jameses', to which Dalyell claims kinship, were descended. But, as Peter Ure notes in 'A pointer to the date of Ford's *Perkin Warbeck*', *Notes and Queries*, new series 17 (1970), 215–17, on the death of Elizabeth in 1355 Robert married a second wife, Euphemia Ross, by whom he had other children, and because his eldest son by Elizabeth had been born before their marriage was solemnised there were arguments about dynastic precedence, arguments which were raised again in 1632 and 1633 over the standing of the Earl of Menteith, who traced his descent from Euphemia. Ford carefully follows the official view; that he introduces such material at all (it is not found in Gainsford or Bacon) may indicate that he was writing the play at the time of the dispute.

I.iii.129–33 *Ten . . . Audley*: this rebellion actually took place in 1497, two years after Clifford's betrayal of the Yorkists, and was caused by resentment over the special taxes levied throughout the kingdom to pay for the forces raised against the Scottish incursions of 1496–7 (see III.i.21–9). A blacksmith named Michael Joseph and a lawyer, Thomas Flammock, were its leaders; they were joined by James Touchet, Lord Audley, at Wells, and were crushed at Blackheath, near London, in June 1497.

III.ii.111 *kingly bug's-words*: inflated language appropriate for a royal occasion. The masque that follows includes no dialogue, so Huntly may be speaking in a generalising way ('This is the usual kind of swaggering royal show'), or else the printed text may provide only a truncated form of the masque as it was actually performed in the play.

III.ii.139 *seal those eyes*: the metaphor comes from the practice of closing a letter or document with a wax seal. However, the audience might hear the verb as 'seel' and take it to mean shut by sewing the eyelids together, a practice used in falconry. Cf. *The Broken Heart*, II.ii.3–5 and note. Either sense expresses Warbeck's general meaning.

III.iii.58 *new creation*: i.e. the death of the present Earl and the revival of the title after the extermination of the family. Warwick, the principal male heir of the house of York, was executed in 1499 (cf. V.iii.192–5), and a marriage between Catherine of Aragon and Henry's son, Prince Arthur, was concluded in 1501.

IV.ii.94–5 *If . . . out*: if this and that may eventuate. But there may have been a loss of text at this point; the original may have read, 'If things may fall in and things may fall out'.

IV.iii.19–26 *King . . . kingdoms*: Anderson points out that this passage would have a special resonance for Ford's audience, since James VI of Scotland, who united the English and Scottish thrones in 1603 as James I, was the great-grandson of Margaret and James IV.

V.i.46–50 *All . . . Taunton*: Warbeck attacked Exeter in September 1497, but was driven back by its citizens and troops led by Sir Edward Courtenay, Earl of Devon. Courtenay was wounded by a Cornish arrow (see V.ii.29–30), but survived. Warbeck then marched on Taunton, a town about thirty miles north-east of Exeter, but his soldiers began to desert and he himself abandoned the remainder and fled to sanctuary at Beaulieu.

V.ii.60–1 *retir'd . . . court*: as Duke of Richmond, Henry had lived in asylum at the court of Francis, Duke of Brittany, since 1471. In 1483 he retired there again after the failure of Buckingham's rising against Richard III, to prepare for the successful invasion of 1485.

V.ii.65–6 *first . . . Haven*: Henry's second and successful invasion of England began with a landing at Milford Haven, a harbour in southern Wales, on 7 August 1485.

V.iii.15–19 *Twice . . . attempt*: Warbeck attempted to escape from Henry's court in 1498, and (with Warwick) from the Tower of London in 1499. Both men were executed in November 1499.

V.iii. 156–86 As usual, Ford has imagined the actions of his characters in detail. While Perkin Warbeck is released from the stocks by the Constable, Daubeney turns to talk to Urswick. His companion Surrey addresses Warbeck as he is freed, and at 159–62 makes it plain that Katherine has taken his hand or is embracing him. At 170 Huntly probably takes the hand of his daughter and her husband, releasing them at 176. At 178 Warbeck embraces Crawford as he takes leave of him. The solemn ritual of farewell is interrupted at 184 as Katherine almost collapses with grief, and is supported first by her attendant Jane, and then by Dalyell.